MW00358431

Azure for Architects

Implementing cloud design, DevOps, IoT, and serverless solutions on your public cloud

Ritesh Modi

BIRMINGHAM - MUMBAI

Azure for Architects

Copyright © 2017 Packt Publishing

All rights reserved. No part of this book may be reproduced, stored in a retrieval system, or transmitted in any form or by any means, without the prior written permission of the publisher, except in the case of brief quotations embedded in critical articles or reviews.

Every effort has been made in the preparation of this book to ensure the accuracy of the information presented. However, the information contained in this book is sold without warranty, either express or implied. Neither the author, nor Packt Publishing, and its dealers and distributors will be held liable for any damages caused or alleged to be caused directly or indirectly by this book.

Packt Publishing has endeavored to provide trademark information about all of the companies and products mentioned in this book by the appropriate use of capitals. However, Packt Publishing cannot guarantee the accuracy of this information.

First published: October 2017

Production reference: 1181017

Published by Packt Publishing Ltd.
Livery Place
35 Livery Street
Birmingham
B3 2PB, UK.
ISBN 978-1-78839-739-1

www.packtpub.com

Credits

Author
Ritesh Modi

Copy Editors
Safis Editing
Juliana Nair

Reviewers
Paul Glavich
Vikram Pendse
Ruben Oliva Ramos

Project Coordinator
Judie Jose

Commissioning Editor
Gebin George

Proofreader
Safis Editing

Acquisition Editor
Shrilekha Inani

Indexer
Tejal Daruwale Soni

Content Development Editor
Abhishek Jadhav

Graphics
Kirk D'Penha

Technical Editor
Aditya Khadye

Production Coordinator
Arvindkumar Gupta

About the Author

Ritesh Modi is a former Microsoft senior technology evangelist currently working as a principal consultant for Infront Consulting Group. He is an architect, a senior evangelist, cloud architect, published author, speaker, and a known leader for his contributions towards datacenter, Azure, bots, blockchain, cognitive services, DevOps, artificial intelligence, and automation. He is the author of multiple books. *Developing Bots using Bot Framework* and *DevOps with Windows Server 2016* are some of his recent books. He has also coauthored another book, titled *Introducing Windows Server 2016 Technical Preview*, along with the Windows Server team.

He has spoken at more than 15 conferences, including TechEd and the PowerShell Asia Conference, and is a published author for MSDN magazine. He has more than a decade of experience in building and deploying enterprise solutions for customers, and more than 25 technical certifications. His interests and hobbies include writing books, playing with his daughter, watching movies, and continuing to learn new technologies. His Twitter handle is @automationnext.

Ritesh currently lives in Hyderabad, India.

Writing this book has been a fantastic experience. I have personally grown as a person who now has more patience, perseverance, and tenacity. I owe a lot to the people who pushed me through their encouragements and motivation. I would like to thank so many people for making this book happen.

I must start with the people who mean the world to me, who inspire me to push myself, and who ultimately make everything worthwhile. I am talking about my mother, Bimla Modi; wife, Sangeeta Modi; and daughter, Avni Modi, the three wonderful ladies in my life. I would also like to thank my father who provided continuous support to ensure that I remained focused on the book.

Thanks, of course, must go to the Packt team. I would like to thank my content development editor Abhishek Jadhav, for taking me in this project and helping me through it. I would like to thank the acquisition editor, Shrilekha Inani, for finding me for this book. I would also like to thank my technical editor, Aditya Khadye, who walked me through the book multiple times and provided me with incredibly useful feedback.

Finally, I would like to apologize to my family, friends, and well-wishers for not being able to spend much time with them during the last year. I am going to make it up to them.

About the Reviewers

Paul Glavich has been an ASP.NET MVP for 13 years and currently works as a principal consultant for Readify. Previously, he was the Chief Technology Officer (CTO) for Saasu, a solution architect at Datacom, then the senior consultant for Readify, and prior to that was a technical architect for EDS Australia. He has over 20 years of industry experience ranging from PICK, C, C++, Delphi, and Visual Basic 3/4/5/6 to his current specialty in .NET with C#, ASP.NET, Azure, Cloud, and DevOps.

Paul has been developing in .NET technologies since .NET was first in beta, and was a technical architect for one of the world's first internet banking solutions using .NET technology.

Paul can be seen on various .NET-related newsgroups, has presented at the Sydney .NET user group and TechEd, and is also a member of ASPInsiders. He has also written some technical articles, which can be seen on community sites such as ASP Alliance. Paul has authored a total of three books, *Beginning AJAX in ASP.NET*, *Beginning Microsoft ASP.NET AJAX*, and the latest book on *.NET Performance Testing and Optimisation*. He is currently focusing on overall architecture, solution design, and Microsoft Cloud solutions.

On a more personal note, Paul is married with three children, three grandkids, holds a 5th-degree black belt in Budo-Jitsu and also practices Wing Chun Kung fu.

There are so many people who have helped me get to where I am today, but it would take another book. So to keep things short, I would like to thank my three children, Kristy, Marc, and Elizabeth for being awesome, my parents for buying me that first computer, my nerd friends for nerding out with me, but mostly I would like to thank my wife, Michele, for supporting me in my life and career, and enduring my never-ending stream of technobabble and Dad jokes.

Vikram Pendse is a Microsoft MVP for Azure and has been a distinguished speaker at various Microsoft events over the last 10 years. He is a very active member of various Microsoft communities in India. He is a cloud solutions architect and is currently working with one of the leading Microsoft Partners in Pune, where he is responsible for building the strategy for moving Amazon AWS workloads to Azure, providing cloud-centric solutions, architecture, supporting RFPs, and global deliveries. You can follow him on Twitter at @VikramPendse.

He has been a technical reviewer in the past with Packt for the following books:

- *Microsoft SharePoint 2010 Enterprise Applications on Windows Phone 7*
- *Microsoft Silverlight 4 Data and Services Cookbook*

I would like to thank my wife, Aarti, and my son, Aditya, for their encouragement and support throughout the process.

Ruben Oliva Ramos is a computer systems engineer from Tecnologico of León Institute with a master's degree in computer and electronic systems engineering, teleinformatics, and networking specialization from the University of Salle Bajio in Leon, Guanajuato Mexico. He has more than 5 years of experience in developing web applications to control and monitor devices connected to Arduino and Raspberry Pi using web frameworks and cloud services to build the Internet of Things applications.

He is a mechatronics teacher at the University of Salle Bajio and teaches students on the master's degree in the design and engineering of mechatronics systems. He also works at Centro de Bachillerato Tecnologico Industrial 225 in Leon, Guanajuato, Mexico, teaching subjects such as electronics, robotics and control, automation, and microcontrollers on the Mechatronics Technician Career, consultant and developer projects include areas such as monitoring systems and datalogger data using technologies such as Android, iOS, Windows Phone, HTML5, PHP, CSS, Ajax, JavaScript, Angular, ASP .NET databases: SQLite, MongoDB, MySQL, WEB Servers: Node.js, IIS, hardware programming: Arduino, Raspberry Pi, Ethernet Shield, GPS and GSM/GPRS, ESP8266, and control and monitor systems for data acquisition and programming.

He has written a book for Packt, titled *Internet of Things Programming with JavaScript*. He has also written *Monitoring, Controlling, and Acquisition of Data with Arduino* and *Visual Basic .NET for Alfaomega*.

I would like to thank my savior and lord, Jesus Christ, for giving me the strength and courage to pursue this project. To my dearest wife, Mayte; our two lovely sons, Ruben and Dario; to my dear father, Ruben; my dearest mom, Rosalia; my brother, Juan Tomas; and my sister, Rosalia, whom I love, for all their support while reviewing this book, for allowing me to pursue my dream and tolerating my not being with them after my busy day job.

I'm very grateful to Packt for giving me the opportunity to collaborate as an author and reviewer, and to belong to this honest and professional team.

www.PacktPub.com

For support files and downloads related to your book, please visit www.PacktPub.com.

Did you know that Packt offers eBook versions of every book published, with PDF and ePub files available? You can upgrade to the eBook version at www.PacktPub.com and as a print book customer, you are entitled to a discount on the eBook copy. Get in touch with us at service@packtpub.com for more details.

At www.PacktPub.com, you can also read a collection of free technical articles, sign up for a range of free newsletters and receive exclusive discounts and offers on Packt books and eBooks.

https://www.packtpub.com/mapt

Get the most in-demand software skills with Mapt. Mapt gives you full access to all Packt books and video courses, as well as industry-leading tools to help you plan your personal development and advance your career.

Why subscribe?

- Fully searchable across every book published by Packt
- Copy and paste, print, and bookmark content
- On demand and accessible via a web browser

Customer Feedback

Thanks for purchasing this Packt book. At Packt, quality is at the heart of our editorial process. To help us improve, please leave us an honest review on this book's Amazon page at `https://www.amazon.com/dp/1788397398`.

If you'd like to join our team of regular reviewers, you can email us at `customerreviews@packtpub.com`. We award our regular reviewers with free eBooks and videos in exchange for their valuable feedback. Help us be relentless in improving our products!

Table of Contents

Preface

Azure, the cloud from the Microsoft stable, is a mature and continually growing cloud platform. It is gaining lots of momentum, traction, and popularity and continues to be the preferred cloud platform for many. Azure is a large platform, but behind this platform are hundreds of Azure resources and services that make the magic happen. All these resources and services are provided to users uniformly using Azure Resource Manager. A cloud platform should respect users and each country's sovereign rules regarding security and data. Azure has more than 35 data centers across the globe and this number keeps on increasing every year. Azure has most of the security certifications that are available in the industry today. Azure provides different levels of control on deployment using different models, such as Infrastructure as a Service, Platform as a Service, and Software as a Service. It also provides rich resources and features to implement hybrid cloud. In fact, with the release of Azure Stack, Azure is one of the most feature-rich and mature platforms to implement hybrid deployments. Azure is an open cloud, allowing any operating system, any programming language, and any runtime to run on it. Azure is flexible and provides multiple resources and options for implementing similar functionalities, although they do have some differences. Azure provides multiple cost and usage models and covers almost every kind of customer—whether in pay-as-you-go mode, enterprise agreements, or a cloud solution provider model. On top of these, it has multiple offers, such as reserved VM instances and Azure hybrid benefits to reduce the overall cost of deployments. Azure provides rich tooling to ensure that customers can automate their deployments and also start their journey on DevOps. DevOps is an emerging paradigm and Azure provides all the features to get it implemented.

With so many options, resources, and different deployment models, it is important that users of Azure understand the purpose, importance, and utility of each resource at the architectural level, and how they compare to their peer resources. Based on requirements, appropriate resources should be deployed. An architecture for a cloud-based solution comprises multiple resources. The choice of resources, their configuration, and interaction must be architected meticulously and appropriately. Azure provides advance platforms, such as IoT, serverless, and big data. These are emerging technologies and each of them is covered in this book.

Azure provides almost all kinds of services to meet the computing needs of any organization and it is important to approach them using the right strategy and architecture. This book is an attempt in this direction, to provide its users enough ammunition to design and architect their solutions, covering design patterns, high availability, security, scalability, cost management, monitoring, and auditing. The topics of all of the chapters in this book demand a complete book of their own. It was extremely difficult to summarize the architectural concerns, best practices, and using Azure features in a single chapter. I would urge all readers to go through each chapter and read the Microsoft online documentation related to each chapter to gain further insights.

What this book covers

Chapter 1, *Getting Started*, introduces cloud computing as a new strategy and paradigm. The focus of this book is Azure and starts with its introduction. It provides details about IaaS, PaaS, and an introduction to some of the important features that help when designing solutions. It will introduce Azure Resource Manager and Resource groups. It will also introduce major Azure resources such as compute, network, storage, functions, IoT, data services, and automation tools and languages.

Chapter 2, *Azure Design Patterns*, talks about Azure cloud patterns related to virtual networks, storage accounts, regions, and availability sets. It also briefly discusses cloud patterns that help in implementing scalability and performance. Messaging patterns help with the building of reliable solutions. Messaging patterns will also be focused in this chapter.

Chapter 3, *Designing High Availability*, focuses on describing the high availability features available on Azure. Enterprises need high availability for their deployments. This chapter will build a solid foundation on high availability concepts and help the user make informed decisions related to IaaS and PaaS deployment strategies.

Chapter 4, *Implementing Scalability*, focuses on designing solutions that can automatically increase and decrease the available resources based on its current consumption to maintain its performance levels. Azure provides virtual machine scale sets (VMSS) for deploying highly scalable solutions. This chapter focuses on VMSS-based architecture and deployment. It will also describe PaaS-based scalability and its strategies.

Chapter 5, *Cloud Security*, introduces important concepts from a security viewpoint. Security is super important in any cloud deployment. Azure provides network security groups, firewalls, NAT, security center, and key vaults features to deploy cyber security applications. This chapter will provide details about these features and architect a solution using them.

Chapter 6, *Designing IoT Solutions*, provides in-depth information about implementing an IoT solution using the Azure cloud. The Azure cloud provides a complete IoT platform for developing device-based solutions. This chapter will show how to architect IoT-based solutions using the Azure cloud. It will also describe architectural concerns that every architect should keep in mind while creating a solution. This chapter will discuss topics related to IoT hubs, event hubs, registering devices, a device to platform conversation, and logging and routing them to appropriate destinations.

Chapter 7, *Designing and Implementing Data Solutions*, dedicates itself to data storage and services. Azure provides multiple features related to data services. This chapter will focus on providing insights about which features and resources to use for different types of solutions, and their pros, cons, and advantages. A complete architecture for ingesting data, cleaning and filtering data, and storing it in appropriate data stores, such as Data Lake and Cosmos DB, and then pushing data to Power BI for visualizing will be part of this chapter.

Chapter 8, *Designing and Implementing Serverless Solutions*, focuses on serverless computing. Azure functions are a versatile platform for hosting small business functionalities as functions and help in weaving solutions together. This chapter will focus on understanding the serverless paradigm, Azure functions, its capabilities, creating solutions by combining multiple functions, understanding triggers and parameters, and different sources of inputs and outputs.

Chapter 9, *Designing Policies, Locks, and Tags*, focuses on using the management features provided by Azure to implement better manage deployments. Tags help by adding additional metadata information to Azure resources. They also help by providing information architecture regarding Azure resources. This chapter provides design guidelines for defining tags for deployments. It also provides details about policies and locks to restrict and control Azure resources regarding their location, usage, size, accessibility, permissions, and so on. It is an important concept, providing management control over Azure resources.

Chapter 10, *DevOps on Azure*, dedicates itself to DevOps. The Azure cloud provides rich tools, utilities, and scripting support to enable automation for DevOps. Azure supports Azure Resource Manager templates, desired state configuration, PowerShell, Rest API, and open source technologies such as Chef, Python, and Linux to devise end-to-end automation of continuous integration, delivery, and deployment. Infrastructure as Code and configuration management is also supported inherently using Azure features such as Azure automation. This chapter will focus on building CI/CD pipelines and configuration management for Azure resources using VSTS.

Chapter 11, *Cost Management*, covers a somewhat different angle compared to the other chapters in this book. It is not a technical chapter but discusses various ways of means to reduce the cost of deployments on Azure. This chapter will focus on calculating the cost of deployment on Azure using the Azure cost calculator. It will also show how changing location, size, and type of resources can affect the cost of the solution, and also provide best practices to reduce the overall cost of Azure deployments.

Chapter 12, *Monitoring and Auditing*, focuses on understanding how Azure services such as Operational Insights and Application Insights provide monitoring and auditing capabilities. This chapter will show how to configure them and utilize them to monitor Azure resources and take actions based on them. This chapter will also focus on architecting monitoring solutions for Azure cloud deployments.

What you need for this book

This book assumes a basic level of knowledge on cloud computing and Azure. All you need is a valid Azure subscription and internet connectivity to use this book. A Windows 10 operating system having 4 GB of RAM is sufficient for using Powershell and executing ARM templates.

Who this book is for

To make use of the content of this book, a basic prior knowledge of cloud and Azure is expected. If you think you do not possess that knowledge, it is always possible to catch up on the basic requirements by quickly reading up on the major components from the Azure documentation at https://docs.microsoft.com/en-us/azure/. This book is essentially intended for cloud architects, developers, consultants, and DevOps engineers who are using Azure to provide their services to end customers and employers. If you are also willing to architect complete solutions on Azure, then this book is ideal for you. If you already have some experience with architecture on Azure, this book can help you to speed up with it in a fast-paced way.

Conventions

In this book, you will find a number of text styles that distinguish between different kinds of information. Here are some examples of these styles and an explanation of their meaning. Code words in text, database table names, folder names, filenames, file extensions, pathnames, dummy URLs, user input, and Twitter handles are shown as follows: "An employee ID in one data store is named EMPIDID in another data store and EID in the third data store within the same organization.

A block of code is set as follows:

```
Import-DscResource -ModuleName 'PSDesiredStateConfiguration'
Node WebServer {
  WindowsFeature IIS
    {
        Name = "Web-Server"
        Ensure = "Present"
    }
```

New terms and **important words** are shown in bold. Words that you see on the screen, for example, in menus or dialog boxes, appear in the text like this: "The first step is to create a data factory resource. After creation, click on the **Copy data** button."

Warnings or important notes appear like this.

Tips and tricks appear like this.

Reader feedback

Feedback from our readers is always welcome. Let us know what you think about this book-what you liked or disliked. Reader feedback is important for us as it helps us develop titles that you will really get the most out of. To send us general feedback, simply email feedback@packtpub.com, and mention the book's title in the subject of your message. If there is a topic that you have expertise in and you are interested in either writing or contributing to a book, see our author guide at www.packtpub.com/authors.

Customer support

Now that you are the proud owner of a Packt book, we have a number of things to help you to get the most from your purchase.

Downloading the color images of this book

We also provide you with a PDF file that has color images of the screenshots/diagrams used in this book. The color images will help you better understand the changes in the output. You can download this file from `https://www.packtpub.com/sites/default/files/downloads/AzureforArchitects_ColorImages.pdf`.

Errata

Although we have taken every care to ensure the accuracy of our content, mistakes do happen. If you find a mistake in one of our books-maybe a mistake in the text or the code-we would be grateful if you could report this to us. By doing so, you can save other readers from frustration and help us improve subsequent versions of this book. If you find any errata, please report them by visiting `http://www.packtpub.com/submit-errata`, selecting your book, clicking on the **Errata Submission Form** link, and entering the details of your errata. Once your errata are verified, your submission will be accepted and the errata will be uploaded to our website or added to any list of existing errata under the Errata section of that title. To view the previously submitted errata, go to `https://www.packtpub.com/books/content/support` and enter the name of the book in the search field. The required information will appear under the **Errata** section.

Piracy

Piracy of copyrighted material on the internet is an ongoing problem across all media. At Packt, we take the protection of our copyright and licenses very seriously. If you come across any illegal copies of our works in any form on the internet, please provide us with the location address or website name immediately so that we can pursue a remedy. Please contact us at `copyright@packtpub.com` with a link to the suspected pirated material. We appreciate your help in protecting our authors and our ability to bring you valuable content.

Questions

If you have a problem with any aspect of this book, you can contact us at `questions@packtpub.com`, and we will do our best to address the problem.

1
Getting Started

Every few years there are technological innovations that change the entire landscape and ecosystem around them. If we go back in time, the 70's and 80's was a time of mainframes. They were huge in size, practically occupying large rooms and almost all computing work was carried out by them. It was difficult to procure one and it was also time-consuming. Enterprises used to order months before they could have an operational mainframe set up.

The first part of the 90's was the era of personal computing and the internet. Computers became much smaller in size and were comparatively easier to procure. Both personal computing and internet innovation changed the entire computer industry. People had a desktop through which they could run multiple programs and could connect to the internet. The rise of the internet also propagated the rise of client-server deployments. Now, there could be centralized servers hosting applications and services that could be reached out by anyone who had a connection to the internet globally. This was also when server technology got a lot of prominences. Windows NT, Windows 2000, and Windows 2003 were launched during this time.

The most remarkable innovation of the 2000's was the rise and adoption of devices, especially smartphones, and with them came a plethora of apps. Apps could connect to centralized servers on the internet and could carry out business as normal. Users were no longer dependent on browsers to make this work. All servers were typically either self hosted or hosted with a service provider, such as an **Internet Service Provider (ISP)**.

Users did not have much control over their servers. Multiple customers and their deployments were part of the same server even without customers knowing about it.

However, there was something else happening towards the mid and later parts of the 2000's. This was the rise of cloud computing and it again rewrote the entire landscape of the IT industry. Although, initially the adoption was slow and people approached it with caution either because the cloud was in its infancy and yet had to mature or people were having multiple varied diverse notions about it.

Nevertheless, today cloud computing is one of the most promising and still upcoming technology and enterprise--no matter how big or small, every company/organization has adopted it as a part of their IT strategy. It is difficult these days to have any meaningful conversation without including cloud computing in the overall solution discussions.

Cloud computing, or simply cloud in layman terms, refers to the availability of resources on the internet. These resources are made available to users on the internet as services. For example, storage is available on-demand through the internet to users for them to store their files, documents, and so on. Here storage is a service provided by a cloud provider.

A cloud provider is an enterprise or consortium of companies that provide cloud services to other enterprises and consumers. They host and manage the services on behalf of the user. They are responsible for enabling and maintaining the health of services. Typically, there are large data centers across the globe opened by cloud providers to cater to IT demands from users.

Cloud resources could be a delivery of hosting services or providing on-demand infrastructures, such as a computer, network, and storage facilities to users for consumption. This flavor of the cloud is also typically known as **Infrastructure as a Service**.

There are three types of services provided by cloud based on their level of abstraction and degree of control on these services by users and cloud providers:

- Infrastructure as a Service (also popularly known as IaaS)
- Platform as a Service (also popularly known as PaaS)
- Software as a Service (also popularly known as SaaS)

IaaS, PaaS, and SaaS differ based on the level of control between a cloud consumer and a cloud provider. With SaaS, a cloud provider has almost complete control over the services with the consumer having control only over its data and application. Similarly, a cloud provider has higher control with IaaS as compared to cloud consumer.

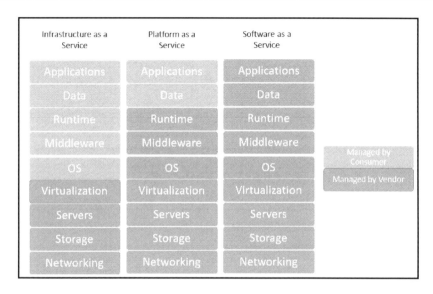

Cloud services- IaaS. PaaS. SaaS

The preceding diagram shows the three categories of service available through cloud providers and the layers that are comprised of each service. These layers are stacked vertically on each other and each layer in the stack is colored differently depending on who manages it, the customer or the provider. From the figure, we see that for IaaS, a cloud provider is responsible for providing, controlling, and managing layers from the network layer up to the virtualization layer. Similarly, for PaaS, a cloud provider controls and manages from the hardware layer up to the runtime layer, while the consumer controls only the application and data layers.

Infrastructure as a Service

As the name suggests, IaaS are infrastructure services provided by a cloud provider. This service includes the physical hardware and its configuration, network hardware and its configuration, storage hardware and its configuration, load balancers, compute, and virtualization. Any layer above virtualization is the responsibility of the consumer. The consumer can decide to use the provided underlying infrastructure in whatever way best suits their requirements. For example, consumers can consume the storage, network, and virtualization to provision virtual machines on top of it. It is then the consumer's responsibility to manage and control the virtual machines and the software deployed within it.

Platform as a Service

PaaS enables consumers to deploy their applications and services on the provided platform, consuming the underlying runtime, middleware, and services. The cloud provider provides the services from infrastructure to runtime. The consumers cannot provision virtual machines as they cannot access and control them. Instead, they can only control and manage their applications. This is a comparatively faster method of development and deployment because now the consumer can focus on application development and deployment. Examples of Platform as a Service include Azure Automation, Azure SQL, and Azure App Services.

Software as a Service

Software as a Service provides complete control of the service to the cloud provider. The cloud provider provisions, configures, and manages everything from infrastructure to the application. It includes the provisioning of infrastructure, deployment, and configuration of applications, and provides application access to the consumer. The consumer does not control and manage the application and can use and configure only parts of the application. They control only their data and configuration. Generally, multi-tenant applications are used by multiple consumers, such as Office 365 and Visual Studio Team Services, which are examples of SaaS.

Last few years have witnessed exponential growth in cloud adoption. While most of the initial growth was from small and medium enterprises, the current adoption is coming from large enterprises. This is happening primarily because of the following drivers mentioned:

- **Cost effective**: Cloud helps in eliminating capital expenditure and instead just incurs an operational cost. Users can stop purchasing physical hardware, expensive software's licenses and set up large data centers. All these are available on the cloud without user spending anything to buy them.
- **Unlimited scale and capacity**: Cloud provides the notion of unlimited availability of resources. This encourages organizations to deploy their workloads on it because they are not constrained by hardware availability limitations.
- **Elasticity**: Cloud computing is elastic in nature. Customers can shrink or increase their Cloud presence based on their needs easily using simple to use user interface. There is no upfront cost, resource availability constraints, and time lag in doing so.

- **Pay as you go**: Using cloud eliminates capital expenditure and organizations pay only for what they use, thereby providing maximum return on investment. Organizations do not need to build additional infrastructure to host their application for times of peak demand.
- **Faster and better**: Cloud provides ready-to-use applications and faster provisioning and deployment of environments. Moreover, organizations get better-managed services from their cloud provider with higher service-level agreements.

What is Azure?

According to Wikipedia:

> *"Azure is a cloud computing service created by Microsoft for building, deploying, and managing applications and services through a global network of Microsoft-managed data centers. It provides software as a service, platform as a service and infrastructure as a service and supports many different programming languages, tools and frameworks, including both Microsoft-specific and third-party software and systems."*

Azure obviously provides all the benefits of cloud, but it is also an open and flexible cloud. Azure cloud supports a variety of operating systems, languages, tools, platforms, utilities, and frameworks. It supports both Linux and Windows, SQL Server, MySQL, Postgres and more, C#, Python, Java, Node.js, Bash, and more languages, MongoDB and DocumentDB NoSQL databases, and Jenkins to VSTS as continuous integration tools. The whole idea behind this ecosystem is to enable users to have their choice and freedom of language, their choice of platform and operating system, their choice of databases, and their choice of storage, their choice of tools and utilities. Users should not be constrained from the technology perspective, instead, they should be able to build and focus on their business solution and Azure provides them with world-class technology stack. Azure is compatible with the user's choice of technology stack.

For example, Azure provides availability of all popular (open source or commercial) database environments. Azure provides Azure SQL, MySQL, and Postgres PaaS service. It provides a Hadoop ecosystem and offers HDInsight, a 100% Apache Hadoop-based PaaS services. It also provides Hadoop on Linux VM implementation for customers who prefer IaaS approach. Azure also provides a Redis cache service and supports other popular database environments, such as MongoDB, Couchbase, Oracle, and many others as an IaaS implementation.

The number of services is increasing by the day and the following figure just provides the rich set of services provided by Azure. Not all services are shown here and it keeps on growing.

Azure services

Azure also provides a unique cloud computing paradigm--the Hybrid cloud. Hybrid cloud refers to a deployment strategy in which a subset of services are deployed on a public cloud, while other services are deployed in an on-premise private cloud or data center. There is a **Virtual Private Network (VPN)** connection between both the public and private cloud. Azure provides users the flexibility to divide and deploy their workload on both public cloud and on-premise data center.

Azure has data centers across the globe. Azure combines these data centers into regions. Each region has multiple data centers to ensure that recovery from disasters is quick and efficient. At the time of writing, there are 38 regions across the globe. This provides users the flexibility to deploy their services at their choice of location and regions. They can also combine these regions to deploy a solution that is disaster resistant and deployed near their customer base.

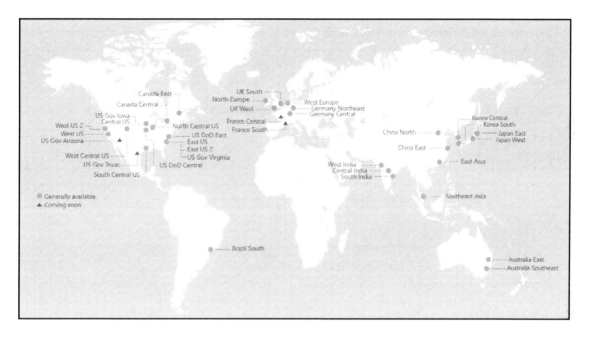

Azure regions and locations

 Azure also has separate clouds for China, Germany, and the governments.

Azure as an intelligent cloud

Azure is not just a cloud; it is an intelligent cloud. Now, you might be wondering what an intelligent cloud is. People consume computing power primarily because of two reasons: Either they are searching for something and after finding what they were looking for, act on it. The entire computing powers are associated with these two purposes. Azure provides infrastructure and services to invest millions and billions of records with hyper-scale processing. It provides multi-petabytes of storages for data. It provides a host of inter-connected services that can pass data among each other. With such capabilities in place, data can be processed to generate meaningful knowledge and insights. There are multiple types of insights that can be generated through data analysis:

- **Descriptive**: This kind of analysis provides details about what is happening or happened in the past
- **Predictive**: This kind of analysis provides details about what is going to happen in the near-future or the future
- **Prescriptive**: This kind of analysis provides details about what should be done to either enhance or prevent the current or future happening
- **Cognitive**: This actually executes the actions determined by prescriptive analytics in an automated manner

While insights are good to them, it is also important to act on them reactively or proactively. Azure provides a rich platform to ingest big data, process and augment data through its rich services, store data in its large data storage systems, conduct analysis on them, generate insights and dashboards, and then execute actions based on it. These services are available to every user of Azure and provide a rich ecosystem to create solutions on top of them. Enterprises are creating applications and services that are completely disrupting industries because of easy availability of these intelligent services from Azure that are easily combined to create meaningful value to end customers. Azure had ensured that services that were commercially unviable to implement by small and medium companies can now readily consume and deploy them in a few minutes.

Azure Resource Manager

Azure Resource Manager is the technology platform and orchestration service from Microsoft that ties up all components discussed earlier. It brings Azure resource providers, resources, and resource groups together to form a cohesive cloud platform. It helps in the registration of resource providers to subscriptions and regions, it makes the resource types available to resource groups, makes the resource and resource APIs accessible to the portal and other clients, and authenticates access to resources. It also enables features, such as tagging, authentication, **Role-Based Access Control** (**RBAC**), resource locking, and policy enforcement for subscriptions and its resource groups. It provides the same deployment and management experience whether through a portal or client-based tools such as PowerShell or a command-line interface.

Azure Resource Manager architecture

The architecture of Azure Resource Manager and its components are as shown in the following figure. As we can see **Azure Subscription** comprises of multiple resource groups. Each resource group contains resource instances that are created from resource types available in the resource provider.

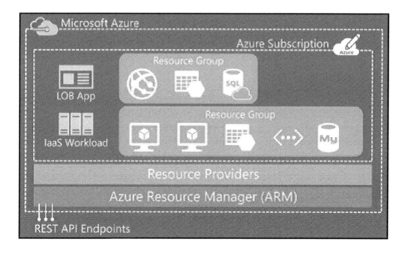

Azure Resource Manager architecture

ARM and ASM

ASM has inherent constraints and some of the major ones are discussed here: ASM deployments are slow and blocking. Operations are blocked if an earlier operation is already in progress:

- **Parallelism**: Parallelism is a challenge in ASM. It is not possible to execute multiple transactions successfully in parallel. The operations in ASM are linear and executed one after another. Either there are parallel operation errors or they will get blocked.
- **Resources**: Resources in ASM are provisioned and managed in isolation from each other, there is no relation between ASM resources. Grouping of services and resources or configuring them together is not possible.
- **Cloud services**: Cloud services are the unit of deployment in ASM. They are reliant on affinity groups and not scalable due to its design and architecture.

Granular and discreet roles and permissions cannot be assigned to resources in ASM. Users are either service administrators or co-administrators in the subscription. They either get full control on resources or do not have access to them at all. ASM provides no deployment support. Deployments are either manual or you will need to resort to writing procedural scripts in PowerShell or .NET.

ASM APIs were not consistent between resources.

ARM advantages

The ARM provides distinct advantages and benefits over ASM.

- **Grouping**: ARM allows grouping of resources together in a logical container. These resources can be managed together and undergo a common life cycle as a group. This makes it easier to identify related and dependent resources.
- **Common life cycle**: Resources in a group have the same life cycle. These resources can evolve and be managed together as a unit.
- **Role-Based Access Control**: Granular roles and permissions can be assigned to resources providing discreet access to users. Users can have only those rights that are assigned to them.
- **Deployment support**: ARM provides deployment support in terms of templates enabling DevOps and **Infrastructure as Code** (**IAC**). The deployments are faster, consistent, and predictable.

- **Superior technology**: Cost and billing of resources can be managed as a unit. Each resource group can provide their usage and cost information.
- **Manageability**: ARM provides advanced features such as security, monitoring, auditing, and tagging features for better manageability of resources. Resources can be queried based on tags. Tags also provide cost and billing information for resources tagged similarly.
- **Migration**: Easier migration and update of resources within, as well as from across resource groups.

ARM concepts

With the ARM, everything in Azure is a resource. Examples of resources are a virtual machine, network interfaces, public IP address, storage accounts, virtual networks, and more. ARM is based on concepts related to resource providers and resource consumers. Azure provides resources and services through multiple resource providers that are consumed and deployed in groups.

Resource providers

These are services responsible for providing resource types through Azure Resource Manager. The top-level concept in the ARM is resource providers. These providers are containers for resource types. Resource types are grouped into resource providers. They are responsible for deploying and managing the resources. For example, a virtual machine resource type is provided by a resource provider called **Microsoft.Compute Namespace**. The REST API operations are versioned to distinguish between them. The version naming is based on the dates on which they are released by Microsoft. It is necessary that a related resource provider is available to a subscription to deploy a resource. Not all resource providers are available to a subscription out of the box. If a resource is not available in the subscription, one must check if the required resource provider is available in each region. If that is available, the user can explicitly register in the subscription.

Resource types

These are an actual resource specification defining it's public API interface and implementation. It implements the working and operations supported by the resource. Similar to resource providers, resource types also evolve over time with regard to their internal implementation and have multiple versions of its schema and public API interface. The version names are based on dates that they are released on by Microsoft as a preview or **General Availability (GA)**. The resource types become available to a subscription after a resource provider is registered to it. Also, not every resource type is available in every Azure region. The availability of a resource is dependent on the availability and registration of a resource provider in an Azure region and must support the API version needed for provisioning it.

Resource groups

Resource groups are a unit of deployment in the ARM. They are containers grouping multiple resource instances in a security and management boundary. A resource group is uniquely named in a subscription. Resources can be provisioned on different Azure regions yet belong to the same resource group. It provides additional services to all resources within it. Resource groups provide metadata services, such as tagging, which enables categorization of resources, policy-based management of resources, RBAC, protection of resources from accidental deletion or updates, and more. As mentioned before, they have a security boundary and users that don't have access to a resource group cannot access resources contained within it. Every resource instance needs to be part of a resource group or else it cannot be deployed.

Resource and resource instances

Resources are created from resource types and should be unique within a resource group. The uniqueness is defined by the name of the resource and its type together. In OOP parlance, resource instances can be referred to as objects, while resource types can be referred to as a class. The services are consumed through the operations supported and implemented by resource instances. They define properties that should be configured before usage. Some are mandatory properties, while others are optional. They inherit the security and access configuration from its parent resource group. These inherited permissions and role assignments can be overridden for each resource. A resource can be locked in such a way that some of its operations can be blocked and not made available to roles, users, and groups even though they have access to it. They can be tagged for easy discoverability and manageability.

Azure Resource Manager features

The following are some of the major features provided by Azure Resource Manager:

- **Role-Based Access Control**: **Azure Active Directory (AAD)** authenticates users to provide access to subscriptions, resource groups, and resources. ARM implements OAuth and RBAC within the platform, enabling authorization and access control to resources, resource groups, and subscriptions based on roles assigned to a user or group. A permission defines access to operations on a resource. These permissions could allow or deny access to the resource. A role definition is a collection of these permissions. Roles map AAD users and groups to the permissions. Roles are subsequently assigned to a scope, which can be an individual, collection of resources, resource group, or subscription. The AAD identities (users, groups, and service principles) added to a role gain access to the resource according to permissions defined in the role. ARM provides multiple out-of-the-box roles. It provides system roles, such as **owner**, **contributor**, **reader**, and more. It also provides resource-based roles, such as SQL DB contributor, virtual machine contributor, and more. ARM allows the creation of custom roles.

- **Tags**: Tags are name-value pairs that add additional information and metadata to resources. Both resources and resource groups can be tagged with multiple tags. Tags help in the categorization of resources for better discoverability and manageability. Resources can be quickly searched and identified easily. Billing and cost information can be fetched for resources that have the same tags applied. While this feature is provided by the ARM, an IT administrator defines its usage and taxonomy with regard to resources and resource groups. Taxonomy and tags, for example, can be defined based on departments, resource usage, location, projects, or any other criteria deemed fit from a cost, usage, billing, and search perspective. These tags can then be applied to resources. Tags defined at the resource group level are not inherited by its resources.

- **Policies**: Another security feature provided by ARM are policies. Custom policies can be created to control access to the resources. Policies are defined conventions and rules and must be adhered to while interacting with resources and resource groups. The policy definition contains an explicit denial of actions on resources or access to resources. By default, every access is allowed if it is not mentioned in the policy definition. These policy definitions are assigned to resource, resource group, and subscriptions scope. It is important to note that these policies are not replacements or substitutes for RBAC. In fact, they complement and work together with RBAC. Policies are evaluated after a user is authenticated by AAD and authorized by the RBAC service. ARM provides JSON-based policy definition language for defining policies. Some of the examples of policy definition are that it must tag every provisioned resource or resources can only be provisioned to specific Azure regions.
- **Locks**: Subscriptions, resource groups, and resources can be locked to prevent accidental deletion and updates by an authenticated user. Locks applied at higher levels flow downstream to child resources. Locks applied at subscription level lock every resource group and resources within it.
- **Multi-region**: Azure provides multiple regions for the provisioning and hosting of resources. ARM allows resources to be provisioned at different locations and yet reside within the same resource group. A resource group can contain resources from different regions.
- **Idempotent**: This feature ensures predictability, standardization, and consistency in resource deployment by ensuring that every deployment will result in the same state of resources and their configuration no matter the number of times it is executed.
- **Extensible**: ARM architecture provides an extensible architecture to allow creation and plugging of newer resource providers and resource types into the platform.

Virtualization

Virtualization was a breakthrough innovation that completely changed the way physical servers were looked at. It refers to the abstraction of a physical object into a logical object.

Virtualization of physical servers enabled the creation of multiple virtual servers, better known as virtual machines. These virtual machines consume and share the same physical CPU, memory, storage, and other hardware with the physical server on which they were hosted. This enabled faster and easier provisioning of application environments on demand, providing high availability and scalability with reduced cost. One physical server was enough to host multiple virtual machines, each virtual machine containing its own operating system and hosting services on it.

There was no longer any need to buy additional physical servers for deploying new applications and services. The existing physical servers were sufficient to host more virtual machines. Furthermore, as part of rationalization, many physical servers were consolidated into a few with the help of virtualization.

Each virtual machine contains the entire operating system and each virtual machine is completely isolated from other virtual machines, including the physical hosts. Although a virtual machine uses the hardware provided by the host physical server, it has full control over its assigned resources and its environment. These virtual machines can be hosted on a network such as a physical server with its own identity.

Azure helps in creating Linux and Windows virtual machines in a few minutes. Microsoft provides its own images along with images from partners and the community. Users can bring in their own images. Virtual machines are created using these images.

Containers

Containers are also a virtualization technology; however, they do not virtualize a physical server. Instead, a container is an operating-system-level virtualization. What this means is that containers share the operating system kernel provided by the host among themselves along with the host. Multiple containers running on a host (physical or virtual) share the host operating system kernel. Containers ensure that they reuse the host kernel instead of each having a dedicated kernel to themselves.

Containers are also completely isolated from the host and other containers, such as a virtual machine. Containers use Windows storage filter drivers and session isolation for providing isolation of operating system services such as the filesystem, registry, processes, and networks. Each container gets its own copy of operating system resources.

The container has the perception that it has a completely new and untouched operating system and resources. This arrangement provides lots of benefits, they are as follows:

- Containers are faster to provision. They do not need to provide the operating system and its kernel services. They are available from the host operating system.
- Containers are lightweight and require fewer computing resources compared to virtual machines. The operating system resource overhead is no longer required in containers.
- Containers are much smaller in size compared to virtual machines.
- Containers help in solving the problems related to managing multiple application dependencies in an intuitive, automated, and simple manner.
- Containers provide infrastructure to define all application dependencies in a single place.

Containers are an inherent part and feature of Windows Server 2016 and Windows 10; however, they are managed and accessed using a Docker client and Docker daemon. Containers can be created on Azure with Windows Server 2016 SKU as an image.

Each container has a single main process that must be running for the container to exist. A container will stop when this process ends. Also, a container can either run in interactive mode or in a detached mode like a service.

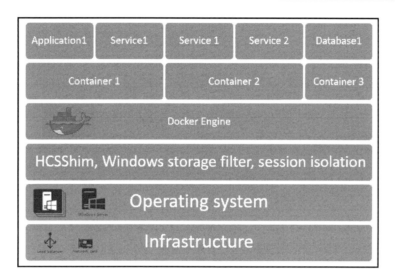

Container architecture

The figure shows all the technical layers that enable containers. The bottommost layer provides the core infrastructure in terms of network, storage, load balancers, and network cards. At the top of the infrastructure is the compute layer, consisting of either a physical server or both physical as well as virtual servers on top of a physical server. This layer contains the operating system with the ability to host containers. The operating system provides the execution driver that the layers above use to call kernel code and objects to execute containers. Microsoft has created **Host Container System Shim** (**HCSShim**) for managing and creating containers and uses Windows storage filter drivers for image and file management.

The container environment isolation ability is provided to the Windows session. Windows Server 2016 and Nano Server provide the operating system and enable the container features and execute the user-level Docker client and Docker engine. The Docker engine uses the services of HCSShim, storage filter drivers, and sessions to spawn multiple containers on the server, each containing a service, application, or database.

Docker

Docker provides management features to Windows containers. It comprises of two executables:

- Docker daemon
- Docker client

The Docker daemon is the workhorse for managing containers. It is a Windows service responsible for managing all activities on the host related to containers. The Docker client interacts with the Docker daemon and is responsible for capturing inputs and sending them across to the Docker daemon. The Docker daemon provides the runtime, libraries, graph drivers, and engine to create, manage, and monitor containers and images on the host server. It also provides capabilities to create custom images that are used for building and shipping applications to multiple environments.

Interacting with intelligent cloud

Azure provides multiple ways to connect, automate, and interact with it. All method require users and codes to be authenticated with valid credentials before they can be used.

- Azure portal
- PowerShell
- Azure **Command Line Interface (CLI)**
- Azure REST API

Azure portal

Azure portal is a great place to get started. With the Azure portal, users can log in and start creating and managing Azure resources manually. The portal provides an intuitive and user-friendly user interface through the browser. The Azure portal provides an easy way to navigate to resources using **blades**. The blades display all properties of a resource, logs, cost, its relationship with other resources, tags, security options, and more. The entire cloud deployment can be managed through the portal.

PowerShell

PowerShell is an object-based command-line shell and scripting language used for administration, configuration, and management of infrastructure and environments. It is built on top of the .NET framework and provides automation capabilities. PowerShell has truly become a first-class citizen among IT administrators and automation developers for managing and controlling the Windows environment. Today, almost every Windows and many Linux environments can be managed by PowerShell. In fact, almost every aspect of Azure can also be managed by PowerShell. Azure provides rich support for PowerShell. It provides a PowerShell module for each resource provider containing hundreds of cmdlets. Users can use these cmdlets in their scripts to automate interacting with Azure. Azure PowerShell module is available through the web platform installer as well as through the **PowerShell Gallery**. Windows Server 2016 and Windows 10 provides package management and PowerShellGet modules for quick and easy downloads and installation of PowerShell modules from the PowerShell gallery. The `PowerShellGet` module provides the `Install-Module` cmdlet for downloading and installing modules on the system. Installing a module is a simple act of copying the module files at well-defined module locations:

```
Import-module PowerShellGet
Install-Module -Name AzureRM -verbose
```

Azure Command-Line Interface (CLI)

Azure also provides Azure CLI 2.0 that can be deployed on Linux, Windows, as well as Mac operating systems. The Azure CLI 2.0 is Azure's new command-line utility for managing Azure resources. Azure CLI 2.0 is optimized for managing and administering Azure resources from the command line, and for building automation scripts that work against the Azure Resource Manager. The command-line interface can be used to execute commands using Bash Shell or Windows command line. Azure CLI is a very famous non-Windows user as it allows us to talk to Azure on Linux and Mac. Steps for installing Azure CLI 2 are available at https://docs.microsoft.com/en-us/cli/azure/install-azure-cli?view=azure-cli-latest.

Azure REST API

All Azure resources are exposed to users through REST endpoints. **Representational State Transfer** (**REST**) APIs are service endpoints that implement HTTP operations (methods), providing **create, retrieve, update,** or **delete** (**CRUD**) access to the service's resources. Users can consume these API's to create and manage resources. In fact, the CLI and PowerShell mechanism uses these REST API's internally to interact with resources on Azure.

Azure Resource Manager templates

In an earlier section, we witnessed deployment features such as multi-service, multi-region, extensible, and idempotent provided by the ARM. ARM templates are primary means of provisioning resources in the ARM. ARM templates provide implementation support for ARM deployment features.

ARM templates provide a declarative model through which resources, their configuration, scripts, and extensions are specified. ARM templates are based on **JavaScript Object Notation** (**JSON**) format. They use the JSON syntax and conventions to declare and configure resources. JSON files are text-based, human-friendly, and easily readable files.

They can be stored in a source code repository and have version control. They are also a means to represent IAC that can be used to provision resources in an Azure resource group again and again, predictably, consistently, and uniformly. A template needs a resource group for deployment. It can only be deployed to a resource group and the resource group should exist before executing a template deployment. A template is not capable of creating a resource group.

Templates provide the flexibility to be generic and modular in their design and implementation. Templates provide the ability to accept parameters from users, declare internal variables, help in defining dependencies between resources, link resources within same or different resource groups, and execute other templates. They also provide scripting language type expressions and functions that make them dynamic and customizable at runtime.

Deployments

PowerShell allows two modes of deployment of templates:

- Incremental
- Complete

Incremental deployment adds resources declared in the template that doesn't exist in a resource group, leaves resources unchanged in a resource group that is not part of a template definition, and leaves resources unchanged in a resource group that exists in both the template and resource group with the same configuration state.

Complete deployment, on the other hand, adds resources declared in a template to the resource group, deletes resources that do not exist in the template from the resource group, and leaves resources unchanged that exist in both the resource group and template with the same configuration state.

Summary

The cloud is not more than 10 years old. It is a new paradigm and still in its nascent stage. There will be a lot of innovation and capabilities added over time. Azure is one of the top cloud providers today and it provides rich capabilities through IaaS, PaaS, SaaS, and hybrid deployments. In fact, Azure stack, which is an implementation of private cloud from Microsoft, will release soon. This will have the same features available on private cloud as that on a public cloud. They both will, in fact, connect and work seamlessly and transparently together. It is very easy to get started with Azure, but also developers and architects can fall into a trap if they do not design and architect their solutions appropriately. This book is an attempt to provide guidance and directions towards architecting solutions the right way using appropriate services and resources. Every service on Azure is a resource. It is important to understand how these resources are organized and managed in Azure. This chapter provided context around Azure Resource Manager and groups--the core framework that provides building blocks for resources. It provides a set of services to resources that help provide uniformity, standardization, and consistency in managing them. The services, such as RBAC, tags, policies, locks, and more are available to every resource provider and resource. Azure also provides rich automation features to automate and interact with resources. Tools such as PowerShell, ARM templates, and Azure CLI can be incorporated as part of release pipelines and continuous deployment and delivery. Users can connect to Azure from heterogeneous environments using these automation tools.

Next chapter will discuss some of the important patterns that help in solving common cloud-based deployment problems and ensure the application is secure, available, scalable, and maintainable in long run.

2
Azure Design Patterns

In the previous chapter, we got an overview of Azure cloud and explained some of the important concepts related to it. This chapter is about Azure cloud patterns related to virtual networks, storage accounts, regions, and availability sets. These are important constructs that affect the final architecture delivered to customers in terms of cost, efficiencies, and overall productivity. This chapter will also briefly discuss cloud patterns that help in implementing scalability and performance within the overall architecture.

In this chapter, we'll cover the following topics:

- Azure virtual network design
- Azure storage design
- Azure zones, regions, and availability sets
- Azure design patterns related to the following:
  - Messaging
  - Performance
  - Scalability

Azure zones and regions

Azure cloud is backed up by large data centers interconnected into a single large network. The data centers are grouped together based on their physical proximity to Azure regions. For example, a couple of data centers in Western Europe together are available to Azure users as the West Europe region. Users cannot control which data center that is, the exact data center for their deployment. They can inform Azure about the region and Azure will pick an appropriate data center.

Choosing an appropriate region is an important architectural decision as it affects the following:

- Availability of resources
- Data and privacy compliance
- Performance of applications
- Cost of running applications

Availability of resources

Not all resources are available in every Azure region. If application architecture demands a resource and it is not available in a region, choosing that region will not help. Instead, a region should be chosen based on the availability of all resources required by the application. It might be so that the resource might not be available while developing the application architecture and could be on the Azure roadmap to make it available subsequently.

For example, log analytics is not available in all regions. Data transfer to log analytics would incur egress network cost if the application is deployed in a region that does not have log analytics (previously known as **operational management suite**). Similarly, Azure key vault provides services to only resources that are co-located in the same region. Another example is that an Azure virtual network can host virtual machines, load balancers from same regions. Virtual machines from different regions cannot be part of the same virtual network.

Data and privacy compliance

Each country has its own rules for data and privacy compliance. Some countries are very specific that their and their citizen's data cannot be stored in any other country. These are legal requirements and should be taken into architectural consideration for an application.

Performance of applications

The performance of an application is dependent on the network route that was taken by requests and response from users. If an Azure region is near the users of the application, users will get better performance from the application compared to users far away from the Azure region. An application deployed in Western Europe for users in south-east Asia will not perform as well as an application deployed at East Asia region for users in in south-east Asia.

Cost of running applications

The cost of Azure services differs from region to region. A region with an overall cheaper cost should be chosen. There is a complete chapter on cost management in this book and it should be referred to for more details from the cost perspective.

Virtual network

A **virtual network** should be thought of as a physical LAN network in your office or home. Conceptually, they both are the same, although the Azure virtual network is implemented as a software-defined network backed up by a giant physical network infrastructure.

A virtual network is required for hosting a virtual machine. They provide a secure communication mechanism between Azure resources to connect to each other. They provide an internal IP address to them, access, and connectivity to other resources including virtual machines on the same virtual network, routing of requests, and connectivity to other networks.

A virtual network is contained within a resource group and is hosted within a region, for example, West Europe. Virtual network cannot span multiple regions, but it can span all data centers with a region. For connectivity across regions, virtual networks can be connected using the VNET-to-VNET connectivity. The virtual network also helps in connecting to on-premise data centers enabling hybrid cloud. There are multiple types of VPN technologies available to connect to on-premise data centers such as site-to-site VPN and point-to-site VPN. There is also a dedicated connectivity available between Azure virtual network and on-premise network using **ExpressRoute**.

A virtual network is free of charge. Every subscription can create up to 50 virtual networks across all regions. However, it can be increased by reaching out to Azure support. There will be no charge for data transfer within a VNET

 Information about networking limits is available at `https://docs.microsoft.com/en-us/azure/azure-subscription-servic e-limits#networking-limits`.

Architectural considerations for virtual networks

Virtual networks like any other resource can be provisioned using ARM templates, REST API's, PowerShell, and CLI. It is quite important to plan the network topology at the beginning stage itself to avoid troubles later in the development life cycle. This is because once the network is provisioned and resources start using it, it is difficult to change it without having a downtime. For example, for moving a virtual machine from one network to another will require the virtual machine to shut down.

- **Regions**: The virtual network is an Azure resource and is provisioned within a region such as West Europe. Applications spanning multiple regions will need separate virtual networks, one per region, and they also need to be connected using the VNET-to-VNET connectivity. There is a cost associated with VNET-to-VNET connectivity for both inbound and outbound traffic. There are no charges for inbound (ingress) data; however, there are charges associated with outbound data.
- **Dedicated DNS**: Virtual networks by default use Azure provided DNS to resolve names within a virtual network and it also allows name resolution on the internet. If the application wants a dedicated name resolution service or wants to connect to the on-premise data centers, it should provide its own DNS server and they should be configured within the virtual network for successful name resolution.
- **Network performance**: Every virtual network has a defined throughput, and it is wise to create a separate virtual network to have a consistent performance instead of putting all network related resources on a single network. This might clog the network.
- **Number of virtual networks**: The number of virtual networks is affected by the number of regions, bandwidth usage by services, cross-region connectivity, and security.

- **Number of subnets in each virtual network**: Subnets provide isolation within a virtual network. It is also a security boundary. Network security groups can be associated with subnets thereby restricting or allowing specific access to IP addresses and ports. Application components having separate security and accessibility requirements should be placed within separate subnets.
- **IP ranges for networks and subnets**: Each subnet has an IP range. The IP range should not be large enough to be underutilized them while other subnets are getting suffocated because of lack of IP addresses. It should have just enough IP addresses to meet current and future requirements. This should be considered after understanding the future IP address needs of the deployment.

Planning should be done for IP addressing and ranges for Azure networks, subnets and on-premise data centers. There should not be an overlap for seamless connectivity and accessibility.

- **Monitoring**: Monitoring is an important architectural facet and is a must to be included in the overall deployment architecture. **Azure Network Watcher** provides logging and diagnostic capabilities with insights into network performance and health. It provides capabilities to watch both inbound or outbound packets to and from virtual machines, whether they are allowed or denied, next hop flow for validating the configuration of user-defined routes, an audit of network security, capturing packets along with subscription limits. It also provides diagnostic logs for all the network resources in a resource group.

Network performance can be monitored through log analytics. The network performance monitor management solution provides network monitoring capability. It monitors the health, availability, and reachability of networks. It is also used to monitor connectivity between public cloud and on-premises and subnets hosting various tiers of a multi-tiered application.

- **Security considerations**: Virtual networks are one of the first components that is accessed by any resource on Azure. Security plays an important role to allow or deny access to the resource. **Network security groups** (NSG) are the primary means of enabling security for virtual networks. They can be attached to virtual network subnets and every inbound and outbound flow is constrained, filtered, and allowed to them.

User-defined routing (UDR) and IP forwarding also helps in filtering and routing requests to resources on Azure.

 You can read more about UDR and forced tunneling at `https://docs.` `microsoft.com/en-us/azure/virtual-network/virtual-networks-udr-` `overview`.

Resources can also be secured and protected by deploying network appliances such as barracuda, F5, and other third-party components.

 You can read more about them at `https://azure.microsoft.com/en-in/solutions/network-appliances` `/`.

- **Deployment**: Virtual networks should be deployed in its own dedicated resource groups. Network administrators should have owner permission on this resource group, while developers or team members should have contributor permissions for allowing them to create another Azure resource in other resource groups consuming services from the virtual network.

It is also good practice to deploy resources with static IP addresses in a dedicated subnet, while dynamic IP address related resources can be on another subnet.

Policies should be created so that only network administrators can delete the virtual network, and it should also be tagged for billing purposes.

- **Connectivity**: Resources in a region on a virtual network can talk seamlessly. Even resources on other subnets within a virtual network can talk to each other without any explicit configuration. Resources in multiple regions cannot use the same virtual network. The boundary of a virtual network is within a region. To make resources available across regions, communicate with each dedicated gateway, which is required on each end to facilitate conversation. The networks on each end are connected to other networks through these gateways.

However, resources on Azure also at times have connectivity needs to on-premise data centers. Azure virtual networks can connect to on-premise data centers using VPN technology and ExpressRoute. In fact, one virtual network is capable of connecting to multiple on-premise data centers and other Azure regions in parallel. As a best practice, each of these connections should be in their dedicated subnets within a virtual network.

Benefits of virtual networks

Virtual networks are a must for deploying any meaningful IaaS solution. Virtual machines cannot be provisioned without virtual networks. Apart from being almost a mandatory component in solutions, it brings great architectural benefits and the most important among them are the following:

- **Isolation**: Most application components have separate security and bandwidth requirements and have different life cycle management. Virtual networks help in creating isolated pockets for these components that can be managed independently of other components with the help of virtual networks and subnets.
- **Security**: Filtering and tracking who is accessing resources is an important feature provided by virtual networks. They can stop access to a malicious IP address and port.
- **Extensibility**: Virtual networks act such as a private LAN on the cloud. It can also be extended into WAM by connecting other virtual networks across the globe and can be extended as an extension to on-premise data centers.

Virtual network design

In this section, we will consider some of the popular design and usage of virtual networks.

There can be multiple usages of virtual networks. A gateway can be deployed at each virtual network endpoint to enable security and transmit packets with integrity and confidentiality. A gateway is a must when connecting to on-premise networks, however, it is optional when using virtual network peering.

Connecting to resources within the same region and subscription

Multiple virtual networks within the same region and subscription can be connected to each other. With the help of virtual network peering, both networks can be connected and would use the Azure private network backbone for transmitting packets among each other. Virtual machines and services on these networks can talk to each other, subject to network traffic constraints.

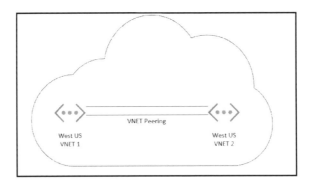

Connecting to resources within the same region in another subscription

This usage is very much like the previous one, however, the additional complexity is that another network is on another subscription. If both the subscriptions belong to the same tenant, then they can be connected using virtual network peering as discussed before. It would also use Azure's private network backbone for transmitting packets among each other.

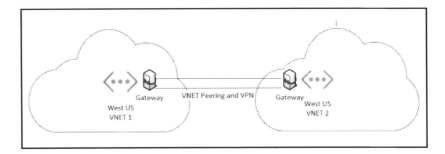

Gateways can be used along with peering

Connecting to resources in different regions in another subscription

In this scenario, the traffic will pass through the public network and the virtual network peering should be deployed along with gateways to encrypt the traffic using VPN.

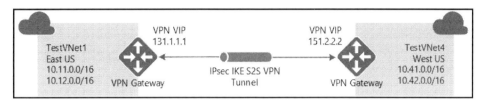

Connecting to on-premise data centers

Virtual networks can be connected to on-premise data centers such that both Azure and an on-premise data center becomes a single **Wide Area Network** (**WAN**). Connecting on-premise network needs deployment on gateways and virtual private networks on both sides of the network. There are three different technologies available for this purpose:

- **Site to site VPN**: This should be used when both Azure network and on-premise should be connected to form a WAN where any resource on both networks can access any other resource on them irrespective of Azure or an on-premise data center. VPN gateways are required to be available on both sides of networks for security reasons. Also, Azure gateways should be deployed on their own subnets on the virtual network connecting to on-premise data centers. Public IP addresses must be assigned to on-premise gateways for Azure to connect to it over the public network.

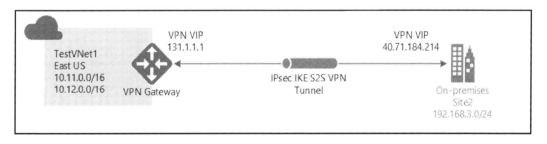

- **Point to site VPN**: This is similar to site-to-site VPN connectivity, however, there is a single server or computer attached to the on-premise data center. It should be used when there are very few users or clients that would connect to Azure securely from remote locations. Also, there is no need for public IP and gateway on the on-premise side in this case.

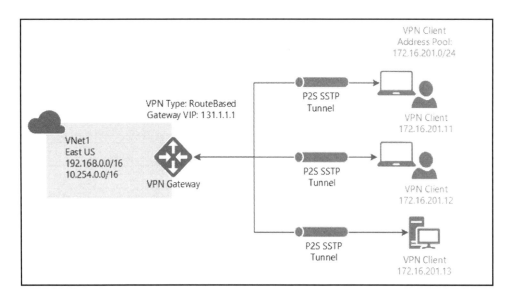

- **ExpressRoute**: Both site-to-site and point-to-site VPN work using the public internet. They encrypt the traffic between the network using VPN and certificates technology. However, there are applications that are deployed in hybrid mode. Some of its resources are hosted on Azure and others on on-premise data center. Even though resources are hosted on Azure, these resources should not use public internet for connectivity to on-premise data center. Azure ExpressRoute is the best solution for them, although a costly option compared to Site to site and point to site VPN connectivity. It is highly secure and reliable connectivity providing much greater speed and reduced latency compared to other VPN technologies. This is because the traffic never uses public internet but rather used dedicated connections with service providers. Azure ExpressRoute helps in extending on-premises networks into Azure over a dedicated private connection facilitated by a connectivity provider

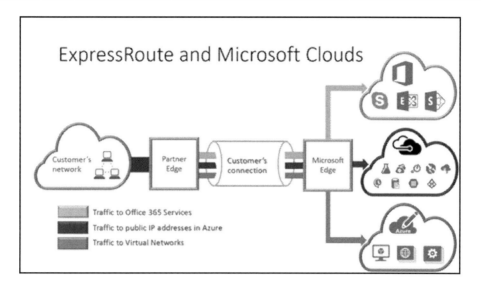

The following figure shows all three types of hybrid networks:

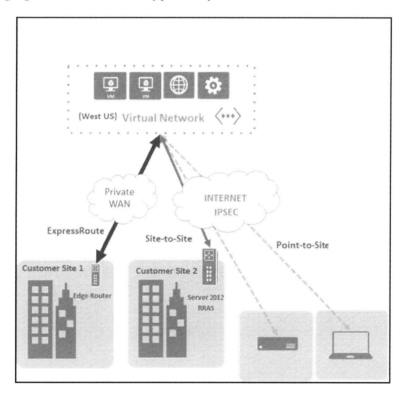

It is a good practice for virtual networks to have separate subnets for each logical component having separate deployments from security and isolation perspectives.

Storage

Azure provides durable, highly available, and scalable storage solutions through storage services.

Storage is used for persisting data for long-term needs. Azure storage is available through the internet from almost every programming language.

Storage categories

Storage has two categories of storage accounts:

- A standard storage performance tier that allows you to store tables, queues, files, blobs, and Azure virtual machine disks.
- A premium storage performance tier supporting Azure virtual machine disks at the time of writing. Premium storage provides higher performance and IOPS compared to standard general storage. Premium storage is currently available as data disks for virtual machines are backed up by SSD's.

Storage types

Azure provides four types of general storage services as shown in the following diagram:

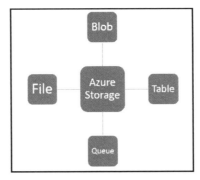

- **Blob storage**: This type of storage is best suitable for unstructured data such as documents, images, and other kinds of files. Blob storage can be hot or cold. Hot means that content within the blob storage is accessed frequently compared to the cold tier.
- **Table storage**: It is a NoSQL key-attribute data store. It should be used for structured data. The data is stored as entities.
- **Queue storage**: It provides reliable message storage.
- **File storage**: This is shared storage based on SMB protocol. It is typically used for storing and sharing files. This also stores unstructured data, but the main distinction is that it is sharable on the SMB protocol.

These four storage types cater to different architectural requirements and cover almost all types of data storage facilities.

Storage features

Azure storage is elastic. It means that you can store as little as a few megabytes to as large as petabytes of data. You do not need to pre-block the capacity and it will grow and shrink automatically. Consumers just need to pay for the actual usage of storage.

Azure storage is secure. It can only be accessed using the SSL protocol. Moreover, access should be authenticated. Azure storage provides the facility to generate an account level **Secure Access Signature** (**SAS**) token that can be used by storage clients to authenticate themselves. It is also possible to generate individual service level SAS tokens for blobs, queues, table, and files. Data stored in Azure storage can be encrypted. This is known as secure data at rest. Azure disk encryption is used to encrypt the OS and data disks in IaaS virtual machines. **Client-side Encryption** (**CSE**) and **Storage Service Encryption** (**SSE**)--are both used to encrypt data in the Azure storage. SSE is a storage account-wide setting that ensures that data is encrypted while writing data to storage and is decrypted while reading by storage engine. This ensures that no application changes are required to enable SSE. In CSE, client applications can use storage SDK to encrypt data before sending and writing to Azure storage. The client application can later decrypt it while reading. This provides both data in transit and data at rest security. CSE is dependent on secrets from the Azure key vault. There is another service Azure disk encryption used to encrypt the OS and data disks in IaaS virtual machines.

Azure storage is highly available and durable. What this means is that Azure always maintains multiple copies of Azure accounts. The location and number of copies depend on the replication configuration. Azure provides four replication settings. These settings have implications on both cost as well as availability during disaster. Locally redundant storage is cheapest and provides least availability compared to others while Read access geo-redundant is costliest and provides high availability.

- **Locally redundant storage**: **Locally redundant storage** (**LRS**) replicates and maintains three copies of storage within same data center of a region. It means data is highly available within a data center only. Storage will be lost or unavailable if for any reason this data center goes down. It follows the synchronous pattern for write operations meaning write to all replicas is regarded as a success. A write request is successful only after it is written to all three replicas. However, Azure ensures fault tolerance from storage disk and rack perspective. It does so by placing the three replicas in different fault and upgrade domains. Fault and upgrade domains are discussed in detail in the next chapter.
- **Zone-redundant storage**: **Zone-redundant storage** (**ZRS**) is costlier than locally redundant storage because apart from three copies in the same data center, it also stores data into another data center as well within a region. Since multiple data center is involved, to maintain performance and latency SLA writes to all storages happens asynchronously.
- **Geo-redundant storage**: **Geo-redundant storage** (**GRS**) provides better durability and availability compared to zone redundancy by replicating storage to another region apart from local redundancy. This is also one of the costliest options but provides disaster recovery at the region level.
- **Read-access geo-redundant storage**: **Read-access geo-redundant storage** (**RAGRS**) is similar to Geo-redundancy but it additionally provides read-only access to replicas.

Architectural considerations for storage accounts

Storage account should be provisioned within the same region as that of other application components. This would help in using the same data center network backbone without incurring any network charges.

Each of the Azure storage services has scalability targets for capacity (GB), transaction rate, and bandwidth. A general storage account allows 500 TB of data to be stored. If there is a need to store more than 500 TB of data, then either multiple storage accounts should be created, or premium storage should be used. General storage performs max at 20000 IOPS or 60 MB of data per second. Any requirement for higher IOPS or data managed per second will be throttled. If this is not enough for applications from the performance perspective, either premium storage or multiple storage accounts should be used.

The size of a virtual machine determines the size and capacity of data disks available. While higher sized virtual machines have data disks with higher IOPS capacity, the max capacity will still be limited to 20000 IOPS and 60 MB per second. It is to be noted that these are maximum numbers and so generally lower levels should be taken into consideration when finalizing storage architecture.

 For more information about bandwidth and storage performance details, check out the link https://docs.microsoft.com/en-us/azure/storage/common/storage-performance-checklist.

Azure storage accounts should be enabled for authentication using SAS tokens. They should not be allowed for anonymous access. Moreover, for blob storage, different containers should be created having separate SAS tokens generated based on different types and categories of clients accessing those containers. These SAS tokens should be periodically regenerated to ensure that these keys cannot be guessed or cracked by anyone.

Generally, blobs fetched for blob storage accounts should be cached and it can be determined that data in a cache is stale by comparing the blob's last modified property to re-fetch the latest blob.

Azure storage account provides concurrency features to ensure that the same file and data is not modified simultaneously by multiple users. It provides the following:

- **Optimistic concurrency**: It allows multiple users to modify data simultaneously, but while writing checks if the file or data has changed. If it has, it informs the users to re-fetch the data and performs the update again. This is the default concurrency for table service.
- **Pessimistic concurrency**: When an application tries to update a file, it places a lock that explicitly denies any updates to it by other users. This is the default concurrency for file services when accessed using SMB protocol.
- **Last writer wins**: In this, the updates are not constrained, and the last user updates the file irrespective of what was read initially. This is the default concurrency for both queue, blob, and file (when accessed using REST) services.

Design patterns

Design patterns are proven solutions to known design problems. They are reusable solutions that can be applied to problems. They are not reusable codes or designs that can be incorporated as is within a solution. They are documented descriptions and guidance to solve a problem. The problem might manifest itself in a different context and design patterns can help solve them. Azure provides numerous services with each service providing a specific feature and capability. Using these services is straightforward, but creating solutions weaving multiple services can be a challenge. Moreover, achieving high availability, super-scalability, reliability, performance, and security for a solution is not a menial task. Azure design patterns provide ready solutions to these problems and provide solutions that can be tailor-made to individual solutions. They help in making highly available, scalable, reliable, secure, and performance-centric solutions on Azure. Although there are many patterns and some of the patterns are dealt in detail in the subsequent chapters, some of the messaging, performance, and scalability patterns are mentioned in this chapter. Also, links are provided for the detailed description of these patterns. These design patterns deserve a complete book by themselves. They have been mentioned here to make the readers aware of their existence and provide links for deeper information.

Messaging patterns

Messaging patterns help in connecting services in a loosely coupled manner. What it means is that services never talk to each other directly. Instead, a service generates and sends a message to a broker (generally a queue) and any other service that is interested in that message can pick it and process it. There is no direct communication between the sender and receiver service. This decouples not only makes services and overall application more reliable, but also more robust and fault tolerant. Receivers can receive and read messages at their own capable speed.

Messaging helps in creating asynchronous patterns. Messaging involves sending messages from one entity to another. These messages are created and forwarded by a sender, stored at durable storage, and finally consumed by recipients.

The top architectural concerns addressed by messaging are the following:

- **Durability**: Messages are stored in durable storage and the application can read it later after they come up in case of prior failure
- **Reliability**: Messages help in implementing reliability with design since messages are not lost because they are persisted in disk
- **Availability of messages**: The messages are available for consumption by applications after restoration of connectivity and prior downtime

Azure provides service bus queues and topics to implement messaging patterns within applications. Storage queue can also be used for the same purpose.

Choosing between Azure service bus queue and storage queue is to decide between how long the message should be stored, size of the message, latency, and cost.

Azure service bus provides support for 256 KB message size, while storage queue provides support for 64 KB message size. Azure service bus can store messages for an unlimited period, while storage queue can store messages for seven days.

The cost and latency are higher in case of service bus queues.

Depending on application requirements and needs the preceding factors should be employed before deciding the best queue.

Competing consumers

A single consumer of messages works in a synchronous manner unless the application itself implements the logic of reading messages asynchronously. Competing consumers pattern helps in implementing a solution in which multiple consumers are ready to process the incoming message and they compete to process it. This helps in architecting solutions that are highly available and scalable. It is scalable because with multiple consumers it is possible to process a higher number of messages in the smaller period. It is highly available because there could be at least one or more consumers to process the messages even if some consumers crash.

This pattern should be used when each message is independent of other messages. The messages by themselves contain complete information for a consumer to complete a task. This pattern should not be used if there is any dependency among messages. The consumers should be able to complete the tasks in isolation. Also, this pattern is applicable if there is variable demand for services. Additional consumers can be added or removed based on demand.

A message queue is required for implementing competing consumers pattern. In this pattern, patterns from multiple sources pass through a single queue that is connected to multiple consumers on another end. These consumers should delete the message after reading it so that it is not re-processed again.

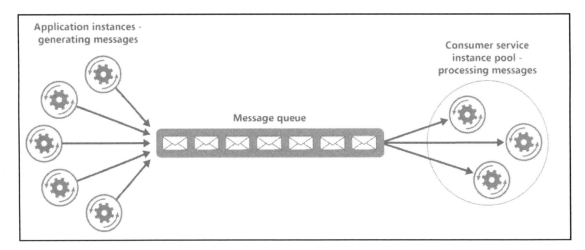

More about this pattern can be read at
`https://docs.microsoft.com/en-us/azure/architecture/patterns/com`
`peting-consumers`.

Priority queue

There is often a need when messages with higher importance should be given priority in processing compared to general messages with lower priority. This pattern is important for applications that provide different **service level agreements** (**SLA**) to consumers, which provide services based on different plans and subscriptions.

Queues follow first-in, first-out patterns. Messages are processed in sequence. However, with the help of this pattern, it is possible to fast-track processing of certain messages due to their higher priority. There are multiple ways to implement it. If the queue provides the capability of assigning priority and based on priority re-order messages, then even a single queue is enough to implement this pattern.

However, if the queue does not have the capability to re-order messages, then separate queues can be created for different priorities and each queue can have separate consumers associated with it.

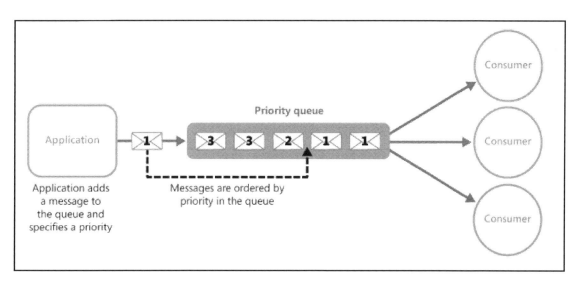

In fact, this pattern can reuse competing consumer patterns if needed to fast-track processing of messages from each queue using multiple consumers.

More about this pattern can be read at
`https://docs.microsoft.com/en-us/azure/architecture/patterns/priority-queue`.

Queue-based load leveling pattern

There are times when the load on an application cannot be determined at all times. Although there is consistent and predictable demand for application for most of the times, there are times when this load can go very high leading to failure of service or providing reduced performance or non-availability. Queue-based load leveling pattern can help during such scenarios. In this pattern, a queue is maintained and all request for the service is stored as messages within this queue. The queue acts as a highly available and durable temporary storage that then sends messages to service at a controlled speed thereby reducing disruption at the service end. The same has been shown in next image. There are multiple tasks sending messages to message queue. The queue stores the messages and ensures that the service gets these messages at a speed consistent with the resources available at the service end.

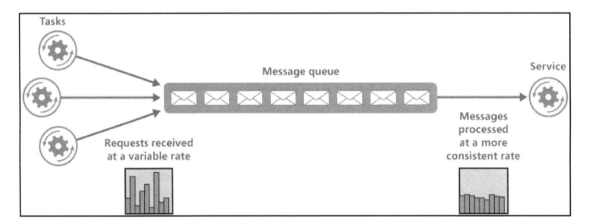

This pattern ensures that there is no unnecessary scaling up and out of resources by provisioning more instances to meet higher service demand. It has a direct impact on cost as well due to predictable usage and instances of resources.

High availability and better scalability are other advantages derived by implementing this pattern.

Performance and scalability patterns

Performance and scalability go hand in hand. Performance refers to the responsiveness of a system to execute any action within a given time interval, while scalability is the ability of a system to handle increases in load without impact on performance. In this section, a couple of design patterns related to performance and scalability are described.

The Command and Query Responsibility Segregation (CQRS) pattern

CQRS is a generic pattern that has applicability in any scenario that has data stored in a data store and it should be accessed in a way to increase the overall performance and responsiveness of the application.

Data operations can broadly be classified into read and write operations. There are multiple ways to read and write to the data store and there is often a data access layer and component responsible for carrying out these operations. This data access component has information about connecting the data store and performs both read and write operations. Performing both operations from within a single interface can be challenging from performance perspective especially if the data is large and the read-write ration is skewed.

Command and Query Responsibility Segregation (CQRS) is a pattern that helps in implementing read and write operations using different interfaces. It means the components implementing the read operations are separate from write operations and can be individually deployed on a separate instance. This helps in providing dedicated resource capacity to them. This pattern also helps in scenarios where execution time for read and write operations is significantly large and consume more resources

CQRS not only helps in improving the performance of the application, but it also helps in design and implementation between multiple teams. Due to its nature of using separate models. CQRS pattern is not a great fit if using model and scaffolding generation tools.

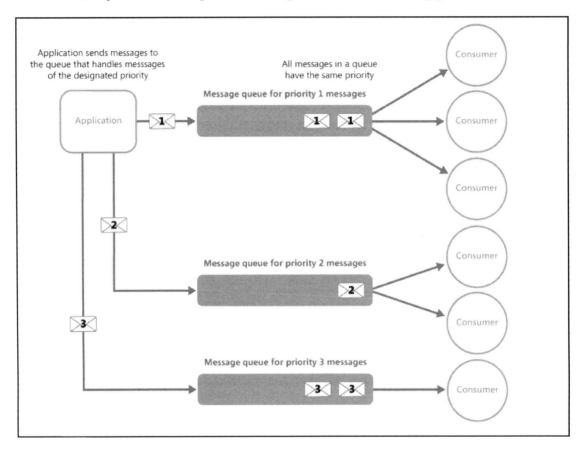

 More about this pattern can be read at
https://docs.microsoft.com/en-us/azure/architecture/patterns/cqr
s.

Throttling pattern

At times, there are applications that have very stringent--SLA requirements from performance and scalability perspective irrespective of a number of users consuming the service. In such circumstances, it is important to implement throttling patterns because they help in limiting the number of requests allowed to be executed. The load on applications cannot be predicted accurately for all circumstances. When the load on application spikes, throttling helps in reducing pressure on the servers and services by controlling the resource consumption.

This pattern should be used when meeting SLA is a priority for applications, to prevent some users to consume more resources than allocated, to optimize spikes and burst in demand, and to cost optimize the resource consumption. These are valid scenarios for applications built to be deployed on the cloud.

There can be multiple strategies used for throttling an application. The throttling strategy can reject newer requests once the threshold is crossed, or it can let the user know that the request is in the queue and will get an opportunity to be executed once the number of requests gets reduced.

The following diagram illustrates implementing throttling in a multi-tenant system where each tenant is allocated a fixed resource usage limit. Once they cross this limit, any additional demand for resources is constrained, thereby maintaining enough resources for other tenants.

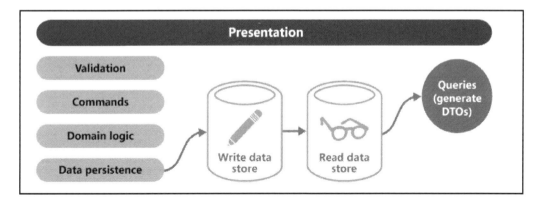

 More about this pattern can be read at
https://docs.microsoft.com/en-us/azure/architecture/patterns/throttling.

Other patterns

Some of the other important patterns are described in this section.

Retry pattern

The retry pattern is an extremely important pattern to make applications and services more resilient to transient failures. Think about a situation that you are trying to connect and use the service, and the service is not available due to any reason. If the service is going to come up in short duration, it makes sense to keep retrying for a successful connection. This will make the application more robust, fault tolerant, and bring instability. In Azure, most of the components are running on the internet and that internet connection can produce transient faults intermittently. Because of these failures that rectify within seconds, an application should not be allowed to crash. The application should be designed in a manner that it can re-try to use the service repeatedly during failures. It should also stop retrying if even after certain number of retries the service is not available.

This pattern should be implemented when an application could experience transient faults as it interacts with a remote server or accesses a remote resource. These faults are expected to be short-lived, and repeating a request that has previously failed could succeed on a subsequent attempt.

The retry pattern can adopt different retry strategies based on the nature of errors and application:

- **Retry a fixed number of times**: It denotes that the application will try to communicate to the service a fixed number of times before it can determine a failure and raise an exception. For example, retry three times to connect to another service. If it is successful in connecting within these three tries, the entire operation is successful, or after the expiry of this count, it will raise an exception.
- **Retry based on schedule**: It denotes that the application will try to communicate to the service repeatedly for a fixed number of seconds or minutes and wait for a fixed number of seconds or minutes before retrying. For example, retrying every three seconds for 60 seconds to connect to another service. If it is successful in connecting within these tries, the entire operation is successful, or after the expiry of 60 seconds, it will raise an exception.

- **Sliding and delaying the retry**: It denotes that the application will try to communicate to the service repeatedly based on schedule and keeps adding an incremental delay in subsequent tries. For example, retrying for a total of 60 seconds where the first retry happens after one second, the second try happens after two seconds from the last retry, the third one after four seconds from the last try, and so on. This helps in reducing the overall number of retries.

The retry pattern is depicted by means of a picture where the first request gets HTTP **500** as a response message, the second retry again gets HTTP **500** as a response, and finally, the request is successful and gets HTTP **200** as a response message.

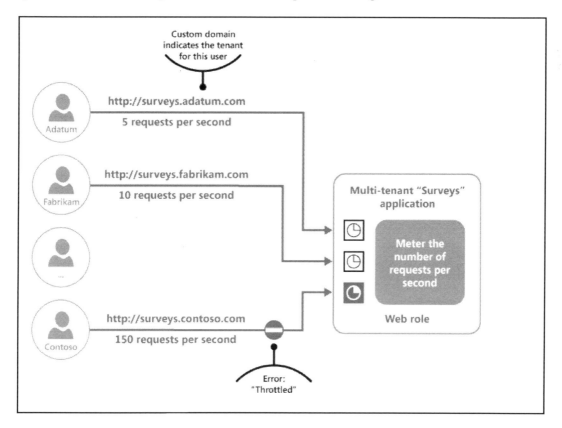

 More about this pattern can be read at
https://docs.microsoft.com/en-us/azure/architecture/patterns/retry.

Circuit breaker pattern

This is an extremely useful pattern. Think again about a situation that you are trying to connect to and use the service, and the service is not available due to any reason. If the service is not going to come up in a short duration, it is no use to keep retrying for connection. Moreover, keeping other resources occupied while retrying wastes a lot of resources that could potentially be used elsewhere.

The circuit breaker pattern helps eliminate such wastage of resources. It can prevent applications from repeatedly trying to connect and use a service that is not available. It also helps applications to detect whether the service is up and running again and eventually allows applications to connect to it.

To implement the circuit breaker pattern, all requests to the service should pass through another service. This service that acts as a proxy to the original service. The purpose of this proxy service is to maintain a state machine and acts as a gateway to the original service. There are three states that it maintains. There can be more states that could be included based on application requirements.

The minimal states needed to implement this pattern are the following:

- **Open**: It denotes that the service is down, and the application is shown an exception immediately instead of allowing it to retry or wait for the timeout. When the service is alive again, the state is transitioned to Half-Open state.
- **Closed**: This state denotes that the service is healthy and that the application can go ahead and connect to it. Generally, a counter is maintained for maintaining the number of failures before it can transition to the Open state.
- **Half-Open**: At some point, as the service is up and running, this state allows a limited number of requests to pass through it. This state is a litmus test checking if the request that passes through it is successful or not. If it is successful, the state is transitioned from Half-Open to Closed. This state can also implement a counter to allow a certain number of requests to be successful before it can transition to the Closed state.

The preceding mentioned states and their transition is shown here:

More about this pattern can be read at
https://docs.microsoft.com/en-us/azure/architecture/patterns/cir
cuit-breaker.

Summary

There are numerous services available on Azure and most can be combined to create real solutions. It was difficult to write about design patterns in 20 pages where there are hundreds of services and multiple ways to bring them together. This chapter explained the three most important services from Azure--regions, storage, and networks. They almost form the backbone of every solution deployed on any cloud. This chapter provided details about these services and how their configuration and provisioning can affect design decisions. The important considerations for both storage and networks were detailed in this chapter. Both networks and storage provide lots of choices and it is important to choose an appropriate configuration based on requirement. Finally, some of the important design patterns related to messaging such as competing consumers, priority queues, and load leveling were described. Patterns related to CQRS and throttling were illustrated and other patterns such as retry, and circuit breaker were discussed.

Next chapter will be an interesting chapter discussing High Availability options available in Azure for deploying workloads.

3
Designing High Availability

Running applications and systems that are available to users for consumption whenever they need is one of the top most priorities for CIO's. They want their applications to be operational, functional, and continue to be available to their customers even when some untoward event happens, and this is the theme for this chapter--High Availability. *Keeping the lights on* is the common metaphor used for High Availability. Achieving High Availability for applications is not an easy task and organizations have to spend considerable time, energy, resources, and money to achieve this. And even when using them, there are still chances and risks that their implementation does not produce the desired results. Azure provides a lot of High Availability features for **virtual machines (VMs)** and PaaS services. In this chapter, we will go through the architectural and design features provided by Azure for ensuring High Availability for applications and services.

In this chapter, we'll cover the following topics:

- Azure availability sets:
  - Fault domain
  - Upgrade domain
- Azure load balancer
- Azure application gateways

High Availability

High Availability is one of the major architectural concerns for any architect. It forms one of the core non-functional technical requirements for any serious service and its deployment. High Availability refers to the feature of a service or application that keeps it operational on a continuous basis, meeting or surpassing its promised defined **service level agreement** (**SLA**). Users are promised certain SLA on the availability of a service. The service should be available for consumption based on its SLA. For example, an SLA can have 99% availability for an application for the entire year (assuming 365 days). It means it should be available for consumption by users for 361.35 days. If it goes less than this, there is a breach of SLA. Most mission-critical applications define their High Availability SLA with five nines for a year. It means the application should be up, running, and available throughout the year, but it can be down and not available only for 5.2 hours.

It is important to note here that High Availability is defined in terms of time that is yearly, monthly, weekly, and so on and it could even be a combination of these.

A service or application is made up of multiple components and these components are deployed on separate tiers and layers. Moreover, it is deployed on an operating system and hosted on a physical or virtual machine. It consumes network and storage services for various purposes. It might even be dependent on external systems. For these services or applications to be highly available it is important that networks, storage, operating system, virtual or physical machines, each component of the application is architected and designed keeping SLA and High Availability in mind. There should be a definite application life cycle process that should be used to ensure High Availability is baked from the start of application planning until its introduction to operations. It also involves architecting for redundancy. There should be redundant resources included in overall application and deployment architecture to ensure that if one goes down, the other takes over and serves the requests of the customer.

SLA

SLA is defined on Wikipedia as:

> *"A service-level agreement is an agreement between two or more parties, where one is the customer, and the others are service providers. Particular aspects of the service - quality, availability, responsibilities - are agreed between the service provider and the service user. The most common component of SLA is that the services should be provided to the customer as agreed upon in the contract".*

Factors affecting High Availability

Planned maintenance, unplanned maintenance, and application deployment architecture are the major factors affecting High Availability of an application.

Planned maintenance

Planned maintenance refers to the process of keeping the application and its surrounding ecosystem comprising of platforms, frameworks, software, operating system, and host and guest drivers up to date with the latest stable releases. It is important to patch software's, drivers, and operating systems with the latest updates as it helps in keeping the environment healthy from a security, performance, and future-ready perspective. Not upgrading an environment is not an option and is a fact of life. Even applications should be upgraded with enhanced functionality, bugs, and hotfixes. Every organization plans for environment and application upgrades and typically these involve shutting down and restarting the application and operating system. It might also involve starting of the physical host operating system that in turn will reboot all guest virtual machines running on top of it.

Unplanned maintenance

As the name suggests, unplanned maintenance refers to maintenance that cannot be planned and is ad hoc in nature. These refer to hardware failures such as storage corruption, network or router failure, power loss, and a host of other failures due to hardware and software. Bugs in underlying platform bringing the application down are also part of unplanned maintenance.

Application deployment architecture

Application architecture plays a crucial role to ensure High Availability of an application. An application whose components are deployed on a single machine is not highly available. When the machine reboots, the application is not available to its users. Similarly, depending on a single instance of a resource can become a single point of failure from a High Availability point of view. Each component of application should be designed in a manner that it can be deployed on multiple machines and redundancy should not be a bottleneck. Some software provides features related to High Availability and are not dependent on host operating systems or other third-party tools. SQL server availability groups is an example of such features.

High Availability versus scalability

High Availability is different than scalability although both are serious architectural concerns. Scalability refers to flexibility and elasticity to add more or reduce resources to existing deployment to accommodate more users than normal without comprising on application performance. Scalability indirectly helps in making an application highly available. However, it does not mean scalability eventually leads to High Availability. High Availability is an architectural concern that is not dependent on the number of users, while scalability rules are determined by a number of users consuming the service. High Availability could be a requirement even if there are very few users. High Availability talks about services being present and operational as and when users demand its consumption. It is a function of consumption based on SLA. Scalability is the topic of the next chapter and it will be discussed in more detail.

High Availability versus disaster recovery

High Availability is again different from disaster recovery; however, the difference could be very subtle. High Availability is a function of the application being in a consumable state as and when the user asks for it. So, it is designed for operations that are before a disaster, while disaster recovery is a function that comes into the picture after a disaster. Disaster recovery refers to the architecture implementation through which services are up and running after a disaster, while High Availability takes care of availability before a disaster. Disaster recovery includes data backup, archived and dormant servers across continents, while High Availability consists of load balancers, distribution of load, active-passive, and active-active redundancy.

Azure High Availability

Achieving High Availability that meets high SLA requirements is a tough requirement. Azure provides lots of features that enable High Availability for applications from the host and guest operating system to applications using its PaaS. Architects can use these features to get High Availability in their applications using configuration instead of building these features by scratch or being dependent on third-party tools.

In this section, we will see features and capabilities provided by Azure to make applications highly available. Before we get into the architectural and configuration details, it is important to understand Azure High Availability related concepts.

Concepts

The fundamental constructs provided by Azure to attain High Availability is through:

- Availability sets
- Fault domain
- Update domain
- Availability Zones

Availability sets

High Availability in Azure is primarily achieved through **redundancy**. Redundancy means that there is more than one resource instance, such that in the event of a failure for a resource, the other takes over. But just having more similar resources does not make them highly available. For example, having more than one virtual machine does not make these virtual machines highly available. Azure provides availability set resources to tag and brings these resources together to form a group. All virtual machines in the availability set become highly available because they are placed on separate physical racks in the Azure data center and each virtual machine is updated one at a time instead of all at the same time. Availability sets provide fault domain and updates domain to achieve this and this is discussed in the next section. In short, availability sets provides redundancy at data center level similar to locally redundant storage.

Fault domain

When a virtual machine is provisioned and assigned to an availability set, it is assigned a fault domain. With **Azure Resource Manager** (**ARM**), each availability set has two or three fault domains by default depending on Azure regions. Some provide two, while others provide three fault domains in an availability set. Fault domains are non-configurable by users. When multiple virtual machines are created, they are placed on separate fault domains. If more than five virtual machines are provisioned on an availability set, they are placed in a round-robin fashion on five fault domains. Fault domains are related to physical racks in the Azure data center. Fault domains provide High Availability from unplanned maintenance due to hardware, power, and network failure. Since a single virtual machine is only placed on a rack, other virtual machines continue running in case the rack in consideration snaps off.

Update domain

Fault domain takes care of unplanned maintenance and updates domain handles planned maintenance. Each virtual machine is also assigned an update domain. There can be as many as 20 update domains in a single availability set. Update domains are nonconfigurable by users. When multiple virtual machines are created, they are placed on separate update domains. If more than 20 virtual machines are provisioned on an availability set, they are placed in a round-robin fashion on these update domains. Update domains take care of planned maintenance.

Availability Zones

This is relatively a new concept introduced in Azure and very similar to zone redundancy we saw for storage accounts. Availability Zones provides high availability within a region by placing virtual machines instances on separate data centers within a region. Availability Zones are applicable to virtual machines, managed disks, virtual machine scale sets and load balancers. This was a gap in Azure for a long time and has been removed recently from computing high availability perspective. More information about Availability Zones is available at `https://docs.microsoft.com/en-us/azure/availability-zones/az-overview`.

Load balancing

Load balancing, as the name suggests, refers to the process of balancing the load among virtual machines and applications. With one virtual machine, there is no need of load balancer because the entire load is on a single virtual machine and there is no other virtual machine to share the load. However, with multiple virtual machines containing the same application and service, it is possible to distribute the load among them through load balancing. Azure provides a couple of resources for enabling load balancing:

- **Load balancers**: Azure load balancer helps in architecting solutions with high availability. Within the TCP stack, it is a layer 4 transport level load balancer. It is a layer 4 load balancer that distributes incoming traffic among healthy instances of services defined in a load-balanced set. Level 4 load balancers work at transport level and have network level information such as IP address and port to decide the target for the incoming request. Load balances are discussed in detail later in this chapter.

- **Application gateways**: Azure application gateways deliver High Availability to your applications. It is a layer 7 load balancer that distributes the incoming traffic among healthy instances of services. Level 7 load balancers can work at the application level and has application level information such as cookies, HTTP, HTTPS, and sessions for the incoming request. Application gateways are discussed in detail later in this chapter.

Virtual machine High Availability

Virtual machines provide compute capabilities. It provides processing power and hosting for applications and services. If the application is deployed on a single virtual machine and that machine is down, then even the application is not available. If the application is composed of multiple tiers and each tier is deployed in its own single instance of a virtual machine, even a downtime in a single virtual machine can render the application non-available. Although Azure tries to make even single virtual machine deployments highly available by placing on different racks as soon as it can figure out, Azure does not ensure or guarantee any SLA on them. Azure provides SLA for those virtual machines that are grouped together in an availability set. It provides 5 nines (99.999%) SLA for the availability of virtual machines if they are part of an availability set and more than two virtual machines are on that availability set.

Computing High Availability

Applications demanding High Availability should be deployed on multiple virtual machines on the same availability set. If applications are composed of multiple tiers, then each tier should have a group of virtual machines on their dedicated availability set. In short, if there are three tiers of an application, there should be three availability sets and minimum six virtual machines (two in each availability set) to make the entire application highly available.

How does Azure provide SLA and High Availability to virtual machines in an Availability set with multiple virtual machines in each availability set? This is the question that might be coming to mind.

Here comes the use of concepts that we considered before: fault and update domain.

When Azure sees multiple virtual machines in an availability set, it places those virtual machines on a separate fault domain. In other words, these virtual machines are placed on separate physical racks instead of the same rack. This ensures that at least one virtual machine continues to be available even if there is a power, hardware, or rack failure. There are two or three fault domains in an availability set and depending on a number of virtual machines in an availability set, the VMs are placed on separate fault domains or repeated in a round robin fashion. This ensures that High Availability is not impacted because of failure of the rack.

Azure also places these VMs on a separate update domain. In other words, Azure tags these VMs internally in such a way that these virtual machines are patched and updated one after another such that any reboot in an update domain does not affect the availability of the application. This ensures that High Availability is not impacted because of the virtual machine and host maintenance.

With the placement of virtual machines in separate fault and update domains, Azure ensures that not all of them are down at the same time and are alive and available for serving requests even though they might be undergoing maintenance or facing physical downtime challenges.

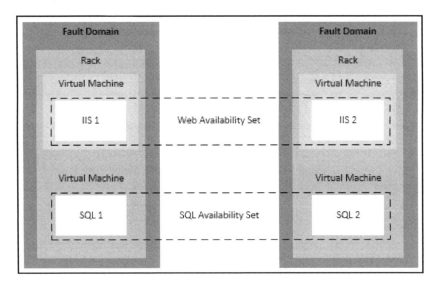

The previous image shows four virtual machines (2 IIS and 2 SQL related). Both IIS and SQL virtual machines are part of their availability set. The IIS and SQL virtual machines are on separate fault domain and different racks in the data center. They would also be on separate upgrade domains.

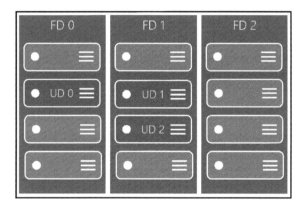

Storage High Availability

Virtual machines are backed up by storage accounts by storing their VHD files on them. While availability sets provide High Availability to compute instance, it does not ensure High Availability of VHD files for virtual machines stored in storage accounts. The VHD files for all VMs might be placed on the same storage cluster and any cluster failure can render all virtual machines non-available or less available than required. In short, it is not only computed services that needs to be highly available, but even storage accounts storing VHD files should be placed on separate clusters such that in an event of failure, at least one or some virtual machines continue to be available both from a computer and storage perspective.

Azure provides managed disks as a concept that provides disk management facilities. Managed disks provide better reliability for availability sets by ensuring that the disks of VMs in an availability set are sufficiently isolated from each other to avoid single points of failure. It does this by automatically placing the disks in different storage clusters. If a storage cluster fails due to hardware or software failure, only the VM instances with disks on those stamps fail. Each virtual machine VHD in an availability set should be placed in a separate storage account. Although, virtual machines from different availability sets can be placed in a storage account.

PaaS High Availability

Azure provides app services and cloud services for hosting managed platforms. Services and applications can be deployed on top of them. They provide flexibility, elasticity, and economies to create and deploy applications. These platforms are managed by Azure and users do not interact with base infrastructure on which they are deployed. They bring in a higher level of abstraction compared to IaaS by letting developers concentrate on their business problem and using the platform to fast track their development and deployment process. This alleviates them to manage, operate, and monitor the base infrastructure. When an application is deployed in-app services or cloud services, Azure provisions virtual machines that are not visible to users. The applications are deployed on these virtual machines and Azure fabric controller is responsible for provisioning, managing, and monitoring them. The fabric controller monitors the status of the hardware and software of the host and guest machine instances. When it detects a failure, it maintains SLAs by automatically relocating the VM instances. When multiple cloud service role instances are deployed, Azure deploys these instances to different fault and update domains.

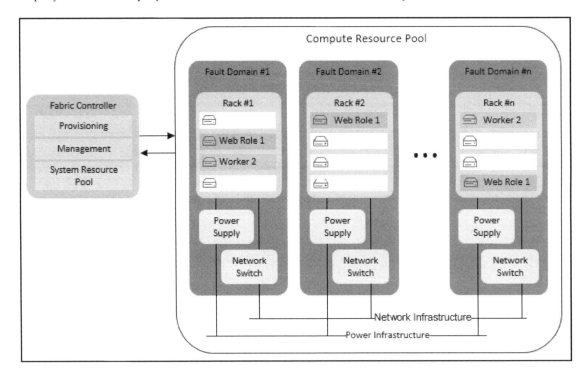

The previous diagram shows that PaaS services with multiple virtual machines instances deploy these web and worker roles on separate fault domains. Deploying on separate fault domains means deploying on separate racks within a data center. It also means that these services have separate network switches and power supply ensuring that even if one of the racks undergoes maintenance, there is disruption of power supply to the rack or failure of the network switch, there are other instances available to serve customer's requests.

Application High Availability

High Availability can be inbuilt within the software used for applications or it can be built from ground-up within applications. One example of the High Availability feature provided by software is SQL server always on availability groups. They help in keeping databases highly available.

Azure Services also have an inbuilt High Availability mechanism. In Azure SQL, data is replicated synchronously within the region. Active geo-replication allows up to four additional database copies in the same region or different regions. Azure storage has its own mechanism to make data available by replicating to multiple data centers and regions.

Load balancing

Azure provides two constructs to provision load balancers. It provides a level-4 load balancer that works at the transport layer within TCP OSI stack and a level-7 load balancer that works at application and session level.

Although both application gateways and load balancer provide basic features of balancing the load, they serve different purposes. There are use cases in which application gateway makes more sense to deploy compared to load balancer.

Application gateway provides the following features that are not available in the Azure load balancers:

- **Web application firewall**: This is an additional firewall on top of operating system firewall and has the capability to peek into incoming messages. This help in identifying and protecting from common web-based attacks such as SQL injection, cross-site scripting attacks, and session hijacks.

- **Cookie-based session affinity**: Load balancers distribute incoming traffic to services instances that are healthy and relatively free. A request can be served by any service instance. There are applications that need advance features in which all subsequent requests following the first request should be processed by same service instance. This is known as cookie-based session affinity. Application gateway provides cookie-based session affinity to keep a user session on the same service instance using cookies.

- **Secure Sockets Layer (SSL) offload**: Encryption and decryption of request and response data are performed by SSL and is generally a costly operation. Web servers should ideally be spending its resources on processing and serving requests rather than encryption and decryption of traffic. SSL offload helps in transferring this cryptography process from the web server to load balancer thereby providing more resources to web servers serving users. The request from the user is encrypted but gets decrypted at application gateway instead of the web server. The request from application gateway to web server is unencrypted.

- **End to end SSL**: While SSL offload is a nice feature for a certain application, there are certain mission-critical secure applications that need complete SSL encryption and decryption even if traffic passes through load balancers. Application gateway can be configured for an end to end SSL cryptography as well.

- **URL-based content routing**: Application gateway are also useful to redirect the traffic to different servers based on the URL content of incoming requests. This helps in hosting multiple services alongside other applications.

Azure load balancers

The Azure load balancer distributes incoming traffic based on transport level information available to it. It relies on the following:

- Originating IP address
- Target IP address
- Originating port number
- Target port number
- Type of protocol--TCP or HTTP

Public load balancing

In this configuration, load balancers are assigned a public IP address. Assigning a public IP address ensures that the load balancer can accept requests coming in from the internet. Without a public IP address, it is not possible to access the resource from the internet. The load balancer can be configured with load balancing rules. Load balancing rules work at the port level. It accepts source and destination ports map them together such that whenever a load balancer receives a request for the source port, the request is forwarded to a virtual machine from a group of virtual machines attached to the load balancer on the destination port. This is shown in the following diagram:

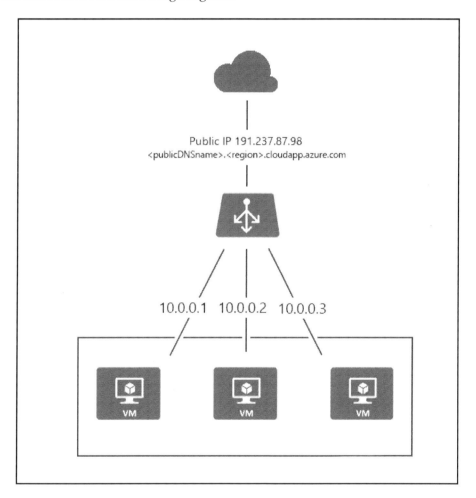

But how does this entire thing work? How is a public IP address assigned to a load balancer? What does the load balancer contain? How is it configured with load balancer rules? How does the load balancer send requests to the virtual machines? How does the virtual machine know that it is attached to the load balancer and more? The answer to all these questions is visible in the following diagram.

In this configuration, the load balancer is assigned a public IP address. The load balancer is accessible from the internet and can accept client requests. The load balancer can be configured with load balancing and NAT rules. Both NAT and load balancing rules are part of the frontend configuration. The frontend configuration sends client requests to one of the IP address available in the backend pool. These IP addresses are associated with the network interface card, which in turn is attached to virtual machines.

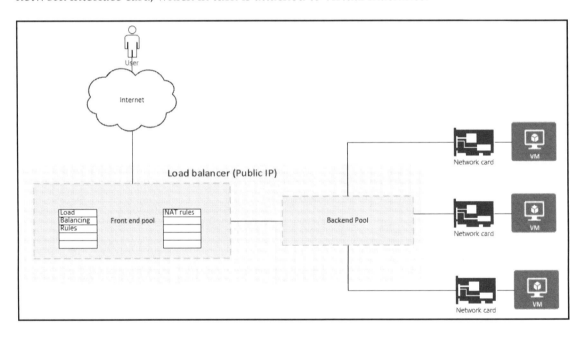

Internal load balancing

The following diagram shows the working of an internal load balancer. You can see that the request comes from resources from Azure itself as it is not accessible on the internet. In this configuration, the load balancer is assigned a private IP address. The load balancer is only accessible within the virtual network to which it is attached. It cannot be accessed through the internet. The rest of its configuration is such as public load balancer. The load balancer can be configured with load balancing and NAT rules.

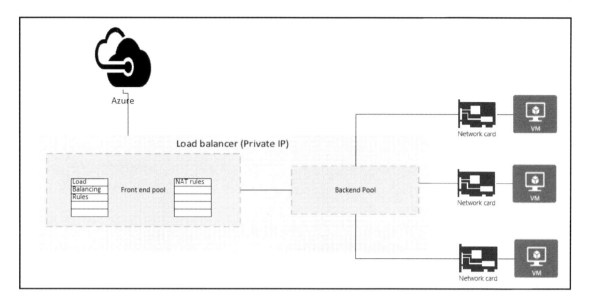

The following diagram shows how multiple load balancers can be deployed to create solutions. In this, there is a public load balancer that accepts client requests and an internal load balancer for the database tier. The database tier virtual machines are not accessible on the internet, but only through the load balancer on port 1433.

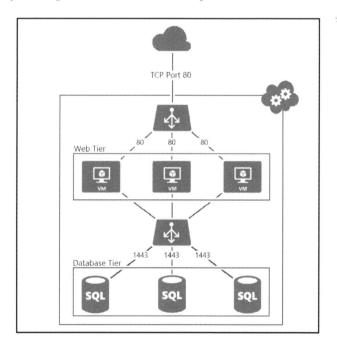

Port forwarding

At times, there is a need where a request should always redirect to a virtual machine. Azure load balancer helps us achieve this with the NAT rules. NAT rules are evaluated after load balancing rules are evaluated and none of its rules are satisfied. NAT rules are evaluated for each incoming request and once it finds them, it forwards the request to that virtual machine through a backend pool. It is to be noted that a virtual machine cannot register the same port for both port forwarding using NAT and load balancing rules.

Azure application gateways

Azure load balancer helps us to enable solutions at the infrastructure level. However, there are times when advance services and features are required from the load balancer itself. These advance services include SSL termination, sticky sessions, advanced security, and more. Azure application gateways are built on top on Azure load balancers to provide these additional features. The Azure application gateway is a level 7 load balancer that works with the application and session payload in a TCP OSI stack. Application gateways have more information compared to the Azure load balancer to take decisions on request routing and load balancing between servers. Application gateways are managed by Azure and are highly available.

An application gateway sits in between the users and virtual machines, as shown in the following figure:

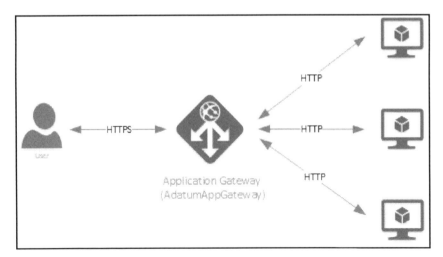

Application gateways are internally implemented using virtual machines. **Internet information service (IIS)** is installed and configured with **Application Request Routing (ARR)** on these virtual machines. These gateways can be installed on multiple virtual machines providing High Availability for the gateways themselves. Although not visible, Azure load balancers distribute loads among multiple application gateway servers. Creating an application gateway needs an internal or public IP address and that is used by users to send requests to it. This public IP or internal IP is provided by the Azure load balancer working at the transport level (TCP/UDP) and having all incoming network traffic being load balanced to the application gateway worker instances. The application gateway then routes the HTTP/HTTPS traffic based on its configuration whether it's a virtual machine, cloud service, internal, or an external IP address.

An application gateway is similar to Azure load balancer from a configuration perspective with additional constructs and features. It provides frontend IP, protocol, certificate and port configuration, backend pool, port, session affinity, and protocol configuration.

Azure Traffic Manager

After having a good understanding of both the Azure load balancer and the application gateway, it's time to get into the details of Traffic Manager. Azure load balancers and application gateways are much-needed resources for High Availability within a data center and region; however, to achieve High Availability across regions and data centers, there is a need for another resource and that is Traffic Manager. Traffic Manager helps us to create highly available solutions that span multiple geographies, regions, and data centers. Traffic Manager is not similar to load balancers. It uses DNS to redirect requests to an appropriate endpoint determined by their health and configuration. Traffic Manager is not a proxy or a gateway. Traffic Manager does not see the traffic passing between the client and the service. It simply redirects the request based on most appropriate endpoints.

Azure Traffic Manager enables you to control the distribution of traffic across your application endpoints. An endpoint is any internet-facing service hosted inside or outside of Azure.

Endpoints are internet facing reachable public URLs. Applications are provisioned within multiple geographies and Azure regions. Applications deployed to each region has a unique endpoint referred by **DNS CNAME**. These endpoints are mapped to Traffic Manager endpoint. When a Traffic Manager is provisioned, it gets an endpoint by default with a `.trafficmanager.net` URL extension.

When a request arrives at the Traffic Manager URL, it finds the most appropriate endpoint out of its list and redirects the request to it. In short, Traffic Manager acts such as a global DNS to identify the region that will serve the request.

However, how does Traffic Manager know which endpoints to use and redirect the client request to? There are two aspects that the Traffic Manager implements to determine the most appropriate endpoint and region.

First, Traffic Manager actively monitors the health of all endpoints. It can monitor the health of virtual machines, cloud services, and app services. If it determines that health of an application deployed to a region is not suitable for redirecting traffic, it redirects the requests to a healthy endpoint.

Second, the Traffic Manager can be configured with routing information. There are four traffic routing methods available in Traffic Manager:

- **Priority**: Should be used when all traffic should go to a default endpoint, and backups are available in case the primary endpoints are unavailable.
- **Weighted**: Should be used to distribute traffic across endpoints evenly or according to defined weights.
- **Performance**: Should be used for endpoints in different regions and users should be redirected to the closest endpoint based on their location. This has direct impact on network latency.
- **Geographic**: This should be used to redirect users from a specific geography to an endpoint (Azure, external, or nested) available in that geography or nearest to that geography. Examples include complying with data sovereignty mandates, localization of content and user experience, and measuring traffic from different regions.

It is to be noted that after the Traffic Manager determines a valid healthy endpoint, clients connect directly to the application.

Architectural considerations for High Availability

In this section, we will go through some of the architectures for High Availability.

High Availability within Azure regions

The architecture shown next, shows High Availability deployment within a single Azure region. High Availability is designed at the individual resource level. In this architecture, there are multiple virtual machines at each tier connected through either application gateway or load balancer and they are part of an availability set. Each tier is associated with an availability set. These virtual machines are placed on separate fault and update domains. While the web servers are connected to application gateways, the rest of the tiers such as application and database tiers have internal load balancers.

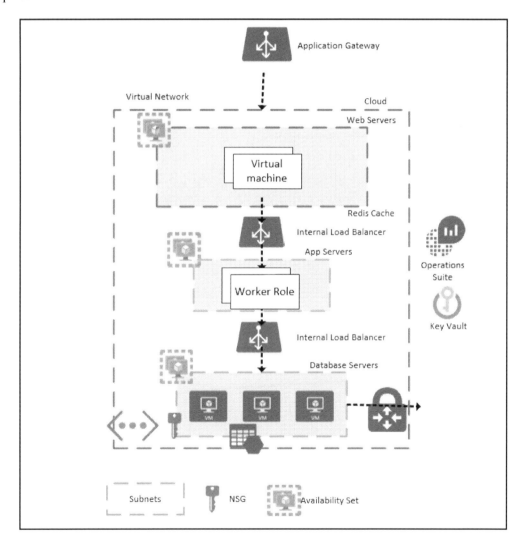

High Availability across Azure regions

The architecture shown next, shows similar deployments on two different Azure regions. Both the regions have the same resources deployed. High Availability is designed at individual resource level within these regions. There are multiple virtual machines at each tier connected through the load balancer and they are part of the availability set. These virtual machines are placed on separate fault and update domains. While the web servers are connected to external load balancers, the rest of the tiers such as application and database tiers have internal load balancers. It is to be noted that application load balancers could have been used for web servers and application tiers instead of Azure load balancer if there is a need for advanced services such as session affinity, SSL termination, advance security using WAF, and path-based routing. Databases in both the regions are connected to each other using VNET peering and gateways. This is helpful in configuring log shipping, SQL Server AlwaysOn, and other data synchronization techniques.

Endpoints of load balancers from both the regions are used to configure Traffic Manager endpoints and traffic is routed based on priority load balancing method. Traffic Manager helps in routing all requests to the East US region and failover to West Europe in case of non-availability of the first region.

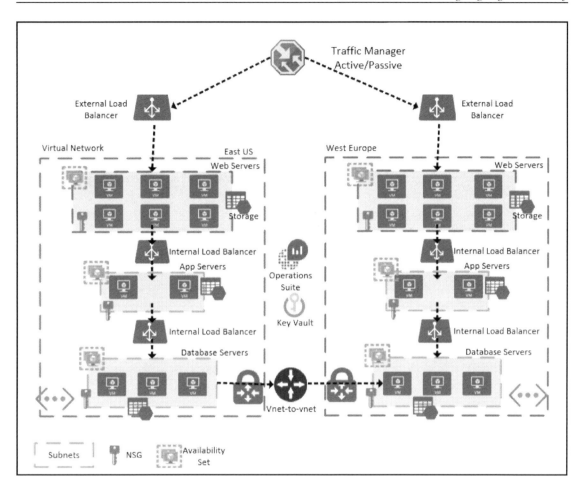

Best practices

This section describes High Availability best practices. They have been categorized into application, deployment, data management, and monitoring.

Application High Availability

An application should be built keeping High Availability as one of the important architectural concerns. Some of the important application related High Availability practices are mentioned next:

- An application should implement appropriate exception handling to gracefully recover and inform stakeholders about the issue
- An application should try to perform the same operation again in the fixed interval for a certain number of times before exiting in an event of an error or exception
- An application should have inbuilt timeout capability to decide that an exception cannot be recovered from
- Maintaining logs and writing logs for all errors, exceptions, and execution should be adopted within the application
- Applications should be profiled to find their actual resource requirements in terms of compute, memory and network bandwidth for a different number of users

 Please refer to `https://docs.microsoft.com/en-us/azure/` `architecture/checklist/availability` for knowing more about application and rest of high availability best practices.

Deployment

Deployment strategy to a large extent affects the availability of application and overall environment. Some of the important things to be taken into consideration are the following:

- Deploy multiple instances of Azure resources including multiple instances for virtual machines, cloud services, and other resources
- Deploy virtual machines on availability sets or availability zones. They cannot be used together
- Deploy multiple instances of virtual machines across multiple regions
- Create multiple environments and keep at least one of them in standby mode

Data management

Some of the important data related best practices for High Availability are the following:

- If possible, store data on Azure provided services such as Azure SQL, Cosmos DB, and table storage
- Use storage accounts that are based on geo-redundant type
- Ensure that data is replicated to multiple regions and not only within zone or data center
- Take periodic backups and conduct restore tests frequently
- If storing data in virtual machines, ensure that there are multiple virtual machines and they are either on availability sets or availability zones
- Use keys and secrets to data stores in Azure key vault

Monitoring

Some of the important monitoring related best practices for High Availability are the following:

- Use OMS (log analytics) for monitoring the environment and enable log auditing
- Use application insights to capture telemetry information from the custom application and environment related to compute, storage and network and other log information
- Ensure alerts are configured on OMS for issues related to availability of environment and application
- Visit Azure monitor frequently to gather recommendation related to high availability

Summary

High Availability is an important and crucial architectural concern. Almost every application and every architect tries to implement High Availability. Traditionally, High Availability was implemented from ground-up without any support from platforms. Azure is a mature platform that understands the need of High Availability for applications and in this bid, provides resources to implement High Availability from granular to data center level. High Availability is not an afterthought and should be part of the application life cycle development from the planning phase itself. Azure provides availability sets that ensure virtual machines are placed on separate fault and update domains. Fault domains ensure that unplanned rack level disruption does not change the availability of an application, while update domains take care of planned maintenance. Even Azure PaaS services use fault and update domains behind the scenes to keep the application up and running. Azure internal and external load balancer is level-4 transport level constructs provided by Azure to distribute load among multiple instances of the application. Similarly, application gateways are level-7 application and session level load balancers that provide advanced functionalities such as SSL termination and sticky sessions. Traffic Managers are global DNS level High Availability constructs to make applications across geographies highly available. Next chapter will focus on scalability which is another important facet for overall architecture on Azure.

4

Implementing Scalability

Running applications and systems that are available to users for consumption is an important consideration for architects for any serious application. However, there is another equally important application feature that is one of the top priorities for architects and it is the scalability of the applications. Imagine situations in which applications are deployed and obtain great performance and availability with few users, but both availability and performance degrade as users start increasing. There are times when an application under normal load performs well but degrades in performance with the increase in the number of users. This happens especially if there is a sudden increase in the number of users and the environment is not built for such large number of users. To accommodate such spikes in the number of users, you might have provisioned the hardware and bandwidth for handling spikes. The challenge with this is that the additional capacity is not used for a majority part of the year and does not provide any return on investment. They are provisioned for use only during few festivals or offers. I hope you are getting the problems architects are trying to solve. All these problems are related to capacity sizing and scalability of an application. The focus of this chapter is to understand scalability as an architectural concern and check out services provided by Azure for implementing scalability.

In this chapter, we'll cover the following topics:

- Scalability
- Scalability in IaaS and PaaS solutions
- Basics of virtual machine scale sets
- Architecture of VMSS
- Auto scaling in VMSS
- Auto scaling rules

- Scaling up and down
- Scaling out and in
- Automation related to VMSS

Scalability

Capacity planning and sizing are one of the top priorities for architects for their applications and services. Architects must find a balance between buying and provisioning too many resources versus less resources. Having fewer resources can lead to not being able to serve all users, turning them off to competition, while having more resources can hurt the budgets and return on investments because most of these resources remain unused most of the time. Moreover, the problem is amplified with varied level of demand during different times. It is almost impossible to predict the number of users for the application round the clock and year. However, it is possible to find an approximate number using past information and continues monitoring.

According to Wikipedia (`https://en.wikipedia.org/wiki/Scalability`), scalability refers to:

> *"Scalability is the capability of a system, network, or process to handle a growing amount of work, or its potential to be enlarged to accommodate that growth. For example, a system is considered scalable if it is capable of increasing its total output under an increased load when resources (typically hardware) are added."*

Scalability refers to the ability in application deployment, process, and technology to handle a growing number of users and providing them the same level of performance when there are fewer users. Scalability might refer to serving more requests without degradation of performance or it might refer to handling larger and more time-consuming work without any loss of performance in both the cases.

Capacity planning and sizing exercises should be undertaken by architects at the very beginning of the project during the planning phase to provide scalability to applications.

Some applications have stable demand patterns while it is difficult to predict others. Scalability requirements are known for stable demand applications while it is a more involved process for variable demand applications. Auto scaling, a concept we will review in the next section, should be used for such applications whose demands cannot be predicted.

Scalability versus performance

It is quite easy to get confused between scalability and performance architectural concerns because scalability is all about ensuring that no matter the number of users consuming the application, all get the same pre-determined level of performance.

Performance relates to application features that ensure that the application caters to predefined response time and throughput, scalability refers to having provision for more resources on a need basis to accommodate more users without sacrificing performance.

It is better to understand them using an analogy. Speed of a train refers to the performance for railway systems, however, accommodating more trains to run in parallel with the same or higher speed will be referred to as scalability of the railway network.

Azure scalability

In this section, we will see features and capabilities provided by Azure to make applications highly available. Before we get into the architecture and configuration details, it is important to understand Azure High Availability related concepts.

Concepts

The fundamental constructs provided by Azure to attain High Availability is through:

- Scaling
- Scaling up and down
- Scaling out and in
- Auto scaling
- Rolling updates

Scaling

Scaling refers to the transformation that either increases or decreases the units of resources used to serve requests from users. Scaling can be automatic or manual. Manual scaling requires an administrator to manually initiate the scaling process, while automatic scaling refers to an automatic increase or decrease of resources based on events available from the environment and ecosystem such as memory and CPU availability. Scaling can be up or down and out or in, which will be explained later in this section.

Scaling up

Scaling up of a virtual machine or service refers to adding up to additional resources to existing servers such as CPU, memory, and disks. It is to increase the capacity of existing physical hardware and resources.

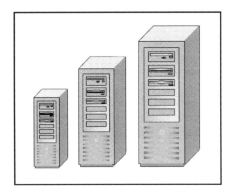

Scaling down

Scaling down of a virtual machine or service refers to the removal of existing resources from existing servers such as CPU, memory, and disks. It is to decrease the capacity of existing physical and virtual hardware and resources.

Scaling out

Scaling out refers to the process of adding additional hardware in terms of additional servers and capacity. This typically involves adding new servers, assigning them IP addresses, deploying applications on them, and making them part of the existing load balancers such that traffic can be routed to them. Scaling out can be automatic or manual as well. However, for better results automation should be used.

Scaling in

Scaling in refers to the process of removal of the existing hardware in terms of existing servers and capacity. This typically involves removing existing servers, de-allocating their IP addresses, removing them from existing load balancer configuration such that traffic cannot be routed to them. Like scaling out, scaling in can be automatic or manual.

Auto scaling

Auto scaling refers to the process of either scaling up/down or scaling out/in dynamically based on application demand and it happens using automation. Auto scaling is helpful because it ensures that deployment always consists of a correct and ideal number of server instances. Auto scaling helps in building applications that are fault tolerant. It not only helps in scalability, but also makes applications highly available. Finally, it provides the best cost management. Auto scaling helps in having the optimal configuration for server instances based on demand. It helps in not over provisioning servers that are underutilized or removes servers that are not needed anymore after scaling out.

PaaS scalability

Azure provides app services for hosting managed applications. App services is a PaaS offering from Azure. It provides the web and mobile platform. Behind these web and mobile platform is a managed infrastructure that is managed by Azure on behalf of its users. Users do not see or manage the infrastructure; however, they have the capability to extend the platform and deploy their applications on top of it. With this, architects and developers can concentrate on their business problems instead of worrying about the base platform and infrastructure provisioning, configuration, and troubleshooting. Developers have the flexibility to choose any language, operating system, and frameworks to develop their applications. App services provide multiple plans and based on chosen plans, capabilities of scalability are available. App services provide five plans. They are as follows:

- **Free**: It uses shared infrastructure. It means multiple applications will be deployed on the same infrastructure from the same or multiple tenants. It gets 1 GB of storage free of cost. No scaling facility is available in this plan.

- **Shared**: It also uses shared infrastructure and gets 1 GB of storage free of cost. Additionally, custom domains are also provided as an extra feature. No Scaling facility is available in this plan.
- **Basic**: It has three different **stock keeping units** (**SKU**)--B1, B2, and B3. They have increasing units of resources available to them in terms of CPU and memory. In short, they provide higher configuration of virtual machines backing these services. Additionally, they provide storage, custom domains, and SSL support. The basic plan provides basic features for manual scaling. There is no automatic scaling available in this plan. Maximum three instances can be used for scaling out of the application.
- **Standard**: It also has three different SKU--S1, S2, and S3. They have increasing units of resources available to them in terms of CPU and memory. In short, they provide higher configuration of virtual machines backing these services. Additionally, they provide storage, custom domains, and SSL support similar to the basic plan. It also provides traffic manager, staging slots, and one daily backup as an additional feature on top of the basic plan. The standard plan provides features for automatic scaling. Maximum 10 instances can be used for scaling out of the application.
- **Premium**: It also has three different SKU--P1, P2, and P3. They have increasing units of resources available in them in terms of CPU and memory. In short, they provide higher configuration of virtual machines backing these services. Additionally, they provide storage, custom domains, and SSL support similar to the basic plan. It also provides traffic manager, staging slots, and 50 daily backups as an additional feature on top of the basic plan. The standard plan provides features for automatic scaling. Maximum 20 instances can be used for scaling out of the application.

PaaS scaling up and down

Scaling up and down of services hosted in-app services is quite simple. The Azure app services menu items to scale up, which opens a new blade with all plans and their SKU's listed. Choosing a plan and SKU will scale up or down the service.

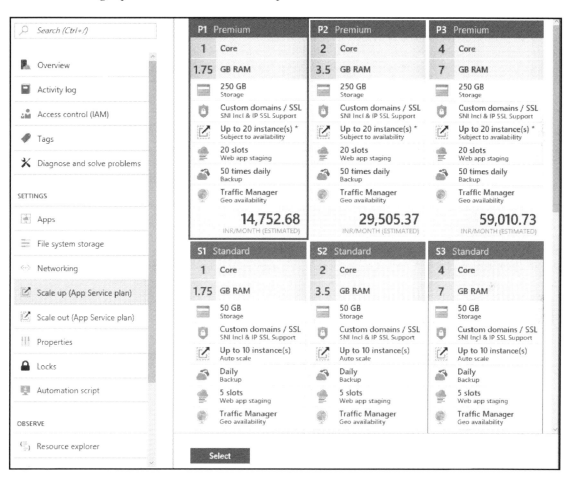

PaaS scaling out and in

Scaling out and in of services hosted in-app services is also quite simple. The Azure app services menu items to scale out, which opens a new blade with scaling configuration options.

By default, auto scaling is disabled for both premium and standard plans. It can be enabled using **Scale Out** menu item and by clicking on the **Enable autoscale** button.

Manual scaling does not need configuration but auto scaling helps in configuring with the help of following properties.

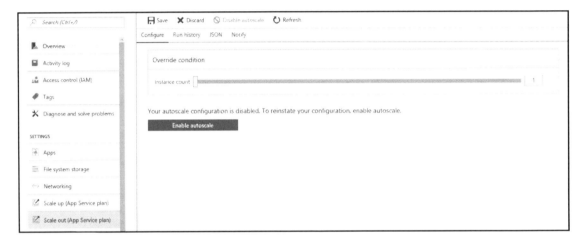

- **Mode of scaling**: Based on some metric such as CPU or memory usage or just scale to specify the number of instances.
- **When to scale**: Multiple rules can be added that determine when to scale out and in. Each rule can determine the criteria such as CPU or memory consumption, whether to increase or decrease instances, how many instances to increase or decrease at a time. At least one rule for scale out and one rule for scale it should be configured. Threshold definition helps in defining the upper and lower limits cross which should trigger auto scale--either increase or decrease the number of instances.

- **How to scale**: Specifies how many instances to create or de-provision in each scale out or in.

IaaS scalability

There are users who want to have complete control over the base infrastructure, platform, and application. They prefer to consume IaaS solutions compared to PaaS solutions. For such customers, when they create virtual machines they are also responsible for capacity sizing and scaling. There is no out-of-the-box configuring for manual or auto-scaling of virtual machines. These customers will have to write their own automation scripts, triggers, and rules to achieve auto scaling. With virtual machines comes the responsibility to maintain them as well. Patching, updates, and upgrades of virtual machines is the responsibility of owners. Architects should think about both planned as well as unplanned maintenance. How these virtual machines should be patched, its order, grouping, and other factors must be thought through to ensure that both scalability and availability of an application is not comprised. To help alleviate such problems, Azure provides virtual machine scale sets as a solution.

Virtual machine scale sets

Virtual machine scale sets (**VMSS**) are an Azure compute resource that you can use to deploy and manage a set of identical VMs. With all VMs configured in the same way, scale sets are designed to support true auto scale, and no pre-provisioning of VMs is required. It helps in provisioning multiple identical virtual machines connected to each other through a virtual network and subnet.

VMSS creates a set that can be created, configured, and managed as a unit. All virtual machines are part of this unit and any changes made are applied to the unit, which in turn applies it to virtual machines using a pre-determined algorithm.

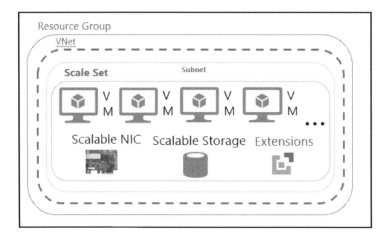

It allows these virtual machines to be load balanced using Azure load balancer or application gateways. All the virtual machines could be either Windows or Linux operating system. They can run automated scripts using a PowerShell extension and they can be managed centrally using desired state configuration. They can be monitored as a unit and individually using log analytics as well.

VMSS can be provisioned from the Azure portal, Azure command-line interface, Azure resource manager templates, REST API's, and PowerShell cmdlets. It is possible to invoke REST API's and Azure CLI from any platform, environment, operating system, and any language.

Already a lot of Azure services use VMSS as its underlying architecture. Major among them are Azure batch, Azure service fabric, and Azure container services. Azure container services in turn provisions Kubernetes and DC/OS on these virtual machine scale sets.

VMSS architecture

VMSS allows for creation of up to 1000 virtual machines in a scale set when using a platform image and 100 virtual machines if using a custom image. If the number of virtual machines are less than 100 in a scale set, they are placed in a single availability set; however, if they are greater than 100, multiple availability sets are created, known as placement groups and virtual machines are distributed among these availability sets. We know from the last chapter that virtual machines in an availability set are placed on separate fault and update domains. Availability sets related to VMSS have five fault and update domains by default. VMSS provides a model that holds metadata information for the entire set. Changing this model and applying changes impact all virtual machine instances. This information includes maximum, minimum virtual machine instances, operating system SKU and version, the current number of virtual machines, fault and update domain, and more.

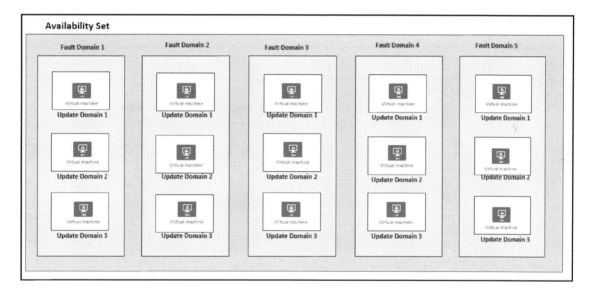

VMSS scaling

Scaling refers to increase or decrease in compute and storage resources. VMSS is a feature rich resource that makes scaling easy and efficient. It provides auto scaling that helps in scaling up or down based on external events and data such as CPU and memory usage.

Horizontal versus vertical scaling

Scaling can be horizontal or vertical or both. Horizontal scaling is another name for scaling out and in, while vertical scaling is about scaling up and down.

Capacity

VMSS have capacity property that determines the number of virtual machines in a scale set. VMSS can be deployed with zero as value for this property. It will not create a single virtual machine; however, if you provision VMSS by providing a number for the capacity property, those number of virtual machines are created.

Auto scaling

Automatic scaling of virtual machines in VMSS refers to the addition or removal of virtual machine instances based on configured environments to meet the performance and scalability demands of an application. Generally, in the absence of VMSS, this is achieved using automation scripts and runbooks.

VMSS helps in this automation process with the help of configuration. Instead of writing scripts, VMSS can be configured for automated scaling up and down.

Auto scaling consists of multiple integrated components to achieve its end goal. Auto scaling continuously monitors the virtual machines and collects telemetry data from it. It stores this data and combines it together and evaluates it against a set of rules to determine whether it should trigger auto scale. The trigger could be to a scale out or scale in. It could also be for scale up or down.

Auto scale uses diagnostics logs for collecting telemetry data from virtual machines. These logs are stored in storage accounts as diagnostics metrics. Auto scale also uses the insight monitoring service that reads these metrics, combines them together, and stores them into its own storage account.

Auto scale background jobs continually run to read the insights storage data, evaluate them based on all the rules configured for auto scaling, and executes the process of auto scaling, if any of the rules or combination of rules returns positive. The rules can take into consideration metrics from guest virtual machine as well as host server.

The rules are defined using the following properties. These properties descriptions are available at `https://docs.microsoft.com/en-us/azure/virtual-machine-scale-sets/virtual-machine-scale-sets-autoscale-overview`.

Rule	Description
`metricName`	This value is the same as the performance counter that you defined in the `wadperfcounter` variable for the diagnostics extension. In the preceding example, the **thread count** counter is used.
`metricResourceUri`	This value is the resource identifier of the VMSS. This identifier contains the name of the resource group, the name of the resource provider, and the name of the scale set to scale.
`timeGrain`	This value is the granularity of the metrics that are collected. In the preceding example, data is collected on an interval of one minute. This value is used with `timeWindow`.
`statistic`	This value determines how the metrics are combined to accommodate the automatic scaling action. The possible values are--`average`, `min`, and `max`.
`timeWindow`	This value is the range of time in which instance data is collected. It must be between 5 minutes and 12 hours.
`timeAggregation`	This value determines how the data that is collected should be combined over time. The default value is `average`. The possible values are--`average`, `minimum`, `maximum`, `last`, `total`, and `count`.
`operator`	This value is the operator that is used to compare the metric data and the threshold. The possible values are--`Equals`, `NotEquals`, `GreaterThan`, `GreaterThanOrEqual`, `LessThan`, and `LessThanOrEqual`.
`threshold`	This value is the value that triggers the scale action. Be sure to provide a sufficient difference between the threshold values for the scale-out and scale-in actions. If you set the same values for both actions, the system anticipates constant change, which prevents it from implementing a scaling action. For example, setting both to 600 threads in the preceding example doesn't work.
`direction`	This value determines the action that is taken when the threshold value is achieved. The possible values are `increase` or `decrease`.

Rule	Description
type	This value is the type of action that should occur and must be set to ChangeCount.
value	This value is the number of virtual machines that are added to or removed from the scale set. This value must be 1 or greater.
cooldown	This value is the amount of time to wait for the last scaling action before the next action occurs. This value must be between one minute and one week.

The auto scale architecture is shown in the following diagram:

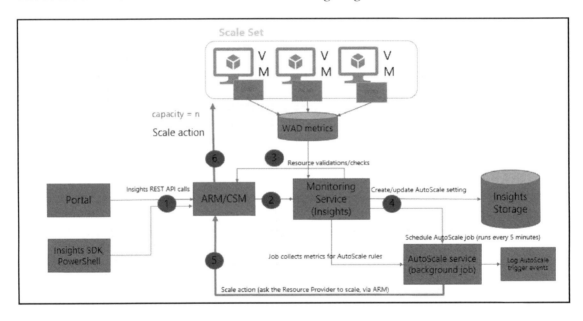

Auto scale can be configured for scenarios that are more complex than general metrics available from environments. For example, scaling could be based on any of the following event:

- Scale on a specific day
- Scale on a recurring schedule such as weekends
- Scale differently on weekdays and weekends
- Scale during holidays that is, one of the events
- Scale on multiple resource metrics

These can be configured using the schedule property of insights resources that help in registering rules.

Architects should ensure that at least two actions--scale out and scale in, should be configured together. Scaling in or scaling out configuration will not help achieve scaling benefits provided by VMSS.

Upgrades

After VMSS and applications are deployed, they need to be actively maintained. Planned maintenance should be conducted periodically to ensure that both environment and application is up to date with latest bits and the environment is current from a security and resilience point of view.

Upgrades can be associated with applications, the guest virtual machine instance, or to the image itself. Upgrades can be quite complex because they should happen without affecting the availability, scalability, and performance of environments and applications. To ensure that updates can take place one instance at a time using rolling upgrade methods, it is important that VMSS supports and provides capabilities for these advanced scenarios.

There is a utility provided by the Azure team to manage updates for VMSS. It's a Python-based utility that can be downloaded from
`https://github.com/gbowerman/vmssdashboard`. It makes REST API calls to Azure to manage scale sets. This utility can be used for starting, stopping, upgrading, and reimaging for virtual machines on a fault domain or group of virtual machines.

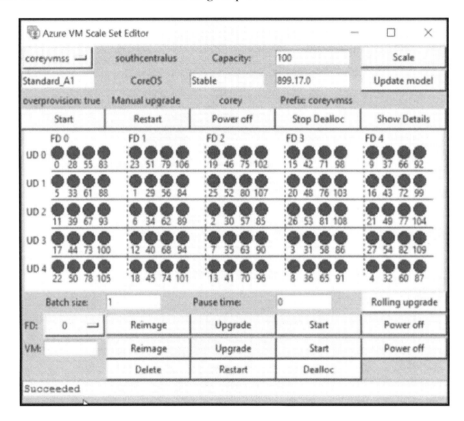

Application updates

Application updates in VMSS should not be executed manually. It must be executed as part of release management and pipeline using automation. Moreover, the update should happen one application instance at a time, not affecting the overall availability and scalability of the application. Configuration management tools such as desired state configuration should be deployed to manage application updates. DSC pull server can be configured with the latest version of the bits and they should be applied on a rolling basis to each instance.

Guest updates

Updates to virtual machine is the responsibility of administrator. Azure is not responsible to patch guest virtual machines. Guest updates are in the preview mode and users should control patching manually or using custom automation such as runbooks and scripts. However, rolling patch upgrades are in preview and can be configured in the ARM template using upgrade policy as shown here:

```
"upgradePolicy": {
"mode": "Rolling",
"automaticOSUpgrade": "true" or "false",
  "rollingUpgradePolicy": {
    "batchInstancePercent": 20,
    "maxUnhealthyUpgradedInstanceCount": 0,
    "pauseTimeBetweenBatches": "PT0S"
  }
}
```

Image updates

VMSS can update the OS version without any downtime. OS update involves changing the version or SKU of the OS or changing the URI of a custom image. Updating without downtime means updating virtual machines one at a time or in groups (such as one fault domain at a time) rather than all at once. By doing so, any virtual machines that are not being upgraded can keep running.

Scaling best practices

In this section, we will go through some of the best practices that applications should implement to take advantages of scalability capability provided by VMSS.

Prefer scaling out

Scaling out is a better scaling solution compared to scaling up. Scaling up or down means re-sizing of virtual machine instances. When a virtual machine is resized, it generally needs to be restarted, which has its own disadvantages. First, there is a downtime for the machine. Second, if there are active users connected to the application on that instance, they might face unavailability of application or they might even have lost transactions. Scaling out does not impact existing virtual machines. It provisions newer machines and adds them to the group.

Bare metal versus dormant instances

Scaling new instances can take two broad approaches. Either create the new instance from scratch, which means to install applications, configure, and test, while on the other hand, there can be dormant instances sleeping and can be started when they are needed due to scalability pressure on other servers.

Configuring maximum and minimum number of instances appropriately

Setting a value of two for both minimum and maximum instance count with current instance count being two, no scale action can occur. There should be an adequate margin between the maximum and minimum instance counts, which are inclusive. Auto scale always scales between these limits.

Concurrency

Applications are designed for scalability to focus on concurrency. Application should use asynchronous patterns to ensure that client requests do not wait indefinitely for acquiring resources if resources are busy serving other requests. Implementing asynchronous patterns in code ensures that threads do not wait for resources and systems gets exhausted of all available threads. Applications should implement the concept of timeouts if there are intermittent failures expected.

Stateless

Applications and services should be designed to be stateless. Scalability can become a challenge to achieve with stateful services and it is quite easy to scale stateless services. With state comes the requirement of additional components and implementation such as replication, centralized or decentralized repository, maintenance, and sticky sessions. All these are impediments in the path to scalability. Imagine a service maintaining active state on a local server. No matter the number of requests on overall application or on individual server, the subsequent requests must be served by the same server. Subsequent requests cannot be processed by other servers. This makes scalability implementation a challenge.

Caching and CDN

Applications and services should take advantage of caching. Caching helps eliminate multiple subsequent calls to either databases of filesystem. This helps in making resources available and free for more requests. **Content Distribution Network (CDN)** is another mechanism for caching static files such as images and JavaScript libraries. They are available on servers across the globe. They also make resources available and free for additional client requests. This makes applications highly scalable.

N+1 design

N+1 design refers to building redundancy within overall deployment for each component. It means to plan for some redundancy even when it is not required. It could mean additional virtual machines, storage, and network interface card.

Summary

Scalability is an important and crucial architectural concern. Almost every application and every architect try to implement scalability along with availability and performance. Azure is a mature platform that understands the need of scalability for applications and provides scalability options for both PaaS as well as IaaS solutions. PaaS app services can be configured to auto scale and virtual machines can be deployed on a scale set to take advantage of scaling. Scaling can be up/down/out/in. Similar to High Availability, scalability is not an afterthought and should be part of the application life cycle development from the planning phase itself. Scaling can be vertical by increasing the size of virtual machine instance or can be horizontal in which additional servers are added to the existing set. VMSS provides a model that holds metadata information for the entire set. Changing this model and applying changes impact all virtual machine instances. This allows upgrading, resizing, stopping, and starting virtual machines on a rolling basis. Finally, some of the important best practices were covered in this chapter related to scalability.

Next chapter deals which security which is the most important architectural concern for cloud deployments.

5
Cloud Security

Security is undoubtedly the most important non-functional requirement for architects to implement. Enterprises prioritize and provide extreme focus on getting their security strategy implemented correctly. In fact, security is one of the top concerns for almost every stakeholder in any application development, deployment, and management. It becomes all the way more important when the same application is built for deployment on cloud.

Running applications and systems that are available to users for consumption is an important consideration for architects for any serious application. However, there is another equally important application feature that is one of the top priorities for architects and it is the scalability of applications. Imagine situations in which applications are deployed and obtain great performance and availability with a few users, but both availability and performance suffers as users start increasing. Another situation in which although the application is performant and available with large number of users but there is certain time in a day or week or there are special events during which the number of user's spikes, and you cannot gauge or predict the number of users. In extension to the previous situation, you might have provisioned the hardware and bandwidth for handling users during these occasions and there are spikes; however, most of the time, the additional hardware is not used and does not provide any return on investment. They are provisioned for usage only during few festivals or offers. I hope you are getting the problems architects are trying to solve. All these problems are related to capacity sizing and scalability of an application. The focus of this chapter is to understand scalability as architectural concern and details out features provided by Azure for addressing these concerns.

In this chapter, we'll cover the following topics:

- Security principles
- Security for Azure
- Compliance and certification

- Directory:
    - Identity--authentication
    - Authorization
    - oAuth and open connect
- IaaS security:
    - Network security
    - Compute security
    - Storage security
- PaaS security:
    - SQL server
    - Key vault
- Security services
- Azure security center
- OMS--monitoring and audit
- Azure trust center

Security

Securing an application means not allowing unknown and unauthorized entities to access the application. It also means that communication with the application is secure and not tempered with.

This includes the following:

- **Authentication**: Authentication refers to establishing the identity of a user and ensuring that the given identity can access the application or service. Authentication is performed in Azure using open connect, also known as **ConnectID**.
- **Authorization**: Authorization refers to allowing and establishing permissions that an identity can perform within the application or service. Authorization is performed in Azure using oAuth technology.
- **Confidentiality**: It refers to that communication between the user and application is secure. The payload exchange between entities is encrypted such that it will make sense only to the sender and receiver, but not otherwise. Confidentiality of messages is performed using symmetric and asymmetric encryption. Certificates are used to implement cryptography--encryption and decryption of messages.

- **Integrity**: Integrity ensures that the payload and message exchange between sender and receiver is not tempered with. The receiver receives the same message as sent by the sender. Digital signatures and hashes are the implementation mechanism to check the integrity of incoming messages.

Security is a partnership between the service provider and the service consumer. Both parties have different levels of control on entire deployment stacks and each should implement security best practices to ensure that all threats are identified and mitigated. We already know from Chapter 1, *Getting Started*, that the cloud provides broadly three paradigms--IaaS, PaaS, and SaaS, each having different levels of collaborative control over deployment stack. Each party should implement security practices for components under its control and ambit. Lack of implementing security at any layer in the stack or by any party would make the entire deployment and application vulnerable to attacks.

Security life cycle

Security is generally regarded as a non-functional requirement for a solution. However, with growing cyber-attacks it is considered as a functional requirement these days.

Every organization follows some sort of application life cycle management for their applications. When security is treated as a functional requirement, it should follow the same process of application development. Security should not be an after-thought, rather it should be part of the application from the beginning. Within the overall planning phase for an application, security should also be planned. Based on the nature of the application, different kinds and categories of threats should be identified and based on these identifications, they should be documented in terms of approach and scope to mitigate them. A threat modeling exercise should be undertaken to illustrate the threat each component can be subjected to. This will lead to designing security standards and policies for the application. This is typically the security design phase. The next phase is called the **Threat Mitigation** or **Build** phase. In this phase, implementation of security in terms of code and configuration is executed to mitigate the security threats and risks.

A system cannot be secure until it is tested. Appropriate penetration tests and other security tests should be performed to identify potential mitigations that are not implemented, missed, or overlooked. The bugs from testing are remediated and the cycle continues till the life of the application. This process of application life cycle management should be followed for security.

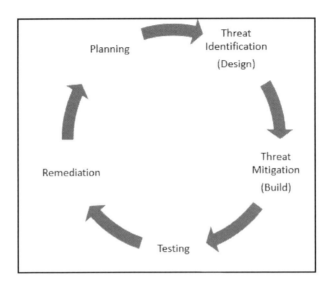

Threat modeling, identification, mitigation, testing, and remediation are iterative processes that continue even when an application or service is operational. There should be active monitoring of entire environments and applications to proactively identify threats and mitigate them. Monitoring should also enable alerts and audit logs to help in reactive diagnosis, troubleshooting, and elimination of threats and vulnerabilities.

The security life cycle for any application starts with the planning phase, which eventually leads to the design phase. In the **Design** phase, application architecture is decomposed into granular components with discreet communication and hosting boundaries. Based on their interaction with other components within and across hosting boundaries, threats are identified. Identified threats are mitigated by implementing appropriate security features within the overall architecture and tested to identify if such vulnerability still exists. After the application is deployed on production and becomes operational, it is monitored for any security breaches and vulnerability and either proactive or reaction remediation is conducted.

Azure security

Azure provides all its services through data centers in multiple regions. These data centers are interconnected within regions as well as across regions. Azure understands that it hosts mission critical and important applications, services, and data for its customers. It must ensure that security is of the utmost importance for its data centers and regions. Customers deploy applications on the cloud based on this trust that Azure will protect their applications and data from vulnerabilities and breach. Customers will not move to the cloud if this trust is broken and hence Azure implements security at all layers from physical data center perimeter to logical software components. Each layer is protected, and even Azure data center team does not have access to them.

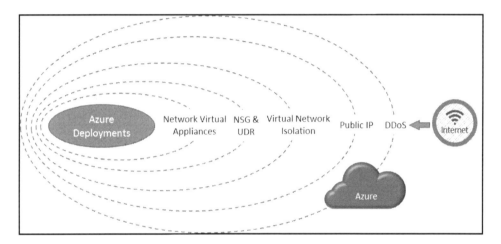

Security is of paramount importance to both Microsoft and Azure. Azure is a cloud platform--a platform hosted by Microsoft. Microsoft ensures that trust is built with its customers and it does so by ensuring that its customer deployment, solutions, and data are completely secure, physically and virtually. People will not use any cloud platform if it is not secure physically and digitally. To ensure that customers have trust on Azure, each activity in development of Azure is planned, documented, audited, and monitored from a security perspective. The physical Azure data centers are protected for any intrusion and unauthorized access. In fact, even Microsoft personnel and operations team do not have access to customer solution and data.

- **Secure user access**: A customer's deployment, solution, and data can only be accessed by the customer. Even Azure data center personals do not have access to any customer artifacts. Customers can allow access to further people; however, that is at the discretion of the customer.

- **Encryption at rest**: Azure encrypts all its management data such that it cannot be read by anyone. It also provides these functionality to its customers as well as those who can encrypt their data at rest.
- **Encryption at transit**: Azure encrypts all data that flows from its network. It also ensures that its network backbone is protected from any unauthorized access.
- **Active monitoring and auditing**: Azure monitors all its data centers actively on an on-going basis. It actively identifies any breach, threat, and risk and mitigates them.

Azure meets both country-specific local, international, and industry-specific compliance standards. Again, they can be found at
`https://www.microsoft.com/en-us/trustcenter/compliance/complianceofferings`.

IaaS security

Azure is a mature platform for deploying IaaS solutions. There are lots of users of Azure who want complete control over their deployments and they typically use IaaS for their solutions. It is important that these deployments and solutions are secure by default and design. Azure provides rich security features to secure IaaS solutions. In this section, some of the major features will be covered.

Network Security Groups

Bare minimum of IaaS deployment consists of virtual machines and virtual networks. The virtual machines might be exposed to the internet by applying a public IP to its network interface or it might be available to internal resources only. The internal resources in turn might be exposed to the internet. In any case, virtual machines should be secured such that unauthorized requests should not even reach them. Virtual machines should be secured using facilities that can filter requests at the network itself rather than them reaching virtual machine and it taking action on them. This is such as creating a ring-fence around virtual machines. This fence can allow or deny requests based on their protocol, origin IP, destination IP, originating port, and destination port. This feature is deployed using the Azure **Network Security Groups** (**NSGs**) resource. NSG is composed of rules that are evaluated for both incoming and outgoing requests. Based on the execution and evaluation of these rules, it is determined if the requests should be allowed or denied access.

NSGs are flexible and can be applied to a virtual network subnet or individual network interfaces. When applying to a subnet, the security rules are applied to any resource, that is, a virtual machines or load balancers on this subnet while applying to a network interface affects the requests only for that network interface. It is also possible to apply NSGs to both network subnet and network interfaces simultaneously. Typically, this design should be used for applying common security rules at network subnet level and unique different security rules at network interface level. It helps in designing modular security rules and applications.

The flow for evaluating NSG is shown in the following figure:

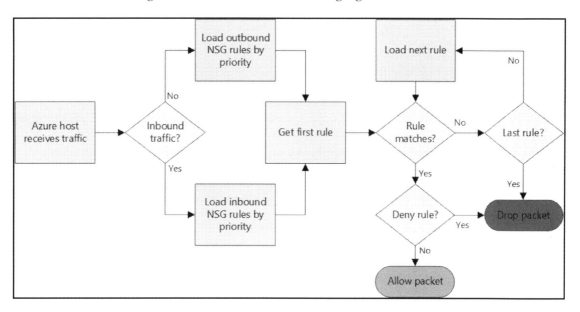

There are a few default rules provided by Azure out-of-the-box. These are very important and come handy when deployments want to use rules related to request from/to the internet, virtual networks, and load balancers. Generally, IP addresses are ever changing for these resources and using these rules provide abstraction to use these IP addresses directly.

Network Security Group design

The first step in designing is to ascertain the security requirements of the resource. The following should be answered:

- Is the resource accessible from the internet only?
- Is the resource accessible from both the internal resources and the internet?
- Is the resource accessible from the internal resource only?
- Determine the resources load balancer, gateways, and virtual machines used
- Configuration of a virtual network and its subnet

Based on answers from these questions, adequate NSG design should be created.

Ideally, there should be multiple network subnets for each workload and type of resource. It is not recommended to deploy both load balancers and virtual machines on the same subnet.

Based on requirements, rules should be determined that are common for different virtual machine workloads and subnets. For example, for a SharePoint deployment, the frontend application and SQL servers are deployed on separate subnets. Rules for each subnet should be determined.

After common subnet level rules are identified, rules for individual resources should be identified and these should be applied to the network interface level.

It is important to understand that if a rule allows an incoming request on a port, that port can also be used for outgoing requests without any configuration.

If resources are accessible from the internet, rules should be created with specific IP ranges and Ports to the extent possible.

Careful functional and security testing should be executed for ensuring that adequate and optimal NSG rules are opened and closed.

Firewalls

NSGs provides external security perimeters for requests. However, it does not mean that virtual machines should not implement additional security measures. It is always better to implement security both internally and externally. Virtual machines whether in Linux or Windows provide a mechanism to filter requests at operating system level. This is known as firewall in both Windows and Linux.

It is advisable to implement firewalls for operating systems. They help in building a virtual security wall that helps in allowing only those requests that are considered trusted. Any untrusted requests are denied access. There are even physical firewall devices, but on the cloud software, operating system firewalls are used.

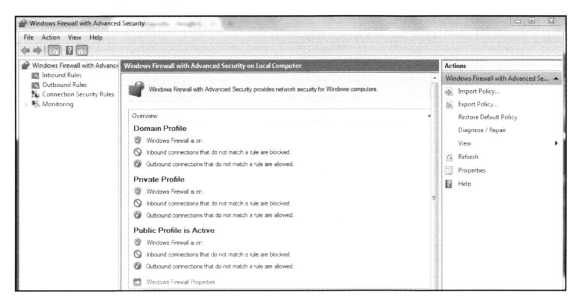

Firewalls help in filtering network packets, identifying incoming ports, and IP addresses. Based on the information from these packets, it evaluates the rules and figures out whether it should allow access or deny it.

Firewall design

As a good practice, firewalls should be evaluated for individual operating systems. Each virtual machine has a distinct responsibility within the overall deployment and solution. Rules for these individual responsibilities should be identified and firewalls should be opened and closed accordingly.

While evaluating firewall rules, it is important to keep network security group rules for both subnet and individual network interface level into consideration. If not done properly, it is possible that rules are denied at NSG level, but left open at firewall level and vice-versa. If a request is allowed at NSG rule level and denied at the firewall level, the application will not work as intended, while the security risks increase if request is denied at the NSG rule level and allowed at the firewall level.

A firewall helps in building multiple networks isolated by its security rules.

Careful functional and security testing should be executed for ensuring that adequate and optimal firewall rules are opened and closed.

Reducing attack surface area

NSGs and firewall help in managing authorized requests to the environment. However, the environment should not be overtly exposed to security attacks. The surface area of the system should be optimally enabled to be able to achieve its functionality but disabled enough that attackers cannot find loopholes and access areas that are opened without any intended use or opened, but not secured adequately. Security should be adequately hardened making it difficult for any attacker to break into the system.

Some of the areas that should be configured include the following:

- Remove all unnecessary users and groups from OS.
- Identify group membership for all users.
- Implement group policies using directory services.
- Block script execution unless it is signed by trusted authorities.
- Log and audit all activities.
- Install malware and anti-virus software's, schedule scans, and update definitions frequently.
- Disable or shut down services that are not required.
- Lock down the filesystem for only authorized access.
- Lock down changes to registry.
- Firewall must be configured according to solution needs.
- PowerShell script execution should be set to restricted or **RemoteSigned**.
- Enabled enhanced protection through Internet Explorer.
- Restrict ability to create new users and groups.
- Remove internet access and implement jump servers for RDP.
- Remove allowing logging into servers using RDP through the internet. Instead use site to site VPN or point to site VPN or express route to RDP into remote machines from within network.
- Regularly deploy all security updates.
- Run security compliance manager tool on the environment and implement all of its recommendations.

- Actively monitor the environment using security center and operations management suite.
- Deploy network virtual appliances to route traffic to internal proxy and reverse proxy.
- All sensitive data such as configuration, connection strings, credentials, and so on should be encrypted.

Implementing jump servers

It is a good idea to remove internet access from virtual machines. It is also a good practice to remove remote desktop services accessibility from the internet, but then how do you access the virtual machines at all. One good way is to allow only internal resources to RDP into virtual machines using Azure VPN options. However, there is also another way--by way of using jump servers.

Jump servers are servers that are deployed on **Demilitarized Zone** (**DMZ**). It means it is on a different network and not on network hosting the core solutions and applications. Instead, it is on a separate network or subnet. The primary purpose of the jump server is to accept RDP requests from users and help them log in to it. From this jump server, users can further navigate to other virtual machines using RDP. It has access to two or more networks--one that has connectivity to the outside world and other internal to the solution. The jump server implements all the security restrictions and provides a secure client to connect to other servers. Normally, access to emails and internet is disabled on jump servers.

An example for deploying a jump server with the **virtual machine scale sets** (**VMSS**) is available at
`https://azure.microsoft.com/en-in/resources/templates/201-vmss-windows-jumpbox/`
using Azure resource manager templates.

PaaS security

Azure provides numerous PaaS services with each having their own security features. In general, PaaS services can be accessed using credentials, certificates, and tokens. PaaS services allow generation of short-lived security access tokens. Client applications can send this security access token to represent trusted users. In this section, we will cover some of the most important PaaS services that are almost used in every solution.

Operations Management Suite (OMS)

Microsoft Management Suite, also known as log analytics, is a new platform for managing cloud deployments, on-premise data centers, and hybrid solutions.

OMS provides multiple modular solutions--specific functionality that helps to implement a feature. For example, security and audit solutions help to ascertain a complete view of security for organizations deployment. Similarly, there are many more solutions such as automation, change tracking, and so on that should be implemented from a security perspective.

The OMS security and audit provides information into four categories:

- **Security domains**: It provides functionality to view security records, malware assessment, update assessment, network security, and identity and access information, computers with security events, and provides access to the Azure security center dashboard.
- **Antimalware assessment**: It helps in identifying servers that are not protected against malware and are having security issues. It helps in providing an overall exposure to potential security problems and its criticality. Users can take proactive actions based on these recommendations. Azure security center sub-category provides information collected by Azure security center.
- **Notable issues**: It helps in quickly identifying active issues and their severity.
- **Detections**: This category is in the preview mode. It enables identification of attack patterns by visualizing security alerts.
- **Threat intelligence**: It helps in identifying attack patterns by visualizing the total number of servers with outbound malicious IP traffic, the malicious threat type, and a map that shows where these IPs are coming from.

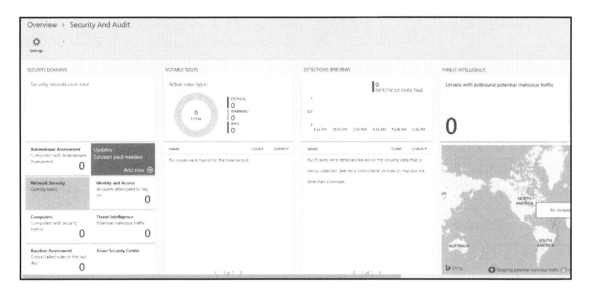

Storage

Storage account plays an important component in the overall solution architecture. Storage accounts can store important information such as user PII data, business transactions, data, and more. It is of utmost importance that storage accounts are secure and allow only restricted access to authorized users. The data stored is encrypted and transmitted using secure channels. Not only the storage, but users and client applications consuming storage account and its data should play a crucial role in the overall security of data. They should also keep data encrypted at all times. This also includes credentials and connection strings connecting to data stores.

Azure provides RBAC control about who can manage Azure storage accounts. These RBAC permissions are allowed to users and groups in Azure **Active Directory** (**AD**). However, when an application to be deployed on Azure is created, it will have users and customers that are not available in Azure AD. For allowing users to access the storage account, Azure storage provides storage access keys. There are two types of access keys at the storage account level--primary and secondary. Users possessing these keys can connect to the storage account. These storage access keys are used in authentication for accessing the storage account. Applications can access storage accounts using either primary or secondary keys. Two keys are provided such that if the primary key is comprised, applications can be updated to use the secondary key, while the primary key is regenerated. This helps in minimizing application downtime. Moreover, it provides and enhances security by removing the comprised key without impacting applications.

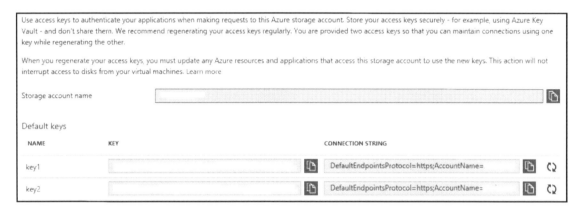

Azure storage provides four services--blob, files, queues, and tables in an account. Each of these services also provides infrastructure for securing themselves using secure access tokens. A **shared access signature** (**SAS**) is a URI that grants restricted access rights to Azure storage services--blob, files, queues, and tables. These shared access signatures can be shared with clients who should not be trusted with the entire storage account key, but only to constrain access to certain storage account resources. By distributing a shared access signature URI to these clients, access to resources is granted for a specified period.

Shared access signature exists at both storage account and individual blob, file, table, and queue levels. Storage account level signature is more powerful and has rights to allow and deny permissions at the individual service level. It can also be used instead of individual resource service levels.

Generating and sharing shared access signatures is preferred as compared to sharing storage account keys. Shared access signatures provide granular access to resources and they can be combined together as well. These include, **read**, **write**, **delete**, **list**, **add**, **create**, **update**, and **process**. Moreover, even access to resources can be determined while generating shared access signatures. It could be for blobs, tables, queues, and files individually or a combination of them. Storage account keys are for the entire account and cannot be constrained for individual services. Neither can it be constrained from the permissions perspective. It is much easy to create and revoke shared access signatures compared to storage access keys. Shared access signatures can be created for use for a certain period of time after which they become invalid automatically.

It is to be noted that if storage account keys are regenerated, then shared access signature based on them will get invalidated and newer shared access signatures should be created and shared with clients.

Cookie stealing, script injection, and denial of service attacks are common means used by attackers to disrupt or disrupt an environment and steal data. Browsers and HTTP protocol implements inbuilt mechanism ensuring that these malicious activities cannot be performed. Generally, anything cross-domain is not allowed both by HTTP and browsers. A script running in one domain cannot ask for resources from another domain. However, there are valid use cases where such requests should be allowed. HTTP protocol implements **Cross Origin Resource Sharing** (**CORS**). With the help of CORS, it is possible to access resources across domains and make them work. Azure storage helps in configuring CORS rules for blobs, file, queue, and table resources. Azure storage allows the creation of rules that are evaluated for each authenticated request. If the rules are satisfied, the request is allowed to access the resource.

Data must not only be protected while in transit, they should be protected while at rest as well. If data at rest is not encrypted, anybody can read the data having access to physical drive in the data center. Although the possibility is next to negligible, customers still should encrypt their data. Storage service encryption also helps in protecting data at rest. This service works transparently and injects itself without users knowing about it. It encrypts data when the data is saved in a storage account and decrypts automatically when it is read. This entire process happens without users performing any additional activity.

Azure account keys must be rotated periodically. This will ensure that an attacker is not able to breach access to storage accounts.

It is also a good idea to re-generate the keys; however, this must be evaluated in regard to its usage in existing applications. If it breaks the existing application, these applications should be prioritized for change management and changes should be applied gradually.

As much as possible, individual service level SAS tokens with a limited time frame should be generated and provided to users who should access them. Permissions must be evaluated and optimum permissions must be provided.

SAS keys and storage account keys should be stored in an Azure key vault. It provides security storage and access to them. These keys can be read at runtime by applications from the key vault instead of storing them in configuration files.

Azure SQL

SQL server helps in storing relational data on Azure. It is a SaaS service that provides highly available, scalable, performance-centric, and secure platform for storing data. It is accessible from anywhere, any programming language and platform. Clients need a connection string comprising of server, database, and security information to connect to it.

SQL server provides firewall settings that disallow access to anyone by default. IP addresses and ranges should be whitelisted for accessing SQL server. Only those IP addresses that architects are confident of belonging to customer or partners should be whitelisted. There are deployments in Azure for which either there are a lot of IP addresses or the IP addresses are not known. For example, applications deployed in Azure functions or logic apps. For such applications to access Azure SQL, Azure SQL provides whitelisting of all IP addresses to Azure services across subscriptions.

It is to be noted that firewall configuration is at the server-level and not database level. It means any changes here affect all databases within a server.

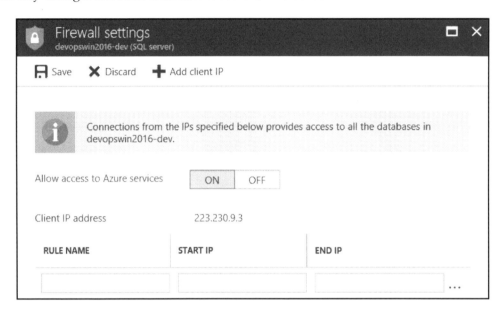

Azure SQL also provides enhanced security by encrypting data at rest. This ensures that nobody, including the Azure data center administrators, can view the data stored in the SQL server. The technology used by SQL server for encrypting data at rest is known as **Transparent Data Encryption** (TDE). There are no changes required at the application level to implement TDE. SQL server encrypts and decrypts data transparently when the user saves and reads data. This feature is available at the database level.

SQL server also provides **Dynamic Data Masking** (DDM), which is especially useful for masking certain types of data, such as credit cards or user PII data. Masking is not the same as encryption. Masking does not encrypt data, but only masks, which ensures that data is not in human-readable format.

Users should mask and encrypt sensitive data in the Azure SQL server.

SQL server also provides **Auditing & Threats Detection** service for all servers. There are advanced data collection and intelligence services running on top of these databases across to find out threats and vulnerabilities and alert users based on them. Audit logs are maintained by Azure in storage accounts and can be viewed by administrators for action. Threads such as SQL injection and anonymous client logins can generate alerts that administrators can be informed about over email.

Data can be masked in Azure SQL. This helps in storing data in a format that does not easily make sense.

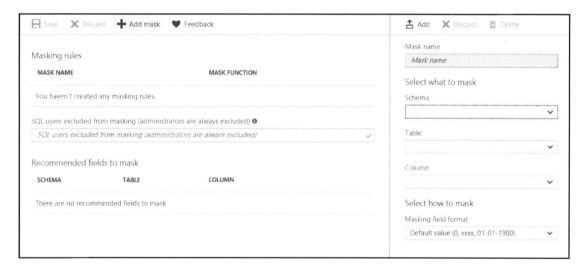

Azure SQL also provides **Transparent data encryption** to encrypt data at rest.

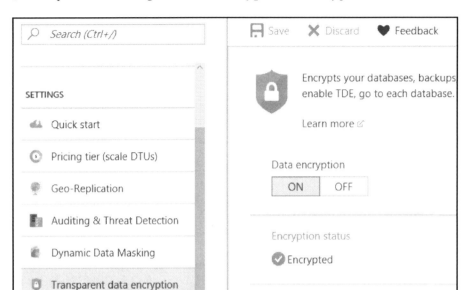

Azure key vaults

Securing resources using passwords, keys, credentials, certificates and unique identifiers are an important element for any environment and application. They are important elements from the security perspective. They need to be protected and to ensure that these resources remain secure and do not get comprised is an important pillar of security architecture. Management and operations that keep the secrets and keys secure while making them available when needed is an important aspect that cannot be ignored. Typically, these secrets are used all over the place--within the source code, configuration file, pieces of paper, and in other digital formats. To overcome these challenges and store all secrets uniformly in a centralized secure storage, Azure key vaults should be created.

Azure key vault is well integrated with other Azure services. For example, using a certificate stored in the Azure key vault and deploying it on Azure virtual machines certificate store can be easily performed. All kinds of keys including storage keys, IoT and event keys, and connection strings can be stored as secrets in the Azure key vault. They can be retrieved and used transparently without anyone viewing them or storing them temporarily anywhere. Credentials for SQL server and other services can also be stored in the Azure key vault.

Azure key vault works on a per region basis. What this means is that an Azure key vault resource should be provisioned at the same region where the application and service is deployed. If a deployment consists of more than one region and needs services from Azure key vault, multiple Azure key vault instances should be provisioned.

Security monitoring and audit

Azure provides two important security resources to manage all security aspects of Azure subscription, resource groups, and resources:

- Azure monitor
- Azure security center

Azure monitor

Azure monitor is a one place stop for monitoring Azure resources. It provides information about Azure resources and their state. It provides a rich query interface using which information can be sliced and diced using data at subscription, resource group, individual resource, resource type, and time interval level.

Azure monitor can be used through the Azure portal, PowerShell, CLI, and REST API.

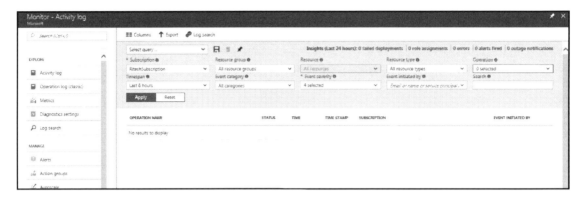

- The **Activity log** provides all management level operations performed on resources. It provides details about the creation time, creator, resource type and status.
- The **Operation log (classic)** provides details of all operations performed on resources within a resource group and subscription.
- **Metrics** helps in getting performance level information for individual resources and sets alerts on them.
- **Diagnostic settings** help in configuring the effects logs by setting up Azure storage for storing logs, stream logs in real-time to Azure event hubs, and send to log analytics (previously known as Operational Management Suite).
- **Log search** helps in integrating the logs analytics with Azure monitor.

Azure monitor can help identify security-related incidents and take appropriate actions based on them. It is important that only authorized individuals should be allowed to access Azure monitor since they might contain sensitive information.

Azure security center

Azure security center as the name suggests is a one place stop for all security needs. There are generally two activities related to security--implementing security and monitoring for any threats and breaches. Security center has been built primarily to help in both these activities. Azure security center enables users to define their security policies and get them implemented on Azure resources. Based on the current state of Azure resources, Azure security center provides security recommendations to harden the solution and individual Azure resources. The recommendations include almost all Azure resources security best practices including encryption of data, disks, network protection, endpoint protection, access control lists, whitelisting of incoming requests, blocking of unauthorized requests, and more. The resources range from infrastructure components such as load balancers, network security groups, and virtual network to PaaS resources such as Azure SQL, storage, and others.

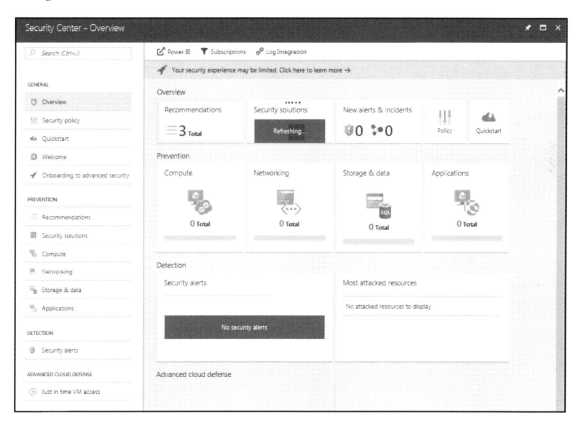

Azure security center is a rich platform and it can provide recommendations for multiple services.

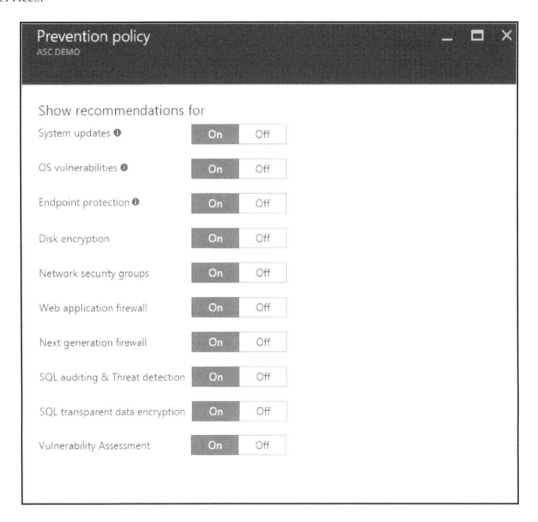

Summary

Security was always an important aspect for any deployment and solution. It has become much more important and relevant because of deployments on the cloud. Moreover, there are increasing events and threats from cybersecurity attacks. In such circumstances, security has become the focal point for organizations. No matter the type of deployment and solution--whether IaaS, PaaS, or SaaS, security is needed across all of them. Azure data centers are completely secure and they have a dozen international security certifications. They are secure by default. They provide IaaS security resources such as NSGs, network address translation, secure endpoints, certificates, key vaults, storage and virtual machine encryption, and PaaS security features for individual PaaS resources. Security has a complete life cycle of its own and it should be properly planned, designed, implemented, and tested just like any other application functionality.

Next chapter onwards, some of technology specific architecture and solution will be the focus of the book. Next chapter discusses **Internet of Things (IoT)** on Azure.

6
Designing IoT Solutions

So far, we have been dealing with architectural concerns and their solutions on Azure in general. This chapter is not based on generalized architecture. This chapter is about one of the most disruptive technology of this century. This chapter will get into the details of IoT architecture on Azure

This chapter will specifically cover the following topics:

- Azure and IoT
- Azure IoT overview
- Device management
    - Registering devices
    - Device to IoT hub communication
- Scaling IoT solutions
- High availability of IoT solutions
- IoT protocols
- Using message properties for routing messages

IoT

IoT is an abbreviation and when expanded is **Internet of Things**. There are two important keywords in this phrase--Internet and Things. To understand it better, let's go back a few centuries in history to relate to the current emergence of this technology.

In the nineties internet was invented and became available generally to everyone although the penetration was less. During this time, almost everyone moved towards having a presence on the internet and started creating static web pages. These static web pages were showing details about various aspects. Eventually the static content became dynamic and content was generated on the fly based on context. In almost all cases, a browser was needed for accessing the internet. There was a plethora of browsers, but without them consuming the internet was a challenge.

During the first decade of this century, there was an interesting development happening-the rise of hand held devices in the form of mobile phones and tablets. Mobile phones started becoming cheaper by the day and available ubiquitously. The hardware and software capabilities of these handheld devices were improving considerably. So much so, people started using browsers on mobile devices rather than desktops. But there was a subtle change that was noticeable and it was the rise of mobile apps. The mobile apps were downloaded from some store and were connected to the internet to talk to backend systems. Towards the end of the last decade there were millions of apps available with almost every conceivable functionality build in them. The backend system for these apps was built on cloud so that they could be scaled rapidly. This was the age of connecting applications and servers.

But, was this the pinnacle of innovation? What was the next evolution in making this better for everyone at large? If you look closely there was another paradigm taking center stage. This was IoT. When apps connected to backend systems, it was basically a device that had compute, storage, and was connected to the internet making requests. How about connecting every device connected to the internet? Instead of just mobile and tablets connected to the internet there can be other devices that can be connected to the internet. These devices were available in select markets, were costly, not available to masses, and had limited hardware and software capabilities. However, during the first part of the current decade commercialization of these devices started in big scale. These devices were becoming smaller and smaller, more capable from hardware and software perspective, had more storage and compute power, could connect to the internet on various protocols, and could be attached to almost anything. This is the age of connecting devices to server, applications, and to other devices.

This led to the formulation of the idea and applications that could change the way industries were operating. Newer solutions that were unheard of before started becoming reality. Now these devices could be attached to anything and they could get information and send it to a backend system that could assimilate that information from all the devices and either take proactive action or report the happenings.

Examples of IoT are vehicle tracking systems that track all vital parameters of a vehicle and send details to centralized data store for analysis, smart city services, such as tracking pollution levels, temperature, street congestion, and so on, and agriculture-related activities related to soil fertility, humidity, and so on.

IoT architecture

Before getting into Azure and its features and services related to IoT, it is important to understand various components needed to create end -to-end IoT solutions.

Imagine IoT devices across the globe sending millions of messages every second to a centralized database. Why is this data collected? This data is collected to extract rich information about events, anomalies, outliers, and happenings within those devices and objects they are connected to.

Let's understand this in more detail.

IoT architecture can be divided into distinct phases:

- Connectivity
- Identity
- Capture
- Ingestion
- Storage
- Transform
- Analytics
- Presentation

The next images show a generic IoT based architecture. Data are generated or collected by devices and send over to cloud gateways. The cloud gateway, in turn, sends the data to multiple backend services for processing. Cloud gateways are an optional component. They should be used when devices themselves are not capable of sending requests to backend services either because of their resource constraints or lack of reliable network. These Cloud gateways can collate date from multiple devices an send to backend services. Data processes by backend services is then shown as insights or dashboards to users.

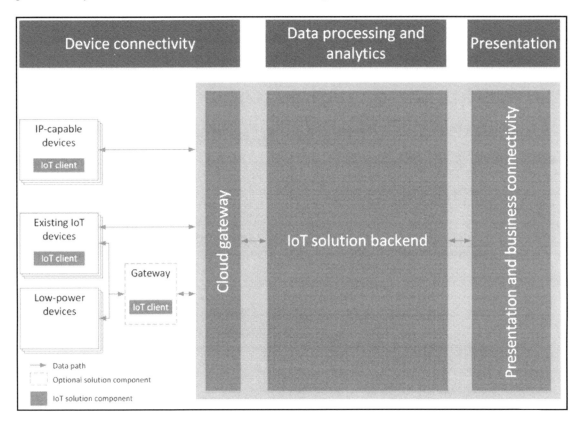

Connectivity

IoT devices need to communicate. There are various connectivity types. It could be between devices in a region, between devices and a centralized gateway, devices to IoT platform, and more.

In all cases mentioned before, IoT devices need connectivity capability. This capability could be in terms of internet connectivity, bluetooth, infrared, or any other near device communication.

Some devices might not have the capability to connect to the internet. In those cases, they can connect through other means to a gateway, which in turn has connectivity to the internet.

IoT devices use protocols to send messages. The major protocols among these are **Advanced Message Queuing Protocol (AMPQ)** and **Message Queue Telemetry Transport (MQTT)**.

Devices data should be sent to IT infrastructure. MQTT protocol is a device to server protocol that devices can use to send telemetry and other information to servers. Once the server receives the message through the MQTT protocol it needs to transport the messages to other servers using a reliable technology based on messages and queues. AMPQ is the preferred protocol to move messages between servers in the IT infrastructure in a reliable and predictable manner.

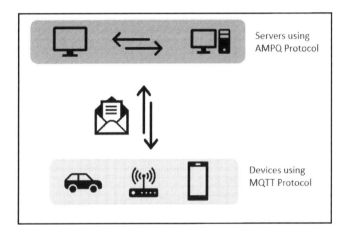

The servers getting initial messages from IoT devices should send messages to other servers for processing, such as saving to logs, evaluation, analytics, and presentation purposes.

Some devices do not have capabilities to connect to the internet or do not support the protocols understood by IT protocols. As mentioned before, IoT devices have various capabilities and some of the features that affect their capabilities are mentioned next. To enable these devices to work with the IoT platform and the cloud, intermediate gateways help in adapting them for sending information to cloud. Gateways help in on-boarding devices that connectivity and networks are slow and not consistent, devices use protocols that are not standard, and their capabilities are limited in terms of resources and power.

In such circumstances when devices need additional infrastructure to participate and connect to backend services, client gateways can be deployed. These gateways receive messages from near devices and forward and push them to IT infrastructure and the IoT platform for further consumption. These gateways are capable of protocol translation if required.

Identity

IoT devices should be registered with the cloud platform. Not every device should be allowed to connect to the cloud platform. The devices should be registered and be assigned an identity. The device should be sending the identity information while connecting and sending information to the cloud. In case the device fails to send this identity information, the connectivity should fail. We will see later in this chapter about how to generate identity for a device using simulation application.

Capture

IoT devices should be able to capture the information from itself and the ecosystem around it. It should have the capability for example to read the moisture content in air or in soil. The information can be captured based on frequency, which could be as low as per second. Once the information is captured, it should be able to send it across to the IoT platform for processing. If a device does not have the capability to connect to the IoT platform directly, it can connect to an intermediary and cloud gateways to push the captured information. The size of captured data and frequency is the most important aspect for the device. Whether the device has local storage and temporarily store the captured data is another important aspect that should be taken care of. The device can work in an offline mode if there is local storage available. Even mobile devices sometimes act as IoT devices connected to various instruments and have the capability to store data.

Ingestion

The data captured and generated by devices should be sent to an IoT platform that is capable of ingesting and consuming that data to extract meaningful information and insights out of it. The ingestion service is an important and crucial service because its availability and scalability effects the throughput of incoming data. If data starts getting throttled due to scalability issues or data is not able to ingest due to availability issues, data would be lost and might get biased or skewed.

Storage

IoT solutions generally deal with millions and billions of records spanning terabytes and petabytes of data. This is valuable data that can provide insights on operations and its health. This data needs to be stored such that analytics can be performed on it. The storage should be readily available for analytics applications and service to consume it. They should provide adequate throughput and latency from a performance perspective, be highly available and scalable, and secure in nature.

Transform

IoT solutions are generally data driven and have considerable high volume. Imagine each car having a device and each one is sending messages every five seconds. If there are a million cars sending messages, it will be equal to 288 million messages per day and 8 billion messages per month. Together this data has lots of hidden information and insights; however, making sense of this kind of data is quite difficult by mere viewing. The data captured and stored can be consumed for solving business problems. Depending on the nature of the problem, not all data captured is of importance. There could be a subset of data that should be used for solving a problem. The data captured and stored could not be consistent as well. To ensure that the data is consistent, not biased or skewed, appropriate transformation should be executed on it for making it readily consumable. This process is typically known as transformation. Here, data is filtered, sorted, removed, enriched, and transformed to a structure; further downstream components and applications can consume readily.

Analytics

The data transformed in the previous step becomes the input and source of data for analytics. Depending on the nature of business and problem at hand there are different multiple types of analytics that can be performed on transformed data.

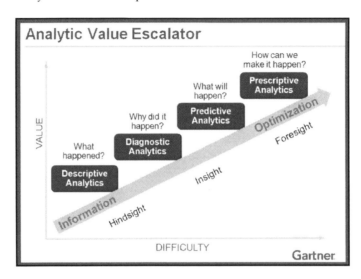

The preceding figure is taken from *Gartner* and it very well depicts the different types of analytics that can be performed:

- **Descriptive Analytics**: This type of analytics helps in finding patterns and details about statuses of IoT devices and overall health. This is generally the first stage of analytics that identifies and summarizes the data for further consumption by more advanced analytics. It will help in finding information such as summarization, statistics related to probability, deviation, and other simple statistical concepts.

- **Diagnostic Analytics**: This type of analytics is more advanced than descriptive analytics. It builds on top of descriptive analytics and tries to answer queries about why things happened. It tries to find the root cause of the events that happened. It tries to find answers using advanced concepts, such as hypothesis and correlation.

- **Predictive Analytics**: This type of analytics tries to predict things that have a high probability of happening in future. It's about prediction based on past data. Regression is one of the examples based on past data, it could, for example, predict the price of a car, stock in the stock market, when the next tire will burst and so on.

- **Prescriptive/Cognitive Analytics**: This analytics are at the highest maturity levels and help take actions automatically. This analytics help in identifying the most appropriate action that should be executed to ensure that health of devices and solution do not degrade and proactive measures can be undertaken. This helps in avoiding and eliminating the problems from the root.

Presentation

Analytics help in identifying answers, patterns, and insights based on data available from the past. These insights also need to be available to all stakeholders in different forms and format in which they can understand. It should be readily consumable and available in multiple formats. Appropriate dashboards and reports can be generated--statistically or dynamically, and then can be presented to stakeholders. The stakeholders can consume these reports for further action and improve continuously on their solution.

Azure IoT

After learning details about the various stages that help in creating end-to-end IoT solutions. Each of these stages are crucial and their implementation is a must for its success. Azure provides lots of services for each of these stages. Apart from these services, Azure provides IoT hubs--the core IoT service and platform that is capable of hosting complex, highly available, and scalable IoT solutions. We will dive deep into IoT hubs after going through other services. This section will detail in brief each of these services.

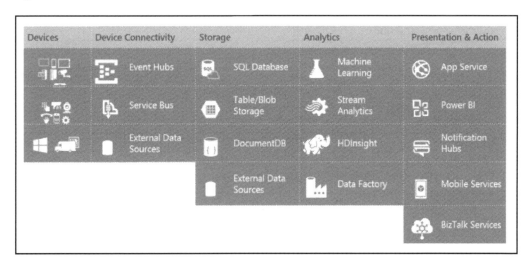

Identity

Azure IoT hubs also provide services for authenticating devices. IoT hubs provide interface for generating unique identity hashes for each device. When devices send their messages containing this hash, the IoT hub can identify them after verification of its own database for existence of such hashes.

Capture

Azure provides IoT gateways that enable IoT hubs non-compliant devices to get adapted and enable pushing of data. There are local or intermediary gateways deployed near devices such that multiple devices can connect to a single gateway to send their information. Similarly, multiple such clusters of devices with a local gateway can be deployed. There can be a cloud gateway deployed on the cloud itself, capable of accepting data from multiple sources and ingesting them for IoT hubs.

Ingestion

Azure provides an IoT hub that becomes a single point of contact for devices and other applications to send data. In other words, ingestion of IoT messages is the responsibility of the IoT hub service. There are other services, such as event hubs and service bus messaging infrastructure that can provide ingestion of incoming messages; however, the benefits and advantages of IoT hubs for ingesting IoT data far outlast compared to event hubs and service bus messaging. In fact, IoT hubs have been made specifically for the purpose of ingesting IoT messages within the Azure ecosystem such that the rest of the services and components can act on them.

Storage

Azure provides multiple types of storage for storing messages from IoT devices. These storage accounts include storing relational data, schema less NoSQL data, and blobs:

- **SQL database**: SQL database provides storing relational data, JSON, and XML documents. It provides rich SQL query language and it uses a full blown SQL server as a service. Data from devices can be stored in SQL databases if data is well defined and expectation is that the schema will not undergo changes frequently.

- **Azure storage**: Azure storage provides table and blob storage. Table storage helps in storing data as entities where schema is not important. It is an implementation of NoSQL databases. Blobs help in storing files in containers as blobs.
- **CosmosDB/DocumentDB**: DocumentDB is a full blown enterprise scale NoSQL database, available as a service capable of storing schema less data. It is a truly distributed database that can span continents providing high availability and scalability of data.
- **External data sources:** Apart from Azure services, customers can bring their own datastores, such as SQL server on Azure virtual machines, and can use them for storing data in relational format.

Transform and analytics

- **Data factory**: Azure data factory is a cloud-based data integration service that allows us to create data-driven workflows in the cloud for orchestrating and automating data movement and data transformation. Azure data factory helps to create and schedule data-driven workflows (called pipelines) that can ingest data from disparate data stores, process/transform the data by using compute services such as **Azure HDInsight Hadoop**, **Spark**, **Azure Data Lake Analytics**, and **Azure Machine Learning**, and publish output data to data stores such as Azure SQL data warehouse for **business intelligence** (**BI**) applications to consume. It's more of an **Extract-and-Load** (**EL**) and then **Transform-and-Load** (**TL**) platform rather than a traditional **Extract-Transform-and-Load** (**ETL**) platform.
- **Azure HDInsight**: Microsoft and Hortonworks have come together to help companies by offering the big data analytics platform on the Azure cloud service. HDInsight is a high-powered, fully managed cloud service environment powered by Apache Hadoop and Apache Spark using Microsoft Azure HDInsight. It helps in accelerating workloads seamlessly with Microsoft and Hortonworks' industry leading big data cloud service.
- **Azure stream analytics**: This is a fully managed real-time data analytics service that helps in performing computation and transformation on streaming data. Stream analytics can examine high volumes of data flowing from devices or processes, extract information from the data stream, and look for patterns, trends, and relationships.

- **Machine learning**: Machine learning is a data science technique that allows computers to use existing data to forecast future behaviors, outcomes, and trends. Using machine learning, computers learn without being explicitly programmed. Azure machine learning is a cloud predictive analytics service that makes it possible to quickly create and deploy predictive models as analytics solutions.

It provides a ready-to-use library of algorithms to create models on an internet-connected PC, and deploy predictive solutions quickly.

Presentation

After appropriate analytics have been conducted on data, the data should be presented to stakeholders in a format that is consumable by them. There are numerous ways insights from data can be presented. This includes presenting data using web applications deployed using Azure app services, sending data to notification hubs that can then notify mobile applications and more. However, the ideal approach for presenting and consuming insights is by way of using **Power BI** reports and dashboards. Power BI is a Microsoft visualization tool for rendering dynamic reports and dashboard on the internet accessible for anywhere on any network.

IoT hubs

IoT projects are generally complex in nature. The complexity arises because of high volume of devices and data, devices are embedded across the world, monitoring and audit of devices, storage of data, transformation and analytics on petabytes of data, and finally taking action based on insights. Moreover, these projects are of long duration, have long gestation periods, and their requirements keep changing because of timelines.

If any enterprise wants to embark on a journey for IoT projects, sooner than later it would be realized that these are not easy problems to solve. These projects need large hardware in terms of compute and storage and services that can work with such high volumes of data.

IoT hub is a platform that is built to help ease and enable IoT projects for faster, better, and easier delivery. It provides all the necessary features and services for the following:

- Device registration
- Device connectivity
- Field gateways
- Cloud gateways

- Implementation of industry protocols such as AMQP and MQTT
- Hub for storing incoming messages
- Routing of messages based on message properties and content
- Multiple endpoints for different types of processing
- Connectivity to other services on Azure for analytics and real-time analytics and more

Protocols

Azure IoT hub natively supports communication over the MQTT, AMQP, and HTTP protocols. In some cases, devices or field gateways might not be able to use one of these standard protocols and will require protocol adaptation. In such cases, custom gateway can be deployed. A custom gateway can enable protocol adaptation for IoT hub endpoints by bridging the traffic to and from the IoT hub.

Device registration

Devices should be registered before they can send messages to the IoT hub. Registration of devices can be done manually using Azure portal or can be automated using IoT hub SDK. Azure provides sample simulation applications, with the help of which it becomes easy to register virtual devices for development and testing purposes. There is also a Raspberry Pi online simulator that can be used as a virtual device and then obviously there are other physical devices that can be configured to connect to the IoT hub.

To simulate a device from a local PC generally used for development and testing purposes, there are tutorials available on Azure documents for multiple languages. They are available at https://docs.microsoft.com/en-us/azure/iot-hub/iot-hub-get-started-simulated.

 Raspberry Pi online simulator is available at https://docs.microsoft.com/en-us/azure/iot-hub/iot-hub-raspberry-pi-web-simulator-get-started and for using physical devices to be registered with IoT hub, steps mentioned at https://docs.microsoft.com/en-us/azure/iot-hub/iot-hub-get-started-physical should be used.

For manually adding a device using the Azure portal, IoT hub provides a **Device Explorer** menu and it can be used for configuring a new device.

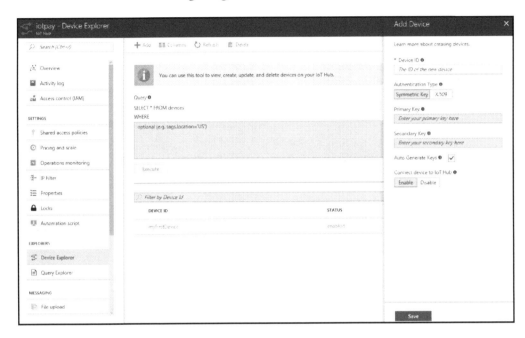

After the device identity is created, primary key connection string for IoT hub should be used in each device to connect to it.

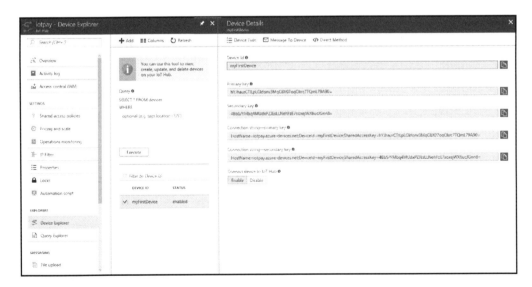

Message management

After devices are registered with the IoT hub, they can start interacting with it. The interaction could be from device to cloud or from cloud to device.

Device to cloud messaging

One of the best practices that must be followed in this communication is that although the device might be capturing a lot of information, only data that is of any importance should be transmitted to the cloud. The size of the message is very important in IoT solutions because of the inherent nature that IoT solutions are generally very high in volumes. Even 1 KB of extra data can result in a gigabyte of storage and processing wasted. Each message has properties and actual payload. Properties define the metadata for the message. This metadata contains data about the device, identification, tags, and other properties that are helpful in routing and identifying messages.

Devices or cloud gateways should connect to IoT Hubs to transfer data. IoT hubs provides public endpoints that can be utilized by devices to connect and send data. IoT hub should be considered as the first point of contact for backend processing IoT hub is capable of further transmit and routing of these messages to multiple services. By default, the messages are stored in Event Hub. Multiple Event Hub can be created for different kinds and types of messages.

Messages can be routed to different endpoints based on message header and body properties and the same is shown in next image.

Message in IoT hub stays within for 7 days by default. Their size can go up to 256 KB.

There is a sample act that acts as a simulator for sending messages to cloud. It is available in multiple languages and the C# version is at

`https://docs.microsoft.com/en-us/azure/iot-hub/iot-hub-csharp-csharp-c2d`.

Cloud to device messaging

Azure IoT hub is a managed service providing bi-directional messaging infrastructure. Messages can be sent from cloud to devices and based on the message the devices can act on them.

There are three types of cloud to device messaging patterns:

- Direct methods require immediate confirmation of the result. Direct methods are often used for interactive control of devices such as opening and closing garage shutters. It follows the request-response pattern.

- Twin's desired properties for long-running commands intend to put the device into a certain desired state. For example, set the telemetry send interval to 30 minutes. Device twins are JSON documents that store device state information (metadata, configurations, and conditions). IoT hub persists a device twin for each device in the IoT hub.

- Cloud-to-device messages for one-way notifications to the device app. This follows the fire and forget pattern.

Security

Security is an important aspect in IoT based applications. IoT based applications comprise of devices that use public internet for connectivity to backend applications. Securing devices, backend applications, and connectivity from malicious users and hackers should be considered a top priority for the success of these applications.

Security in IoT

IoT applications are primarily built around the internet, and security should play a major role to ensure that the solution is not comprised from an identity, confidentiality, and integrity point of view. Some of the important security decisions affecting IoT architecture are the following:

- Devices using HTTP versus HTTPS rest endpoints--rest endpoints secured by certificates ensure that messages transferred from device to cloud and vice versa are well encrypted and signed. The messages should make no sense to an intruder and should be extremely difficult to crack.

- If devices connected to a local gateway, the local gateway should connect to the cloud using a secure HTTP protocol.

- Devices should be registered to cloud IoT hubs before they can send any messages.

- The information passed to cloud should be persisted into storage that is well protected from a confidentiality, integrity, and identity perspective. Appropriate SAS tokens or connection strings that are stored in the Azure Key vault should be used for the connection.

- Azure key vault should be used to store all secrets, passwords, and credentials including certificates.

Scalability

Scalability for IoT hub is a bit different than other services. In IoT hub, there are two types of messaging:

- **Incoming**: Device to cloud messages
- **Outgoing**: Cloud to device messages

And both need to be accounted for in terms of scalability.

IoT hub provides a couple of configuration options during provision time to configure scalability. These options are also available post provisioning and can be updated to better suit the solution requirements in terms of scalability.

The scalability options available for IoT hub are:

- The Sku edition that is the size of the IoT hub
- Number of units

Sku edition

The Sku in IoT hub determines the number of messages it can handle per unit per day and this include both incoming as well as outgoing messages. There are four Sku's defined. They are as follows:

- **Free**: It allows for 8000 messages per unit per day and allows both incoming and outgoing messages. Maximum 1 unit can be provisioned. This edition is suitable for gaining familiarity and testing out the capabilities of the IoT Hub service.
- **Standard (S1)**: It allows for 400,000 messages per unit per day and allows both incoming and outgoing messages. Maximum 200 units can be provisioned. This edition is suitable for a small number of messages.
- **Standard (S2)**: It allows for six million messages per unit per day and allows both incoming and outgoing messages. Maximum 200 units can be provisioned. This edition is suitable for a large number of messages.
- **Standard (S3)**: It allows for 300 million messages per unit per day and allows both incoming and outgoing messages. Maximum 10 units can be provisioned. This edition is suitable for a very large amount of messages.

An astute reader would have noticed that Standard S3 Sku allows for a maximum of 10 units only compared to other standard units that allow for maximum 200 units. This is directly related to the size of the machines running behind. The size and capability of virtual machines for Standard S3 is significantly higher compared to other Sku's where the size remains same.

Units

Units define the number of instance of each SKU running behind the service. For example, 2 units of Standard S1 Sku will mean that the IoT hub is capable of handling *400K * 2 = 800K* messages per day.

Units increase the scalability of the application.

High availability

IoT hub is a PaaS service from Azure. Customers and users do not directly interact with underlying number and size of virtual machines on which IoT hub service is running. Users decide on the region, the Sku of the IoT hub and number of units for their application. The rest of the configuration is determined and executed by Azure behind the scenes. Azure ensures that every PaaS service is highly available by default. It does so by ensuring that multiple virtual machines provisioned behind the service are on separate racks in the data center. It does this by placing those virtual machines on an availability set and on a separate fault and update domain. This helps in high availability for both planned as well as unplanned maintenance. Availability sets take care of high availability at data center level.

To achieve high availability across multiple data centers in a region or across regions, customers should take additional action to provision additional IoT hub services in different regions, ensure that devices are registered at all IoT hub services, and each have the same identifier. Create a separate monitoring application on each region such as a web application, all tied up using a traffic manager and continually monitoring the traffic manager endpoint for current location unavailability to redirect traffic to other IoT hubs, and write logic to route the device messages to the new IoT hub.

Summary

IoT is one of the biggest upcoming technologies of this decade and is already disrupting the industries with the type of solutions they can create. Things that sounded impossible are possible to track, monitor, and take actions remotely. IoT hub acts as a platform that eases creating and delivering IoT solutions to the customer in a faster, better, and cheaper way. It provides implementation of all industry protocols such as MQTT and AMQP, along with field gateways that can adapt non-standard devices. It provides high availability, scalability, and security features to both messages and overall solution. It provides connectivity to a large number of Azure services, helps in routing messages to multiple different endpoints--each capable for processing messages. IoT can fast track the entire development life cycle and help faster go-to-market strategies for companies.

Azure provides numerous data storage options and services. Next chapter will be a primer on data storage and services on Azure.

7

Designing and Implementing Data Solutions

Data is the new currency is becoming true these days. Any organization that has any considerable data is sitting on a pile of intelligence and insights that can turn the future around. During the last decade there have been innovations that have contributed massively to data explosion. The first among them is the popularity of social platforms. There are platforms, such as Facebook, LinkedIn, and Twitter that have millions if not billions of users across the globe, generally this means millions of content every day. There is lots of wisdom and insights into this social networking content. Another big data changer paradigm is IoT. IoT devices are generating billions of messages every day for a variety of industries. Hardware is becoming cheaper; this further fuels its usage for IoT scenarios. It is also quite clear that traditional methods and tools are not appropriate to load such large volume of data and generate insights from it. They are not made for big data analysis. Availability of such large volumes of data led to innovation in storage of large data. Big data systems, such as Hadoop, have become quite popular for storing large volumes of data, advance analytics, and streaming live data systems then became the focus of innovation. Machine learning, artificial intelligence, and deep learning have taken center stage for finding insights from big data.

Data is characterized by volume, velocity, and varied format. There is a need for a variety of services that can come together to create complete solutions for data that is of huge volume, has high velocity and is available in multiple formats. These services should be enterprise class and scale with high availability, performance-centric, and secure. Azure is a mature platform for handling the complete life cycle of data--from storage to analytics to visualization--all are available with multiple choices for each stage in the life cycle.

In this chapter, we will go into detail about the following:

- Azure SQL
- Azure SQL stretching and sharding
- Azure NoSQL Cosmos DB
- Azure SQL versus Cosmos DB
- Azure data factory
- Azure stream analytics
- Data Lake
- Table storage
- SQL data warehousing

Azure SQL

Azure SQL is a cloud database as a service available in Azure. Microsoft's flagship database technology SQL Server has been available for more than 20 years and Microsoft provides the same on the cloud and provides complete database instances to its users. Azure SQL is a completely managed, relational database service providing higher productivity, faster and easier provisioning, and cheaper alternatives. It provides almost all features of a full-blown SQL Server without any need for managing infrastructure and licenses.

Azure SQL is based on a SQL Server database engine and provides a relational database as its core feature. Data is stored in a tabular format, in rows and columns. A combination of columns forms the schema for the table and rows are stored in a tabular form. Azure SQL is one of the most popular data destinations on Azure. Almost every application needs data to be persisted over time and Azure SQL provides data stores for these applications.

Azure SQL is a transaction based database. It means that it provides support for transactions. There are four major tenets of transactions, also known as **ACID properties**. They are as follows:

- Atomicity
- Consistency
- Isolated
- Durable

Azure SQL is composed of two important components:

- **Azure SQL logical server**: This is equivalent to a SQL Server instance in the on-premise data center or Azure virtual machines. A server is a physical and logical boundary consisting of multiple databases. It provides a security boundary with its own set of users, groups, and permissions. Users must be authenticated with the server before they can access databases within it. The server provides all the management functions and features for managing and maintaining Azure SQL.
- **Azure SQL databases**: This is the core component of Azure SQL because it is here that the data is stored. Each database is composed of multiple tables with each table consisting of columns and columns together holding rows.

Azure SQL columns provide multiple datatypes to support varied types of data. It includes general datatypes, such as char, varchar, integer, and so on, and more advanced ones, such as JSON, XML, and Spatial. Tables can be normalized such that both writing and reading data can be extremely fast, however it adds redundancy of data. It also allows the creation of multiple types of indexes on columns--clustered, non-clustered, covering, unique, and so on to improve the performance of queries.

It provides **Transact-SQL** as a language to issue data manipulation and data definition statements. The SQL data engine takes the heavy lifting of parsing, tokenizing, storing, finding an optimal execution plan, and actual execution of queries. It also interacts with the storage engine to fetch data from storage to memory and vice-versa. It provides and implements transactional capabilities and provides management features, such as logs, jobs, agents, backup, restore, and always-on.

Azure SQL performance is measured in **Database Transaction Units** (**DTU**). For Azure to guarantee a minimum performance **service level agreement** (**SLA**), a combination of compute, memory, and storage resources are calculated together to form DTU. Each DTU confirms and guarantees certain levels of performance.

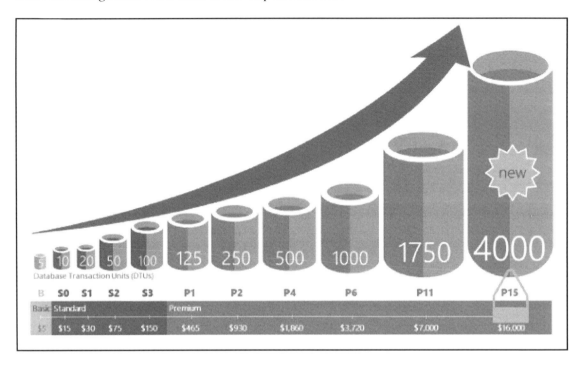

Azure SQL provides four levels of performance. They are as follows:

- **Basic**: This is for the less demanding workloads providing 5 DTUs of performance
- **Standard**: This is for general production workloads and provides anything between 10 to 3,000 DTUs
- **Premium**: This is for IO-intensive workloads providing DTUs between 125 to 4,000
- **PremiumRS**: This is again for IO-intensive workloads but with reduced availability and durability and provides between 125 to 1,000 DTUs

Users should decide the best DTU needs based on their application requirements. They can start with low DTUs and eventually scale up with increased demand for their application. Scaling of DTU adds more compute, memory, and IOPS resources without stopping database. The scale up and down happens transparently without affecting the availability of the database. Storage can also be scaled up and down based on requirements.

Azure SQL availability

Azure ensures that data is highly available. Even in case of disaster or hardware failure, data is still available, and it provides multiple capabilities to ensure high-availability.

Azure SQL performs automatic backup of the user's database. These databases are backed up in a manner to minimize the time to recover in case of a disaster. It performs a full weekly backup, hourly differential backups, and backup of transaction logs every five minutes. These backups are then stored in a geo-redundant storage which keeps multiple copies across geographies. In case of a disaster, Azure support can help get these backups and restore them.

Azure SQL also provides geo-replication of databases with up to four readable secondary databases in different regions. All these primary and secondary databases are continuously synchronized using asynchronous replication. It also provides capability for auto-failover to another database in another region.

Azure SQL provides point-in-time recovery and restores databases as well.

Azure SQL security

Azure provides advance secure features to ensure that data is never comprised.

Azure SQL transparently encrypts and decrypts all data, backups, log files using **Transparent Data Encryption** (**TDE**) automatically. Applications are not aware of this behind the scene encryption and decryption. They use data as they do normally, however, data at rest in a SQL Server cannot be comprehended by anyone having access to them using database tools. The encryption keys can be managed and stored in the Azure key vault.

Azure SQL also takes care of protecting data in flight that is getting transmitted over a network. It provides an **Always Encrypted** feature that keeps data encrypted even while in storage at rest, during query processing, and on network.

Another great security feature provided by Azure SQL is **dynamic data masking**. It helps in exposing data to non-privileged users by hiding sensitive data in query results. This also works transparently without changing the application.

Azure SQL users and groups can be managed using the Azure **Active Directory** (**AD**). Users from Azure active directory can be providing access to server and database and this simplifies the overall management of identities by centralizing and out sourcing it.

Azure SQL security goes down from the server to rows in tables. It provides row-level security wherein users can access only those rows that they are authorized to.

It also allows access to those IP addresses that are whitelisted explicitly by the administrator. It also provides advance auditability in terms of who is accessing the server and database logging for every writing and reading data activity.

Elastic pools

Azure DTUs are great to guarantee a minimum level of performance and resource consumption, however, Azure SQL dedicated the resources for a given DTU for a SQL database and remains the same even if the resources are under-utilized. In case, there are large numbers of databases, each database will have its own dedicated DTU, although some of the databases might not be utilized at all or remain under-utilized. Azure provides a better alternative for such scenarios of having a large number of databases. Azure provides elastic pools that help in hosting multiple databases on the same SQL Server and puts them on the same pool. Each pool has dedicated DTUs assigned to them known as **eDTU**. Within this pool there might be databases that consume more resources than the estimated, while there are others that do not consume many resources. An elastic pool helps in aggregating the DTUs utilized by each of these databases in the pool and ensures that over-utilized databases are not throttled and under-utilized databases are not over charged. The cost of eDTU gets amortized over multiple databases in spite of some databases having a sudden jump in demand. Elastic pools help in reducing the overall cost for multiple databases while ensuring that demanding databases get more resources in times of need.

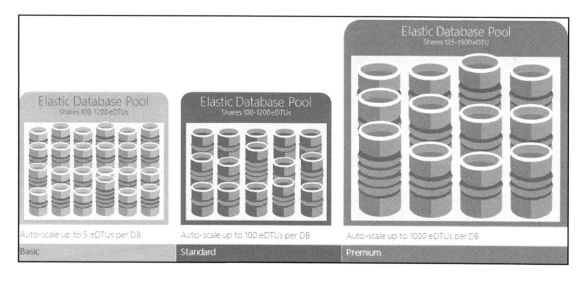

Azure SQL scaling out

Azure SQL is a versatile platform and provides features to cater to different needs. Azure scale out is one such feature, also known as **sharding**. Imagine a situation of having a very large database containing millions of rows. The performance of queries is degrading because of a large number of writes and reads have to traverse through large recordsets. It is a better design to break this large database into multiple smaller databases and distribute data among them. However, to write such a controller or manager is a difficult and herculean task. Azure provides scaling out features to cater to this need of horizontally partitioning data between multiple databases. Client applications connect to the primary Azure database that is responsible for querying data from appropriate databases, collating the information and send it back to the client application. The same process is followed for write operations as well. Azure SQL also provides the facility to merge back these shards into one database.

The table must have partitioned horizontally based on pre-determined keys and the primary database has to maintain details about the range of keys with each database. There are additional management tasks that are also performed by this primary database. The image shown next shows a typical sharding strategy. Each color shows a database that has been partitioned. While some of them are elastic pools, the rest of them consume their dedicated DTUs.

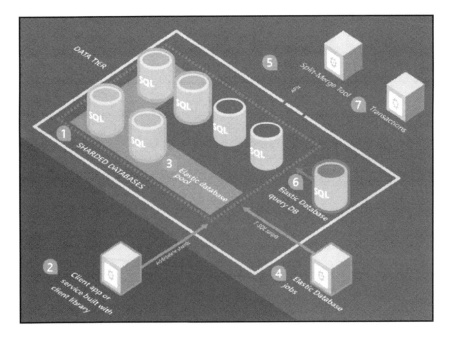

Azure portal does not provide the necessary user interface to shard databases. The scaling out and sharding is done using REST API, PowerShell, or any programming language consuming the Azure SQL SDK and elastic database client library.

 The tools for managing sharding are available at
`https://docs.microsoft.com/en-us/azure/sql-database/sql-database`
`-elastic-scale-get-started`.

These tools consume Azure SQL SDK and elastic database client libraries to provide different options to manage the process of sharding and merging.

It provides options for splitting and merging databases, creating a new shard, adding databases to shards, executing queries against all shards, and deleting the shard. The previous image shows these client applications interacting with Azure SQL.

Stream analytics

Stream analytics is a fully managed data and event processing engine that helps in providing real-time analytics on the data getting streamed. While Cosmos DB and Azure SQL provide data that is already available in their storage, stream analytics provides analytics computation on data that is getting streamed live as they are ingested. They are not queries against data stored in permanent storage. This is an extremely powerful capability for getting real-time insights instead of finding insights much after the event occurred.

The beauty of stream analytics lies in the fact that the data can come from anywhere-- applications, IoT devices, other Azure services, such as event hubs or any other system.

The other fundamental core tenet of stream analytics is the processing of a large volume of data. It has been created to process a huge quantity of data and extract insights and information out of it in real-time.

It also allows necessary integration with other systems and services to act on the extracted insights, such as sending notifications, raising alerts, logging into multiple log analytics services, and reporting using visualization tools.

The crux of stream analytic lies in the fact that data of a high volume, velocity, and multiple format can be processed by a single service in real-time and means actions can be taken on the same.

The architecture of stream analytics is shown in the following diagram:

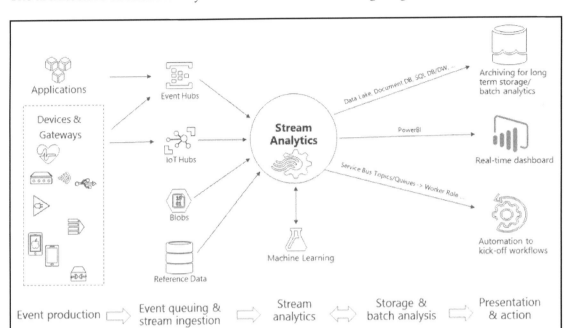

Stream analytics provides **Extract-Transform-Load** (**ETL**) functionality for real-time processes. It defines a job that is configured with incoming data along with source of data, transformations, and the output data log with destinations.

There are many use cases for implementing stream analytics. They are as follows:

- Many industries need real-time analytic solutions, such as parking system, highway toll-booth systems, movie ticket sales, and so on
- Social media sentiment analysis
- Web traffic analysis
- Log analytics for security and other breaches and more
- Infrastructure monitoring

There are multiple components that are part of the Azure stream analytics service.

Data sources

Stream analytics works on data. Data is extracted from the source location and after transformation, data is loaded into the target location. Both the source and destination locations are termed as data sources in Azure analytics parlance. There are data sources, such as Azure event hubs and IoT hubs that can provide data to Azure analytics. There can be other data sources, such as IoT devices that can send data directly to stream analytics and ones that are on-premise or on different cloud platforms. The data sources could either be a place where the data or the event is generated or it could be from storage, such as Azure storage, IoT hubs, and so on.

Data integration

Data sources are providers and receivers of data. However, the glue that helps connecting Azure stream analytics with them is data integration. Azure stream analytics provides integration for both source and destination data sources. This integration queries data within the specified time-range and provides them to the stream analytics engine for processing.

Data transformation

Incoming data is processed to gather insights. This process of transformation involves data to be filtered, augmented, and enriched. Not every data that comes in might be of interest. There might be data that is incorrect or missing. To ensure that insights are not biased and skewed, data needs to be brought into a stage that will provide accurate results. This is the job of transformation. Azure stream analytics provides SQL type query language that helps in grouping, aggregation, joining, and filtering data according to business requirements.

Stream analytics engine

This is the core component of stream analytics. It is here that the stream analytics jobs are executed and every component interacts together to ETL the data. This engine keeps running and continuously executes jobs over time-series windows to ensure that real-time insights can be gathered.

Storage and presentation

The analytics engine can also help act on the gathered insights. It can send data to durable storage to Azure blob storage or present data using visualization tools, such as Power BI or use it to send notifications.

Architecture

Azure stream analytics is a mature platform and service for real-time analytics. It provides features for multiple inputs and outputs. In the image shown next, there are multiple **Event Hub**, **IoT hubs**, and **Blob storage** as input data sources. These can be joined together, grouped, and aggregated within the same **Stream Analytics** job and insights generated.

There is the **Data Egress** (out-going) cost in Azure, however, the cost is not applicable within a region. If data transfer happens within a region, the egress cost is not applicable. It is applicable when data transfer happens between regions. It is for this reason, as a good practice data sources in Azure should ideally be located within the same region as that of Azure stream analytics.

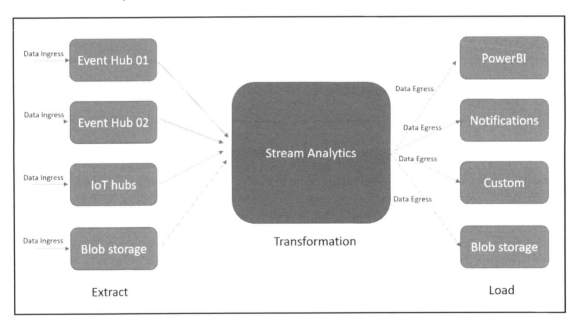

On the Azure portal, the Azure stream analytics dashboard provides the number of inputs and outputs.

Azure data factory

Data is generally stored in flat files, relational databases, NoSQL databases and other locations in multiple formats, such as JSON, XML, CSV, text files, and binary. Moreover, each data store defines its own model to store data. An employee ID in one data store is named EMPIDID in another data store and EID in the third data store within the same organization. There are multiple facets for the same data within different data stores. Azure data factory is a data integration service that helps in authoring orchestration and workflow scenarios for the ETL of data. Azure data factory works with data from any location-cloud, on-premise, and works at the cloud scale. It works with large volumes of data with varied formats.

The workflows in Azure data factory are known as data pipelines and Azure data factory helps in creating, deploying, monitoring, and scheduling these data pipelines easily. Azure data factory is a managed PaaS service providing high availability, scalability, and fault tolerance to data pipelines.

Azure data factory can ingest from multiple locations and load the final transformed data to multiple different target locations and types. From the onset, data factory looks like just another ETL service, however, there is a big difference. The main difference between data factory and other ETL tools is based on **transformation**. The transformation executed by data factory is based on compute services, such as HDInsight Hadoop, Azure Data Lake analytics, Spark, and Azure machine learning, whereas the transformation executed by other ETL tools are related to transformation of rows and columns, filtering and aggregation of rows and column, and enrichment of data. Azure data factory prepares the data by filtering, aggregating, grouping, joining, and enriching data, and then applies transformation using compute services. The output of this transformation are insights, information that can further be consumed by visualization tools, such as Power BI and other custom applications.

Azure data factory provides connectors for almost every major data store including SAP, Oracle, MongoDB, Cassandra, and supports multiple types of protocols and drivers for connectivity to these data stores including ODBC, OLEDB, ODATA, and HTTP.

The data factory pipelines can be scheduled to run daily, hourly, and weekly.

The main difference between Azure data factory and Azure stream analytics is that while Azure data factory works on a snapshot of data that is already available on durable storage, Azure stream analytics works on transient real-time data that is processed as and when it is generated.

There are two versions of Azure data factory--V1 and V2. V2 is currently in preview and only available in East US and East US 2 regions. V1 is generally available and is available in East US, West US, West Central US, and North Europe. As a good practice, data sources in Azure should ideally be located within the same region as that of the Azure data factory.

The architecture of Azure data factory is shown in the following image:

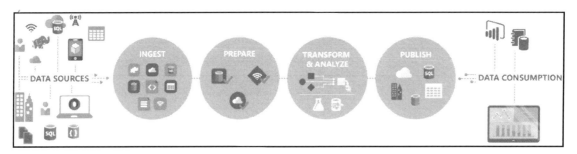

There are multiple components that are part of the data factory service.

Data sources

Data should first be ingested within the data factory. Data can be either be on cloud or on-premise. The data needs to move within Azure data factory. Azure data factory provides linked services and dataset constructs for connecting and fetching data into the data factory.

Datasets refer to actual data stored at the data source or data location. It could be a comma separated value file on the on-premise server or a file in a container in the Azure storage account as blob or in the Azure SQL. The possibilities are endless. Linked services refer to the process of connecting to the data source by using a data source specific connection string and using it to fetch datasets into the data factory. For example, if you are copying data from the Azure blob file to Azure SQL, two datasets, and two linked services are needed. One linked service would consist of the connection string to the Azure storage account while the other would contain the connection string for Azure SQL. The dataset related to Azure blob would consist of files containing the data, and the dataset related to Azure SQL would consist of tables where data would be written. The data pipeline uses activities (for example, copy activity) to connect to data sources using linked services and copy datasets from source location to data factory.

Data factory consists of multiple pipelines and each pipeline consists of activities. Pipelines are made up of multiple activities where each activity is responsible for executing a single responsibility. For example, copy activity is responsible for copying data from a data location using linked services and datasets to another data location using target linked services and datasets.

The relationship between activities, pipeline, linked services, and dataset is shown next.

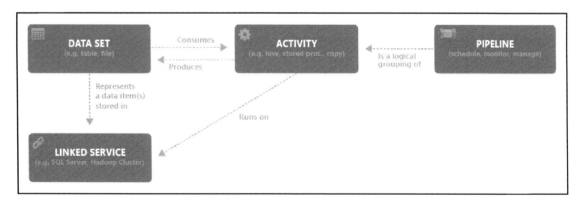

The dataset types available in the data factory are available at
`https://docs.microsoft.com/en-us/azure/data-factory/v1/data-factory-create-datasets#Type`.

Azure data factory pipelines can be executed manually or scheduled to run periodically.

Data transformation

Now that the data is available in the data store, it can be processed using compute services, such as Azure HDInsight Hadoop, Spark, Data Lake analytics, and machine learning. The data output from transformations can be published for further consumption.

Publish and presentation

The transformation output can be stored in durable storage, such as Cosmos DB, Azure SQL, Azure data warehouse, or any custom analytics tools. Also, Power BI can be connected to the durable storage for creating reports, dashboards, and visualization.

Using data factory

This section will show step-by-step details about how to use Azure data factory to create datasets, linked services and pipelines, and transfer data from one storage account to another.

Data factory provides numerous data stores from which data can be read and transferred to. Data factory provides enormous flexibility in terms of choosing a source and target data store. The next screenshot shows the number and type of data stores available in the data factory. You can choose any of them as a source and target.

Azure data factory also provides a wizard interface for identifying a source data store and its data along with target data store and data. The same is shown in the next screenshot:

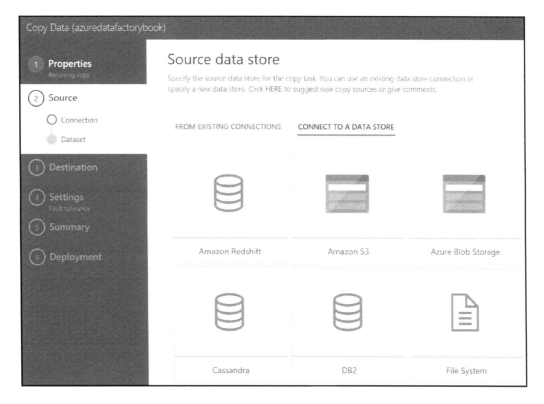

1. The first step is to create a data factory resource. After creation, click on the **Copy data** button:

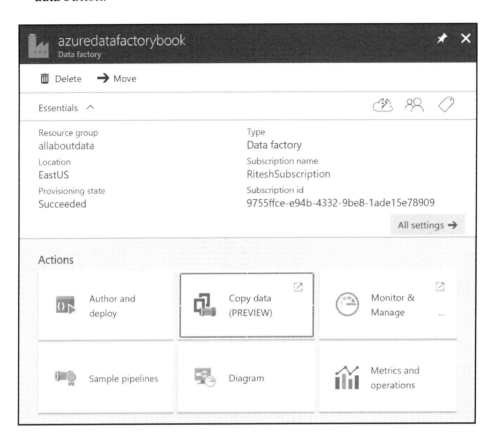

2. This will open a browser window and navigate to
`https://datafactory.azure.com/`. This URL provides a wizard-based user
interface to configure the data factory:

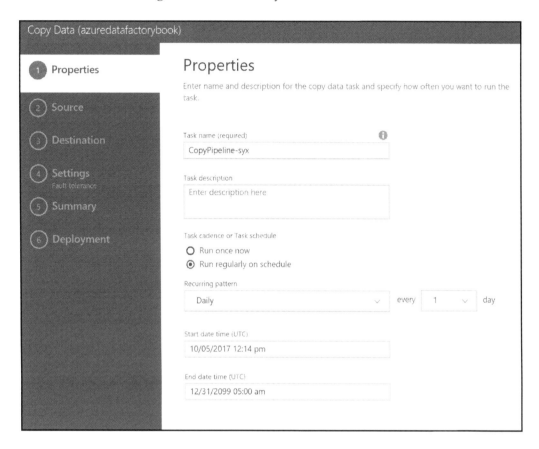

3. Fill in all the details, such as the name of the task, scheduling information,
recurring pattern, start date, and end date. Click on **Next**.

4. Select **Azure Blob Storage** as the source data store. This could be any data source and the next step that the wizard will ask for is the value for constructing the connection string and linked service to connect to it. This is shown in the next screenshot. Click on the **Next** button:

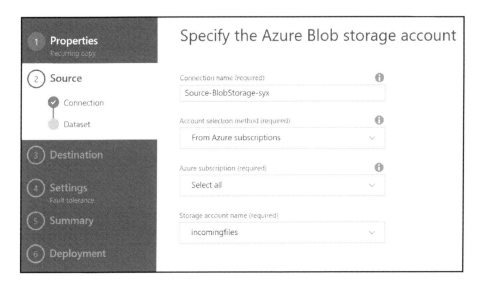

5. The next step asks the user to select the file in the source data store. This activity creates a dataset for the data factory:

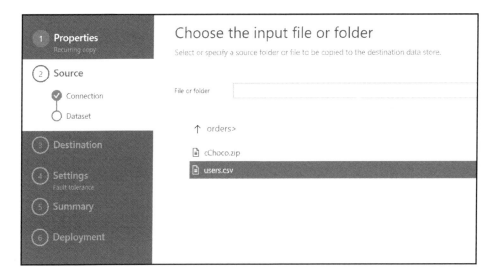

6. The `users.csv` file is a simple file containing some representative data however, in a real-life scenario, millions and billions of records with terabytes of data might be available.

7. The `users.csv` looks as shown next. It has a header as the first row and the rest of the rows contain comma-separated data. Choose the compression type if the file is already compressed.

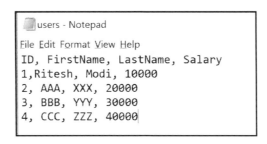

8. Clicking on **Next** will identify the file format and show that to the user. It is here where the user can change the settings for the file format. This is shown in the next screenshot:

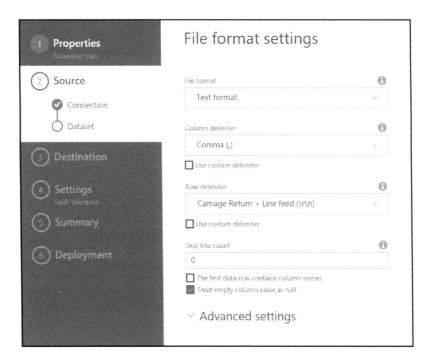

9. Clicking on **Next**, it will ask for the **Destination data store** configuration. This is similar to the source data store. Choose an appropriate target data store as shown next:

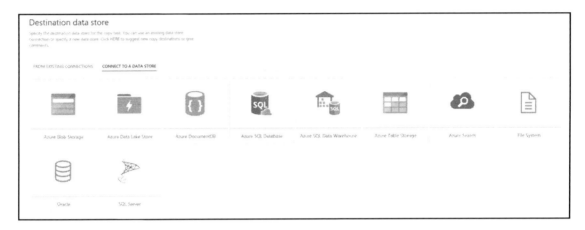

10. In our sample, we are selecting **Azure Blob Storage** but users are advised to play with all kinds of data stores, such as **Azure Data Lake Store**, **Azure DocumentDB**, **Azure SQL Data Warehouse**, **Azure Table Storage**, **Azure Search**, **Oracle**, and **SQL Server**.

11. Specify the connection string details for the target data store as shown next and then click on **Next**.

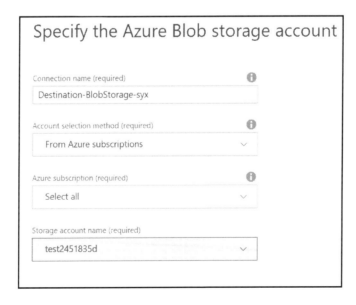

12. Provide appropriate details for the target dataset, such as container name and file name as shown in the next screenshot and click on **Next**:

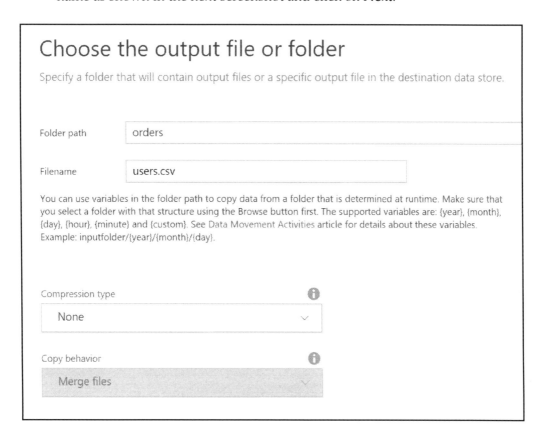

Choose the output file or folder

Specify a folder that will contain output files or a specific output file in the destination data store.

Folder path   orders

Filename   users.csv

You can use variables in the folder path to copy data from a folder that is determined at runtime. Make sure that you select a folder with that structure using the Browse button first. The supported variables are: {year}, {month}, {day}, {hour}, {minute} and {custom}. See Data Movement Activities article for details about these variables. Example: inputfolder/{year}/{month}/{day}.

Compression type

None   ⌄

Copy behavior

Merge files   ⌄

13. Configure the **File format** setting for the destination data store as shown in the next screenshot and click on **Next**:

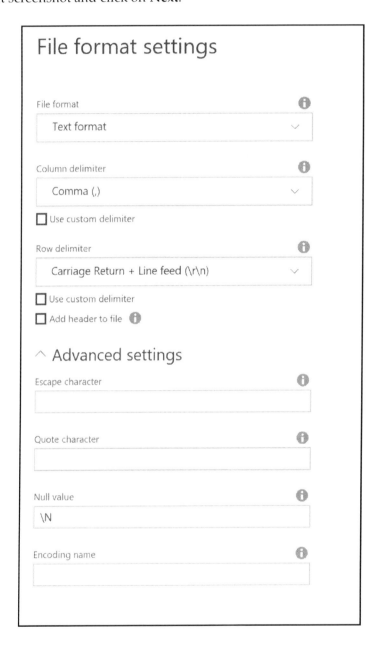

14. Configure the tolerance and performance (using parallel writes) settings as shown next and click **Next**:

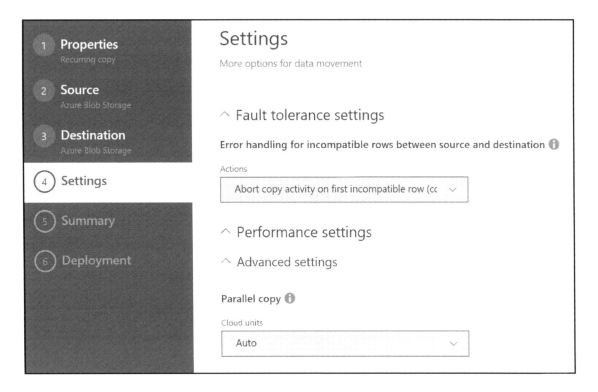

15. Validate all the details as shown in the **Summary** window. This is shown in the next screenshot, then click on **Next**:

16. This will start the deployment process. The next screenshot shows that the deployment is successful and the data was transferred from the **West Central US** to the **South Central US** from one **Azure Blob Storage** to another.
17. This will be a scheduled activity if scheduling was configured earlier.

Azure Data Lake

Azure Data Lake is an Azure hosted service providing end-to-end services for storing big data, transforming it, and performing analysis on top of it. It comprises multiple services:

- Azure Data Lake store
- Azure Data Lake analytics

It provides enterprise grade scalability, performance, and security for data storage and processing. It helps in the massive execution of parallel workloads and is a much sought service for data scientists and analysts.

Azure Data Lake store

Azure Data Lake store provides storage for big data. It provides petabyte scale of storage and is highly optimized for storing data that has high volume, velocity, and comprises multiple types and format. Data of various format and size can be co-stored within the same Data Lake.

Traditional storage, such as filesystems, relational databases, and other storage are general purpose storage accounts and are not suitable for storage of big data that is accessed for analytics purposes. The repository should be optimized for faster and efficient querying and should be able to store data in raw as well as processed format. Azure Data Lake has been created specifically for this purpose.

Azure Data Lake is accessible by a variety of tools and services including HDInsight Hadoop, Azure machine learning, stream analytics, data factory, event hubs, and more.

Data comes from a variety of sources and devices, such as social media, IoT devices, line of business applications, relational and non-relational databases, web scraping, and many more.

It is currently available only at three Azure locations--East US 2, North Europe, and Central US.

Eventually, Azure Data Lake is a hierarchical file-based storage just as a Windows, Linux, or Hadoop filesystem that has been optimized for efficient querying and storage for big data workloads.

The data in Azure Data Lake is highly available as it is replicated into multiple replicas and stored in different data centers.

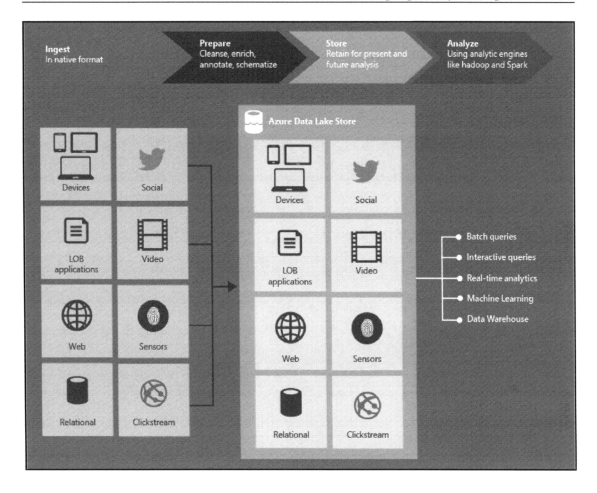

Data Lake security

Security aspects are supremely important when dealing with data. Azure Data Lake is a secure repository, access to which is managed by Azure AD. Users, groups, and service applications that are provisioned and enabled in Azure AD are allowed to access the Azure Data Lake store. Moreover, after authentication the identity should have adequate permissions to perform activities on the Azure Data Lake store. **Role-Based Access Control (RBAC)** from **Azure Resource Manager** (**ARM**) is responsible for enforcing permission checks and authorization for an identity. There is additional authorization security available in terms of **Access Control Lists** (**ACLs**). The ACLs can be applied with read, write, and execute permissions of folders, sub-folders, and files.

Similar to Azure SQL, Data Lake store can only be accessed by those IP addresses that are explicitly allowed by whitelisting them in the Data Lake store configuration. Since, Azure Data Lake is frequently accessed by services in Azure itself, additional configuration is available to provide access to them without knowing their IP addresses.

Data stored in Azure Data Lake store can be encrypted. Data at rest can be in an encrypted form, such that it cannot be read by anyone having access to it. Similar to SQL Azure TDE, the data in Data Lake store can be encrypted before storing and decrypted after retrieval transparently, without the application knowing about it. It is good practice to keep data encrypted at rest. The encryption and decryption keys can be stored in the Azure key vault.

Data Lake performance

Performance is another very important aspect for solutions based on Data Lake store. Since Data Lake store is a repository, it should be storage intensive providing high throughput in terms of higher IOPS for reads and writes. Traditional storages does not consume the entire throughput available from the storage and hardware. Instead, Azure Data Lake store provides higher throughput by parallelizing the access to data and consuming the bandwidth available from hardware.

It is to be noted that for end-to-end solutions, it is just not the performance of Azure Data Lake store that is important, in fact the performance of all data sources from where data is ingested into Azure Data Lake store is also important along with services that accesses data for analytical purposes.

Azure Data Lake analytics

Azure Data Lake analytics is one of the flagship services from Azure to execute analytics jobs. Azure Data Lake stores took care of storing big data in an optimized way. However, for an end-to-end scenario, the data in storage is useful if it is read by a service and that service can perform analytics on it and gain meaningful insights. The analytics service is compute intensive in nature because of deep processing of a large quantity of data. To setup an environment for such a service involves provisioning and configuring virtual machines, tune them for performance and maintain them. Azure Data Lake analytics provides platform as a service capability for running analytics jobs. It means users no more need to think about provisioning and configuring infrastructure and hardware, rather, they can concentrate on writing their analytics job and focus on the business problem.

Azure Data Lake analytics provides its own SQL-style language U-SQL that has a capability to integrate code generally written using programming languages, such as C#. It's a versatile language that can query multiple types of databases, such as Azure SQL, IaaS SQL Server, and Azure SQL data warehouse.

Another important benefit, apart from low maintenance, is that it provides the pay-as-you-go model from a cost perspective. Users pay only when the analytic jobs are running and not otherwise. There is no charge for provisioning Azure Data Lake analytics if it is not running.

Azure Data Lake analytics is a scalable service. It means that when a job executes in Azure Data Lake analytics, it provisions compute and memory resources behind the scene and dynamically keeps scaling out as more demand for resource happens. After the job completes, the resources are scaled down automatically. All this happens transparently without the knowledge of the user.

Azure Data Lake analytics just as Azure Date Laka store, is integrated with Azure AD for authentication purpose. Users, groups, and service applications available in Azure AD can access Azure Date Laka analytics. ARM's RBAC is also applied from an authorization perspective to determine the permissions applicable for users and Azure Date Laka analytics.

Azure SQL data warehouse

Azure SQL is a highly scalable, durable, performance centric, highly available service for transactional data. This has traditionally been called **Online Transaction Processing (OLTP)** applications. There is another set of applications popularly known as the **Online Analytics Processing (OLAP)**. Typically, OLAP applications are based on a data warehouse that stores massive amounts of data in a format readily consumable by analytics engine as the **SQL Server Analysis Services (SSAS)**. The data warehouse stores data that is de-normalized for efficient querying.

Data warehouses are categorized into read major data stores. The write to this data store happens periodically contrary to OLTP applications where both writes and reads are comparable. Generally, applications that provide reporting, visualization, and analytics services connect to a data warehouse to load and generate analytical insights out of it.

Date warehouses are also characterized by their massive need for storage and compute power. They generally consist of terabytes and petabytes of data and perform aggregation and grouping of millions and millions of records.

Azure provides SQL data warehouse as a service on the cloud that is massively scalable, has high adjustable performance, is highly available and secure. It is built on top of the Azure SQL Server and databases and so it gets all goodness and features from it. It also stores data into Azure blob storage services that helps in storing a virtually unlimited amount of data into them.

The architecture of Azure SQL data warehouse is shown next. Azure SQL data warehouse comprises of two kinds of nodes:

- **Control node**: This node is responsible for all interaction with users and applications interacting with Azure SQL data warehouse. It is the main brain and engine behind the execution of Azure SQL data warehouse. It is responsible for coordinating with all worker or compute nodes for storage and compute requirements. It also helps in distributing the load between them.
- **Compute nodes**: These nodes are the actual workhorses of Azure SQL data warehouse. They are the ones that store and retrieve data from Azure blob storage and provide compute power by executing SQL statements against the data. They implement a technology called **PolyBase** that helps in executing SQL statements against data stored in the non-relational stores, such as Azure blob storage service.

Both control and compute nodes are based on Azure SQL database and host on the Azure logical SQL Server.

There is another important component called **Data Movement Service** (**DMS**) available on all nodes in Azure SQL data warehouse irrespective of control and compute nodes. This is the glue that actually helps in the movement of data, combining, and aggregating data from multiple compute nodes, and presenting uniform data to the requestor.

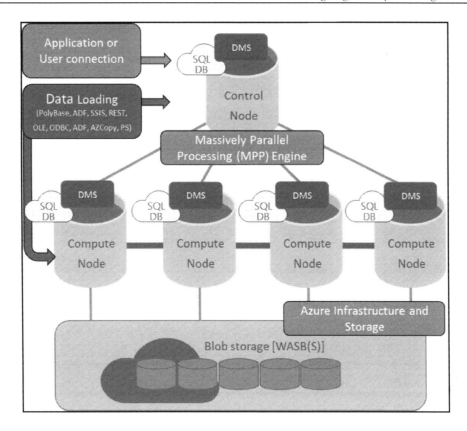

Some of the important characteristics of Azure SQL data warehouse are as follows:

- **Massively Parallel Processing** (**MPP**) system providing features to implement parallel data warehousing.
- The interaction is based on Transact-SQL. Ability to connect using SQL drivers and tools.
- Available virtually at all Azure locations to help data sovereignty and governance.
- Completely elastic from a storage perspective. Virtually unlimited storage available.
- The compute layer is different from the storage layer. This helps in scaling them independently.

- Provides the querying capacity and power of an SQL Server.
- Provides all benefits of Azure SQL:
    - FIP-based firewall access control list
    - Always on scalability and availability
    - Horizontal sharding
    - Pooling for cost optimization
    - Security

An important aspect of Azure SQL data warehouse is adjustable performance configuration. The performance is defined using a **Data Warehouse Unit** (**DWU**). Each DWU provides SLAs in terms of compute, IOPS, and memory. The cost of Azure SQL data warehouse goes higher with a higher configuration for DWU. This is similar to the DTUs provided by Azure SQL. Users can decide the best performance requirements for their application and accordingly adjust the performance scale. There are two different ways performance can be adjusted. They are as follows:

- **Optimized for Elasticity**: According to Azure this separates compute and storage for independent, elastic sizing of resources. It is designed for frequent scaling operations to manage the compute spend and cloud burst scenarios. It offers the lowest starting scale point.
- **Optimized for Compute (Preview)**: It is coming soon.

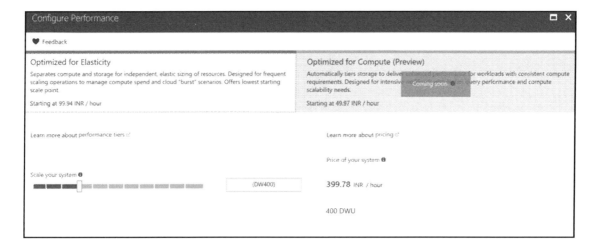

Azure SQL data warehouse can be integrated to a host of services on Azure as the following:

- Machine learning
- Power BI
- Stream analytics
- Data factory

Table storage

Azure table storage service is available as part of the Azure storage account. Azure storage provides multiple types of storage and table service is one among them. Azure table service is a fully managed, secure, scalable, highly available petabyte-scale storage service that helps in storing data in the NoSQL format. As we know, NoSQL helps in building schema-less design, Azure table service is also schema-less. It helps in storing documents using key-attribute pairs. What this means is that table service does not enforce any schema on entities. Entities can have different properties for each entity at the same time without modification.

Data in Azure tables is stored as entities. Data is stored in tabular format where entities form the rows and properties form individual columns. An entity is very similar to a row in a relational database and each table service consists of multiple entities and each entity consists of a pair of keys that help uniquely identify the entity. The relationship between table service, entities, and the key-value store is shown next. The entities are referred using partition and row keys. The values for both partition and row keys should come from the data itself.

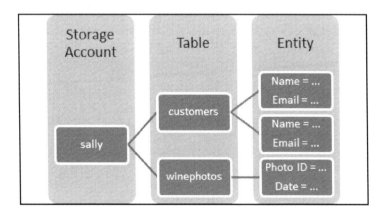

Partitions should be thought of dividing a table into separate logical structure for fast and easy querying. A partition is uniquely identified using storage account name, table name and partition name. It is very important the partition and row keys are decided appropriately. They can be a maximum 1 KB in size each. Their combination should be unique across the table so that any entity can be uniquely identified, and they are also indexed. Partitions help to scale tables into terabytes without sacrificing query performance. It is very similar to sharding in Azure SQL.

Details about designing tables in Azure is available at
`https://docs.microsoft.com/en-us/azure/cosmos-db/table-storage-d`
`esign-guide`.

It is to be noted that table services are part of the storage account. Each general storage account has a maximum limit of 20,000 operations/second. Based on requirements of operations this might be an overkill or over-utilized. If these numbers of operations are not enough, Cosmos DB should be considered. Another aspect is the storage limit in table service which is maxed at 500 TB. For storage greater than 500 TB, Cosmos DB should be considered.

Another constraint of table services is that it allows indexing only on partition and row keys. This makes them less efficient when querying based on other columns in table service. Writing complex queries using joins are difficult with table service.

Table services stores data as properties in tabular format whereas Cosmos DB stores data as JSON-document objects and the whole object can be indexed instead of just a few select columns.

Summary

Data is one of the most crucial elements for a solution. Data has value and they need to be protected and secured. The nature of data has changed over the last few years. Data has grown exponentially in terms of volume, and the velocity of generation of data has also increased manifold. Data is also stored on-premise and on the cloud, in PaaS and IaaS services and there are a ton of drivers and protocols to access them. The data can be in any format and so parsing and understanding data across all formats is a challenge by itself. Azure provides rich services to handle all these newer facets of data. Azure provides Azure SQL, SQL on IaaS, elastic pools, sharding, data factory, stream analytics, Data Lake store and analytics, data warehouse, machine learning, and Power BI to architect end-to-end data solutions from ingestion of data to processing, transformation, loading, and analytics. This chapter was an introduction to these services on Azure and they should be read further using the Azure documentation.

Next chapter will discuss one of most emerging deployment patterns on cloud known as Serverless.

8
Designing and Implementing Serverless Solutions

Serverless is one of the hottest buzzwords in technology these days and everyone wants to ride this bandwagon. Serverless brings a lot of advantages in overall computing, software development processes, infrastructure, and technical implementation. There is a lot going on in the industry--at one end of the spectrum is infrastructure as a service and serverless at the other end. There is PaaS and containers in between. I have met many developers and it seems to me that there exists some level of confusion among them about IaaS, PaaS, containers, and serverless computing. Also, there is much confusion about use cases, applicability, architecture, and implementation for the serverless paradigm. Serverless is a new paradigm that is changing not only technology but also culture and processes within organizations.

This chapter will concentrate on the following topics related to serverless:

- What is serverless architecture?
- What are Azure functions?
- Creating your first Azure function
- Types of Azure functions
- Creating a connected function
- Creating an event-driven function
- Creating a solution comprising of multiple functions

In this chapter, we will go into detail about the following:

- Azure billing
- Invoicing

- Usage and quotas
- Usage and billing API
- Azure pricing calculator
- Best practices

A short history of serverless

Before we understand serverless, its architecture, and implementation, it is important to understand its history and how it evolved.

At the beginning there were physical servers. Although users had complete control over physical servers, there were lots of disadvantages:

- Long gestation period between ordering and actual deployment of the server
- Capital intensive in nature
- Waste of resources
- Lower return on investment
- Difficult to scale out and up

A natural evolution to physical servers was virtualization. Virtualization refers to the creation of virtual machines on top of physical servers and deploying applications within them. Virtual machines provide advantages in terms of the following:

- No need to procure physical hardware
- Comparatively easier to create newer virtual machines
- Complete isolation of environments
- Lower costs compared to physical servers

However, virtualization had its own set of disadvantages. They are the following:

- Still dependent on physical procurement of the server for scaling out after a number of virtual machine instances.
- Still costly because of human and hardware dependence.
- Wastage of compute resources. Each virtual machine runs a complete operating system in it.
- High reliance and costs in maintenance.

The next evolution was IaaS from cloud providers. Instead of procuring and managing data centers and infrastructures, the strategy was to create virtual machines, storages, and networks on the cloud. The cloud provides software-defined infrastructure services and hides all the details related to physical servers, networks, and storage. This had some advantages:

- No capital expenditure. Only operational expenses.
- No gestation time to create new virtual machines. New virtual machines can be provisioned within minutes rather than hours.
- Flexible size of virtual machines.
- Easier scaling up and out of virtual machines.
- Completely secure.

The disadvantages of virtual machines on the cloud are the following:

- Requires active monitoring and auditing.
- Requires active maintenance of virtual machines.
- Scalability, high-availability, and performance of virtual machines should be managed by users. Any degradation and subsequent improvement is the user's responsibility.
- Costly option because users pay for the entire machine whether it is used or not.

The cloud also provides another pattern for deploying applications, popularly known as PaaS. PaaS provides abstraction from the underlying infrastructure in terms of virtual machines, virtual networks, and storage on the cloud. It provides a platform and an ecosystem where users do not need to know a thing about the infrastructure at all; they can bring and deploy their application on these platforms. There are definite advantages using PaaS compared to IaaS but there are still possible better options. The main disadvantages of PaaS are the following:

- PaaS applications are deployed on virtual machines behind the scenes and the payment model is not granular. It is still at the deployment level.
- It still demands monitoring for scaling out and in.
- Users still needs to identify the requirements for their platform. There are limited options available for different types of platform. Azure provided the Windows environment for a long time and only recently was Linux available. Moreover, installation of packages, utilities, and software is the responsibility of its users.

Further, a new paradigm emerged known as containers, which was primarily popularized by Docker. Containers provide a lightweight, isolated, and secure environment that have all the benefits of virtual machines minus their disadvantages. They do not have a dedicated operating system and instead rely on a base server operating system. Containers come in both IaaS and PaaS patterns. Containers provide a large number of advantages:

- Faster provisioning of environments
- Consistent and predictable creation of environments
- They help in creating microservices architectures
- Rich ecosystem with advance services from Kubernetes, Swarm, and DC/OS

The disadvantages of containers are the following:

- They require active monitoring and auditing.
- They require active maintenance.
- Scalability, high-availability, and performance of virtual machines should be managed by users or advance tools, such as Kubernetes. Any degradation and subsequent improvement is the user's responsibility.

And this leads to serverless as the current state of evolution for deployment and consumption of applications.

Serverless

Serverless refers to a deployment model in which users are responsible for only their application code and configuration. Customers of serverless do not have to bother about the underlying platform and infrastructure and can concentrate on solving their business problems by writing code against them.

Serverless does not mean there are no servers. Code and configuration needs some server to run them. Serverless is from the customer's perspective. From the customer perspective, serverless means that they do not see the server at all. They do not care about the underlying platform and infrastructure. They do not need to manage and monitor them. Serverless provides an environment that can scale up and down, out and in, automatically, without the customers even knowing about it. All operations related to platforms and infrastructures happen behind the scenes, transparently, without the user knowing about them. Customers are provided with performance **service level agreements (SLA)** and Azure ensures that it meets that SLA irrespective of the number or size of the servers required.

Customers are required to bring in their code only and the rest of the artifacts needed to run the code is the responsibility of the cloud provider.

Principles of serverless technology

Serverless technology is based on the following principles.

Lower cost

Cost is based on the actual consumption of the compute resources and power. There is no cost associated to them if there is no consumption.

Event-driven

Serverless functions should be able to execute based on certain events happening. The event should trigger the execution of the function. In other words, serverless should allow functions to decouple themselves from other functions and instead rely on the firing of certain events in which they are interested in.

Single responsibility

Serverless should implement a single functionality and responsibility and it should do that well. Multiple responsibilities should not be coded or implemented within a single function.

Execute quickly

Serverless functions should not take a long time to complete a job. They should be able to execute quickly and return back.

Azure functions or functions as a service - FaaS

Azure provides *functions* as a resource. They are serverless implementations from Azure. With Azure functions, code can be written in any language the user is comfortable with and an Azure function will provide a runtime to execute them. Based on the language chosen, an appropriate platform is provided to users for bringing their own code. They are a unit of deployment and can automatically be out and in. When dealing with functions, users cannot view the underlying virtual machines and platform but Azure functions provide a small window to see them in terms of the **Kudu** console.

Azure functions runtime, bindings, and triggers

There are two main components of Azure functions.

Azure function runtime

The core and brain of Azure functions is its Azure runtime. The pre-cursor to Azure functions is Azure web jobs. The code for Azure web jobs also forms the core for Azure functions. There are additional features and extensions added to Azure web jobs to create Azure functions. The function runtime is the magic behind making the function work. Azure functions are hosted within Azure app services. Azure app services load Azure runtime and either wait for an external event to occur or for any HTTP requests. On arrival of a request or occurrence of a trigger, it loads the incoming payload, reads the function's `function.json` file to find the function's bindings and trigger, maps the incoming data to incoming parameters, and invokes the function with parameter values. Once the function completes its execution, the value is again passed backed to Azure function runtime by way of an outgoing parameter defined as binding in the `function.json` file. The function runtime returns the values to the caller. Azure function runtime acts as a glue that enables the entire functioning of functions.

Azure function binding and triggers

If Azure function runtime is the brain of Azure functions, then function bindings and triggers are the heart of Azure functions. Azure functions promote loose-coupling and high cohesion between services using triggers and bindings. Generally, the application implements code using imperative syntax for incoming and outgoing parameters and return values. This generally results in hardcoding the incoming parameters. Since Azure functions should be capable of invoking any function defined, they implement a generic mechanism to invoke functions by means of triggers and binding.

Binding refers to the process of creating a connection between the incoming data and the Azure function, mapping the data types. The connection could be a single direction from runtime to the Azure function, Azure function to runtime for return values, or multi-direction--the same binding can transmit data between Azure runtime and Azure functions. Azure functions use a declarative way to define bindings.

Triggers are a special type of binding through which functions can be invoked based on external events. Apart from invoking the function, it also passed the incoming data, payload, and metadata to the function.

Bindings are defined in the `function.json` file:

```json
{
  "bindings": [
    {
      "name": "checkOut",
      "type": "queueTrigger",
      "direction": "in",
      "queueName": "checkout-items",
      "connection": "AzureWebJobsDashboard"
    },
    {
      "name": "Orders",
      "type": "table",
      "direction": "out",
      "tableName": "OrderDetails",
      "connection": "<<Connection to table storage account>>"
    }
  ],
  "disabled": false
}
```

In this example, a trigger is declared that invokes the function whenever there is a new item in the storage queue. The `type` is of `queueTrigger`, the `direction` is `in`, `queueName` is `checkout-items`, and details about the target storage account connection and table name are also shown. All these values are important for the functioning of this binding. The name `checkOut` can be used within the functions code as a variable.

Similarly, a binding for return values is declared. Here the return value is named as `Orders` and the data is the output from the Azure function. It writes the return data into the Azure table storage using the connection string provided.

Both bindings and triggers can be modified and authored using the **Integrate** tab in Azure functions. Behind the scene, the `function.json` file is updated. The trigger `checkOut` is declared, as shown here:

And the output **Orders** is shown next:

The authors of Azure functions do not need to write plumbing code to get data from multiple sources. They just decide the type of data expected from the Azure runtime. This is shown in next code segment. Notice the checkout is available as a string to the function. Functions provide multiple different types to be able to send to a function. For example, a queue binding can provide the following:

- **Plain old simple object (POCO)**
- String
- Byte[]
- CloudQueueMessage

The author of the function can use any one of these datatypes and Azure function runtime will ensure that a proper object as a parameter is sent to the function:

```
using System;
public static void Run(string checkOut, TraceWriter log)
{
    log.Info($"C# Queue trigger function processed: { checkOut }");
}
```

It is also important to know that in the previous images, the storage account names are `AzureWebJobsStorage` and `AzureWebJobsDashboard`. These are keys that are defined within the Azure functions `appSettings` setting.

For more information on Azure bindings and triggers, refer to the following link: `https://docs.microsoft.com/en-us/azure/azure-functions/functions-bindings-storage-queue`.

Azure function proxies

Azure function proxies are one of the latest additional features to Azure functions. After starting using Azure functions, there will be a time when there might be lots of function implementation and it will be difficult to integrate them together in a workflow by clients. Instead of letting clients weave these functions together, Azure proxies can be used. Proxies help in providing clients with a single function URL and then in turn invoke multiple Azure functions behind the scenes to complete workflows. It is important to understand that proxies are applicable in those cases where functions accept requests on demand instead of driven by events. These internal functions connected to a proxy can be within a single function app or on multiple separate apps. Proxies get requests from clients, convert, override, and augment the payload and send them to backend internal functions. Once they get a response from these functions, they can again convert, override, and augment the response and send it back to the client.

More information about Azure functions can be found at
`https://docs.microsoft.com/en-us/azure/azure-functions/functions-proxies`.

Monitoring

Complete log information is provided for each request or trigger in the **Monitor** tab of Azure functions. This helps in identifying issues and auditing any risks, bugs, or exception in Azure functions.

Authentication and authorization

Azure functions rely on Azure app services for their authentication needs. App services have rich authentication features where clients can use OpenConnectID for authentication and OAuth for authentication. Users can get authenticated using Azure AD, Facebook, Google, Twitter, or Microsoft accounts.

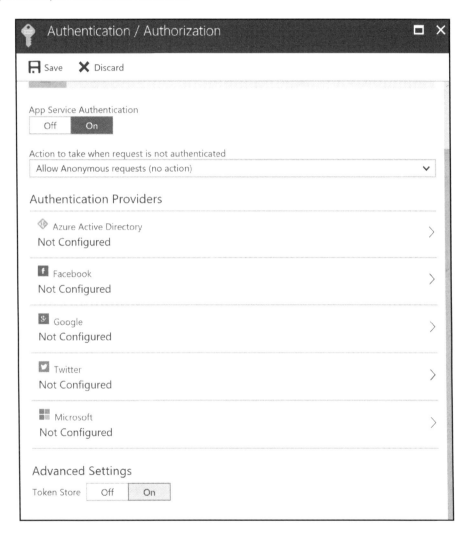

Azure functions that are based on HTTP can also incorporate usage of keys that should be sent along with HTTP requests. These keys are available from the **Manage** tab in the functions.

Function keys allow authorization to individual functions. These keys should be sent as part of the HTTP request header.

Host keys also allow authorization to all functions within a function app. These keys should be sent as part of the HTTP request header.

The default keys are used when using function and host keys. There is an additional host key named **_master** that helps in administrative access to the Azure function runtime API.

Azure function configuration

Azure functions provide configuration options at multiple levels. They provide configuration for the following:

- The platform itself
- The function app services

These settings affect every function contained by them. More information about these settings are available at https://docs.microsoft.com/en-us/azure/azure-functions/functions-how-to-use-azure-function-app-settings.

Platform configuration

Azure functions are hosted within Azure app services, so they get all of its features. Diagnostic and monitoring logs can be configured easily using platform features. Furthermore, it provides options for assigning SSL certificates, using a custom domain, authentication, and authorization (using Azure AD, Facebook, and other OAuth and OpenConnectID protocols) as part of the networking features.

Although customers are not concerned about the infrastructure, operating system, filesystem, platform on which the functions actually execute, the Azure function provides the necessary tooling in place to peek within the underlying system to change and tweak them. The console and Kudu console are tools used for this purpose. They provide a rich editor to author Azure functions and edit their configuration.

Azure functions, just like app services, allow storing configuration information within the `web.config` application setting section, which can be read on demand.

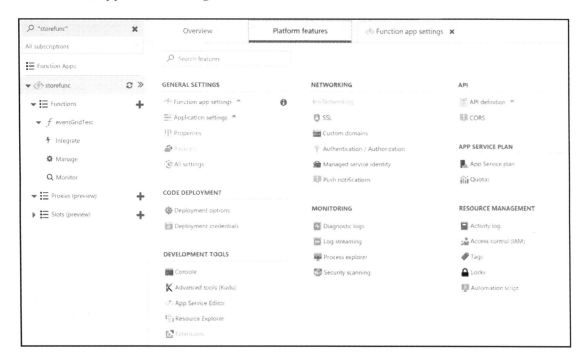

App services function settings

These settings affect all functions. Application settings can be managed here. Azure function proxies can be enabled and disabled. We will discuss proxies later in this chapter. They also help in changing the edit mode of a function app and the deployment to slots.

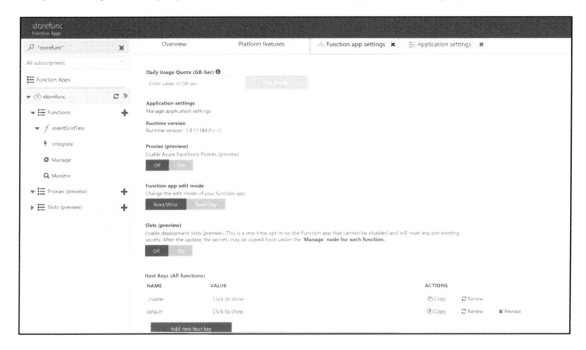

Azure function cost plans

Azure functions are based on Azure app services and provide a better costing model for the users. There are two cost models:

- **Consumption plan**: This is based on the actual consumption and execution of functions. This plan calculates the cost based on the compute usage during actual consumption and execution of the function. If a function is not executed, there is no cost associated with it. However, it does not mean that performance is compromised in this plan. Azure functions will automatically scale out and in based on demand to ensure basic minimum performance levels are maintained. A function execution is allowed 10 minutes for its completion.

- **App service plan**: This plan provides complete dedicated virtual machines behind the scene to functions and so the cost is directly proportional to the cost of the virtual machine and its size. There is a cost associated with this plan even if functions are not executed at all. Function code can run for as long it is needed to complete. There is no time limit. Within the app service plan, the function runtime goes idle if not used within a few minutes and can be awoken only using a HTTP trigger. There is an **Always On** setting that can be used for not letting the function runtime to go idle. Scaling is either manual or based on auto-scale settings.

Azure functions advantages

Serverless computing is a relatively new paradigm in server technology and helps organizations convert large functionalities into smaller discrete on-demand functions that can be invoked and executed through automated triggers and scheduled jobs. They are also known as FaaS, in which organizations can focus on their domain challenges instead of the underlying infrastructure and platform. It also helps in democratizing solution architecture into smaller reusable functions deriving higher value for their investments.

There is a plethora of serverless compute platforms available on the internet. Some of the important ones are:

- Azure functions
- AWS Lambda
- IBM OpenWhisk
- Iron.io
- Google Cloud functions

In fact, every few days there is a new framework getting introduced and it is becoming increasing difficult for enterprises to decide and choose the framework that works best for them.

Azure provides a rich serverless environment known as Azure functions and I would like to point out a few features that it supports to make them enterprise-ready:

- **Large choice of triggers**: Triggers act as events and execute serverless compute functions automatically. These triggers pass the raw data, the action, and event important to the functions. The serverless compute platform should provide different types of triggers enabling enterprises with multiple choices for their solution architecture. It should also provide facilities to execute the functions periodically as a scheduled task.

- **Webhooks**: A webhook helps in advanced integration with third-party services. It places hooks so that any change in a third-party service will start executing the serverless compute functions. It provides a rich infrastructure that can collaborate with important services such as version control systems and social media platforms.

- **On-demand execution**: The functions should not only be executed based on triggers but also have a mechanism to be executed manually. This brings flexibility during the development and testing of the functions.

- **Unlimited scalability**: A serverless compute platform should scale out and in functions dynamically based on their demand. Serverless compute functions are generally reachable through the internet and it is difficult to predict the number of users that could potentially connect to them. It is very important that they scale up automatically with more instances during high demand and scale down when demand reduces. This would help enterprises to reduce capital expenditure on an infrastructure that remains idle for a large part of the year.

- **High availability**: This is a no-brainer. Serverless functions should be highly available. Enterprises do not like unplanned downtime and it is extremely important for serverless functions to be available all the time (24x7x365). If a serverless compute platform does not guarantee more than five nines in terms of availability (99.999%), enterprises should look for another platform.

- **Security**: The platform should provide an appropriate infrastructure for providing security to serverless functions. There should be provision to authenticate, authorize, and maintain the confidentiality and identity of the users. Moreover, the platform should provide provisions to authenticate using the new age OAuth-based authorization protocols. The platform should also allow **Cross-Origin Resource Sharing** (**CORS**). CORS allows JavaScript code running in a browser on an external host to interact with serverless functions for functions accessible through the internet.

- **Industry standards**: The platform should use industry standards rather than proprietary technology. JSON is becoming the de-facto standard for message payload exchange on REST endpoints. It should support both HTTP and HTTPS protocols. This allows cross-platform applications to invoke and consume these services.

- **Monitoring, logging, and auditing**: Any serverless platform should provide infrastructure to monitor functions at the operational level, generate alerts, and inform teams to take corrective actions on them. The platform should provide a rich logging mechanism to capture activities in functions and provide telemetry metrics to its owner. This should include availability, scalability, and performance details among others. The logs should be easily accessible in the form of dashboards, making an audit exercise easy for administrators. Enterprises want to optimize time, effort, and money spent on keeping serverless functions operational. They should choose a serverless platform that provides rich operational information through monitoring, logging, and audit capabilities.

- **DevOps friendly**: Enterprises have caught up big time with DevOps. Large enterprises have already adopted DevOps; the small and medium enterprises are not far behind. Every company wants to deploy technologies in their landscape and ecosystem that are automatable from continuous integration, deployment, and delivery processes. The platform should not only provide automation endpoints and utilities but it should also be easy for developers to configure DevOps-related practices for function development.

- **Language support**: A serverless platform should provide multiple language options for the development of functions. Gone are the days when enterprises used a single popular language for all their development activities. Today, companies deploy languages known well to their developers. They also use heterogeneous languages in their landscape for higher productivity and affinity to the type of application getting developed. It could be C#, JavaScript, Bash, PowerShell, or a combination of any such technologies.

- **Advance tools for authoring, testing, and deployment**: Tools should make developing, testing, and debugging easy for the function developer. Apart from providing quick start wizards, tools should increase developer productivity by providing an integrated environment for developing and debugging, executing unit and integration tests, the ability to mock objects, and help in automated deployments. The authoring editor should provide templates and scaffolding code to fast-track development. It should also provide emulators that help in testing the function without hosting on the real environment.

- **Fault tolerant**: Serverless functions should not crash or die due to errors or exceptions in user code or server infrastructure. They should log the exceptions, inform the user, and elegantly continue to execute the next request.
- **Long running activities**: A serverless platform should provide flexibility to run long running activities. After the long running activities complete their execution, the serverless platform should pick up the execution and return to the user.
- **Ability to configure**: Although a serverless compute means no access to the underlying platform, there should be adequate touchpoints through which administrators can peep and change the configuration of the underlying platform. This will help enterprises to troubleshoot, conduct advance deployments, and tweak the platform according to their needs.
- **Set quotas**: The serverless compute platform should have flexibility to determine quotas for execution. This would help in constraining mindless usage of a serverless compute.
- **Multiple hosting plans**: The platform should provide options for multiple usage plans depending upon the resource consumption and executions. Enterprises can choose the plan that best fits their needs and optimize their expenditure while ensuring cost benefits.
- **Rich integrations**: The serverless compute platform should be able to integrate with other services, such as cognitive services, analytics services, communication services, and other transaction-based services, to provide rich and contextual services to customers. This will help enterprises to create solutions that are innovative and relevant to the industry.
- **Massive parallelism**: The serverless platform should be capable of executing requests synchronously as well asynchronously. This eventually helps in writing patterns that can help in massive scalability of functions by optimally utilizing the platform resources.
- **Multi-level configurations**: The platform should provide options to configure at the individual function level, function grouping level and platform level. This will help enterprises to change the overall behavior of their functions, including platform behavior, with minimal effort.

Azure functions use cases

There are many valid use cases for using and implementing Azure functions.

Implementing microservices

Azure functions help in breaking down large applications into smaller discreet functional code units. Each unit is treated independent of the other and evolves in its own life cycle. Each such code unit has its own compute, hardware, and monitoring requirements. Each function can be connected to all other functions. These units are weaved together by orchestrators to build complete functionality. For example, in an e-commerce application, there can be individual functions (code units) each responsible for listing catalogs, recommendations, categories, subcategories, shopping carts, checkouts, payment types, payment gateways, shipping addresses, billing addresses, taxes, shipping charges, cancellations, returns, emails, SMS, and so on. Some of these functions are brought together to create use cases for e-commerce applications such as product browsing, checkout flow, and so on.

Integration between multiple endpoints

Azure functions can build overall application functionality by integrating multiple functions. The integration can be based on the triggering of events or it could be on a push basis. It helps in decomposing large monolithic applications into small components.

Data processing

Azure functions can be used for processing incoming data in batches. They can help in processing data coming in multiple formats such as XML, CSV, JSON, text, and so on. They can also run conversion, enrichment, cleaning, and filtering algorithms. In fact, multiple functions can be used, each doing either conversion or enrichment, cleaning or filtering. Azure functions can also be used to incorporate advance cognitive services such as **optical character recognition** (OCR), computer vision, image manipulation, and conversion.

Integrating legacy applications

Azure functions can help in integrating legacy applications with newer protocols and modern applications. Legacy applications might not be using industry standard protocols and formats. Azure functions can act as a proxy for these legacy applications, accept requests from users or other applications, convert the data into a format understood by a legacy application, and talk to it on protocols it understands. This opens a world of opportunity for integrating and bringing old and legacy applications into the mainstream portfolio.

Scheduled jobs

Azure functions can be used to execute continuously periodically for certain application functions. These application functions can range from periodically taking backups, restoring, running batch jobs, exporting and importing data, bulk emails, and so on.

Communication gateways

Azure functions can be used in communication gateways such as using notification hubs, **short messaging service (SMS)**, and email.

Types of Azure functions

Azure functions can be categorized into three different types:

- **On demand functions**: These are functions that are executed when they are explicitly called or invoked. Examples of such functions include HTTP-based functions and webhooks.
- **Scheduled functions**: These functions are like timer jobs and execute functions on fixed intervals.
- **Event-based functions**: These functions are executed based on external events. For example, uploading a new file to Azure blob storage generates an event which can start execution of the Azure function.

Creating your first Azure function

Azure functions can be created using the Azure portal, PowerShell, Azure CLI, and REST API's. Steps to create a function using the ARM template is already detailed at `https://docs.microsoft.com/en-us/azure/azure-functions/functions-infrastructure -as-code`. In this section, Azure functions will be provisioned using the portal.

Azure functions are hosted within Azure app services. Users create a new function app which in turn creates an app service plan and app service. The app service plan is configured based on the following:

- **Name**: Name of app service. The name should be unique within the `.azurewebsites.net` domain.
- **Location**: Location for hosting the Azure function app service.

- **Hosting plan**: This is also known as the pricing plan. Here, two options, as discussed previously, are available--consumption and app services plan.
- **Resource group name**: The name of the resource group containing both the app service plan and app service.
- **Storage account**: Azure functions needs an Azure storage account to store their internal data and logs.
- **Enable application insights**: To capture telemetry information from Azure functions.

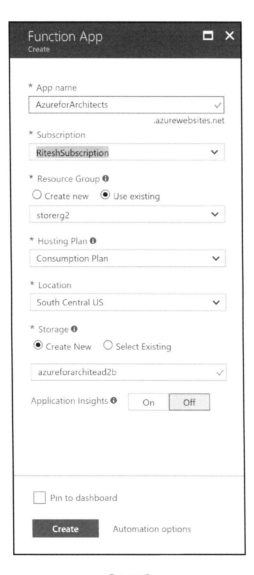

Creating an Azure function app will provide a dashboard after provisioning.

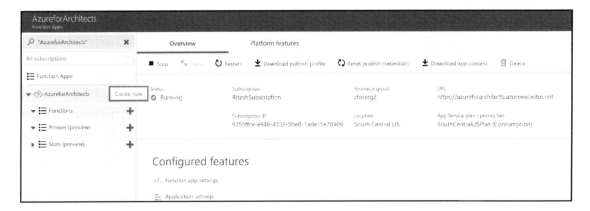

Clicking on the plus button next to the functions will show a wizard for creating a new function. This wizard shows quick templates for creating the **Webhook + API**, **Timer**, and **Data processing** functions. It will create the necessary scaffolding code and structure for getting started. This scaffolding code is also generated for default bindings and triggers. It also allows for the selection of a language for implementation of the function. Azure functions allow the following:

- C#
- JavaScript
- F#
- PowerShell
- Bash
- Python languages

This wizard also allows for creation of custom functions from scratch.

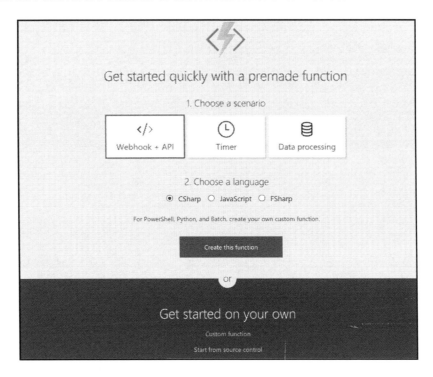

There are many more options provided for creating a custom function.

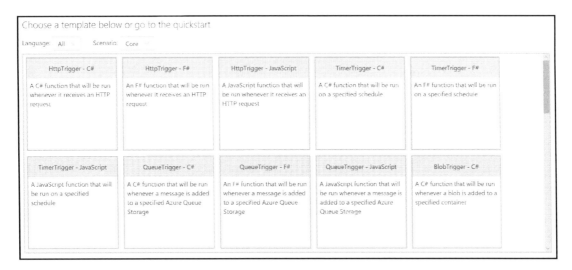

In this section, a custom Azure function will be created using the PowerShell language, which can be executed whenever it receives a HTTP request. Provide an appropriate name, in this case `FirstFunction,` and choose **Anonymous** as the authorization level. Authorization levels will be discussed later in this chapter.

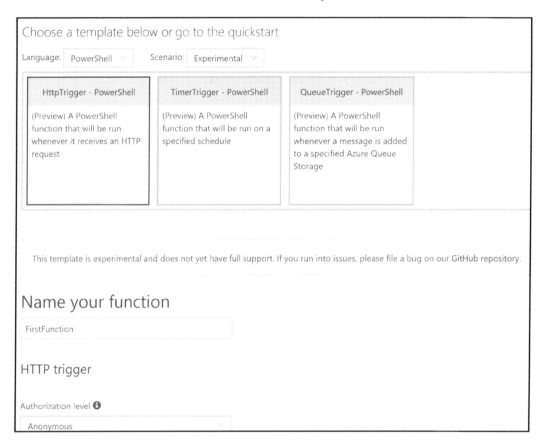

Creating this function provides a complete function authoring integrated environment along with some code. This code gets the raw content from the incoming `req` parameter, which is filled up by Azure runtime with incoming data (query string, form values, and so on), and it converts it in the PowerShell object. There could be multiple types of data within this incoming parameter, and a single `name` value is extracted out of it. Azure functions runtime also creates a new variable for every incoming `querystring` with an HTTP request and appends it with `$req_query_`. So sending the name as `querystring` will provide an out-of-the-box variable, `$req_query_name`, containing the value for the name `querystring` and will be consumed within the function. The response for this function is written to a file that the Azure function runtime reads and sends back to the browser.

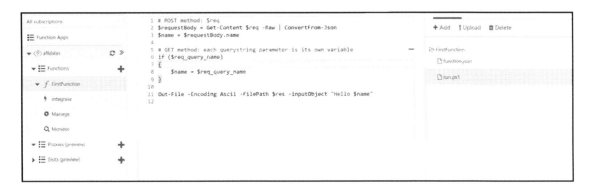

This function that can be invoked using an HTTP request from the browser. The URL for this function is available from the environment and is composed of the function app name along with the function name. The format is `https://<<function app name>>.azurewebsites.net/api/<<function name>>`. In this case, the URL will be `https://azureforarchitects.azurewebsites.net/api/FirstFunction`.

For sending parameters to this function, additional query string parameters can be appended at the end of the URL. For example, for sending name parameters to this function, the `https://azureforarchitects.azurewebsites.net/api/FirstFunction?name=rit esh` URL can be used. The output of the function is shown in the following figure:

```
←  →  ○  ⌂       🔒  azureforarchitects.azurewebsites.net/api/FirstFunction?name=ritesh

"Hello ritesh\r\n"
```

For HTTP-based functions, the Azure function already provides triggers and binding within the `function.json` file. This file is used for defining all function level triggers and bindings and there is one associated with every function.

```
function.json        Save              ▶ Run                        </> Get function URL
 1 {
 2    "bindings": [
 3      {
 4        "name": "req",
 5        "type": "httpTrigger",
 6        "direction": "in",
 7        "authLevel": "anonymous"
 8      },
 9      {
10        "name": "res",
11        "type": "http",
12        "direction": "out"
13      }
14    ],
15    "disabled": false
16 }
```

The HTTP template creates a trigger for all incoming requests. The trigger invokes the Azure function and passes in the entire incoming data and payload as a parameter named as `req`. This parameter is available within the Azure function. The response from the function is a binding that takes output from the `res` variable from the Azure function and sends it back to the HTTP channel as a response.

Creating an event-driven function

In this example, an Azure function will be authored connected to the Azure storage account. The storage account has a container for holding all blob files. The name of the storage account is `incomingfiles` and the container is orders:

Create a new Azure function from portal.

As of now, this Azure function does not have connectivity information to the storage account. Azure functions need connection information for the storage account and that is available from the **Access keys** tab in the storage account. The same information can be obtained using the Azure function editor environment. In fact, it allows for the creation of a new storage account from the same editor environment.

This can be added using the new button beside the **Storage account connection** input type. It allows for selecting an existing storage account or creating a new storage account. Since I already have a couple of storage accounts, I am reusing them. Readers should create a separate Azure storage account. Selecting a storage account will update the settings in the **appsettings** section with the connection string added to it.

Ensure that a container already exists within the blob service of the target Azure storage account. The path input refers to the path to the container. In this case, the orders container already exists within the storage account. The **Create** button will provision the new function monitoring the storage account container.

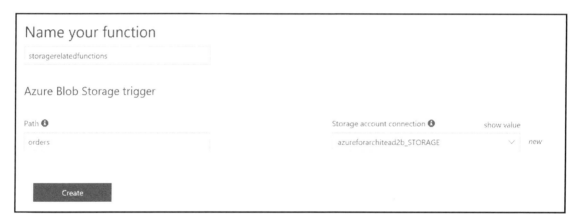

The code for the Azure function is as follows:

```
public static void Run(Stream myBlob,  TraceWriter log)
{
    log.Info($"C# Blob trigger function Processed blob\n  \n Size:
{myBlob.Length} Bytes");
}
```

The bindings are shown next:

```
{
  "bindings": [
    {
      "name": "myBlob",
```

```
        "type": "blobTrigger",
        "direction": "in",
        "path": "orders",
        "connection": "azureforarchitead2b_STORAGE"
    }
  ],
  "disabled": false
}
```

Now, uploading any blob file in the orders container should trigger the function:

Creating a connected architecture with functions

A connected architecture with functions refers to creating multiple functions, whereby the output of one function triggers another function and provides data for the next function to execute its logic. In this section, we will continue with the previous scenario of the storage account. In this case, the output of the function getting triggered using Azure storage blob files will write the size of the file to Azure **Cosmos DB**.

The configuration of Cosmos DB is shown next. By default, there are no collections created in Cosmos DB. A collection will automatically be created while creating a function that will get triggered when Cosmos DB gets any data.

Create a new database `testdb` within Cosmos DB and a new collection named `testcollection` within it. You need both the database and collection name while configuring Azure functions.

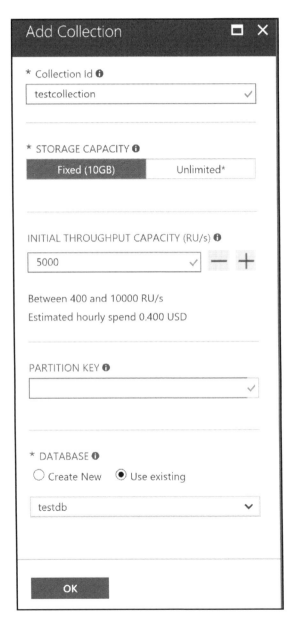

It's time to revisit the `storagerelatedfunctions` function and change its binding to return the size of the data for the uploaded file. This returned value will be written to Cosmos DB. This will demand a change to the bindings as well with an additional one responsible for capturing output values. This binding will eventually write to the Cosmos DB collection. Navigate to the **Integrate** tab and click on the **New Output** button following the **Outputs** label and select **Azure Cosmos DB**.

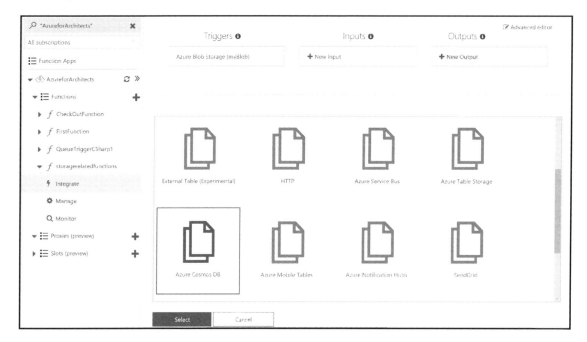

Provide the appropriate names for the database and collection (check the checkbox to create the collection if it does not exist), click on the **New** button to select our newly created Azure Cosmos DB, and leave the parameter name as `outputDocument`.

Modify the function as shown next.

```
1  public static void Run(string  myBlob, out object outputDocument, TraceWriter log)
2  {
3          log.Info($"C# blob trigger function processed: {myBlob.Length}");
4          log.Info($"C# blob trigger function processed: {myBlob}");
5      outputDocument = new {
6          id = myBlob.Length.ToString(),
7          len = myBlob.Length,
8          data =  myBlob
9      };
10
11 }
12
```

Now uploading a new file to the orders collection in the Azure storage account will execute a function that will write to the Azure Cosmos DB collection. Now another function can be written with the newly created Azure Cosmos DB as a trigger binding. It will provide the size of files and the function can act on it. This is shown next:

Summary

Serverless is a new deployment unit in today's world. The evolvement of functions from traditional methods has led to designing loosely coupled, independently evolving, self-reliant architecture that was only a concept in earlier days. Functions are a unit of deployment and provide an environment where users do not need to manage the environment at all. All they have to care about is the code written for the functionality. Azure provides a mature platform for hosting functions and integrating them seamlessly based on events or on demand. Nearly every resource in Azure can participate in an architecture composed of Azure functions. The future is functions, as more and more organizations want to stay away from managing infrastructures and platforms. They want to offload this to cloud providers. It is an essential feature to master by every architect dealing with Azure.

Next chapter is an interesting one as it deals with Azure Resource Manager concepts such as policies, locks, and tags in details.

9
Designing Policies, Locks, and Tags

Azure is a versatile cloud platform. Customers can not only create and deploy their application, they can also actively manage and govern their environments. Clouds generally follow a pay-as-you-go paradigm where a customer subscribes for an Azure subscription and virtually can deploy anything on it. It could be as small as a small basic virtual machine to thousands of virtual machines with higher Sku's. Azure will not stop any customer from provisioning any resources or constraint them in terms of numbers. Within an organization there could be a large number of people having access to the Azure subscription. There is a need to have a governance model in place such that only the required adequate resources are provisioned by people who have rights to create them. Azure provides resource management features, such as Azure **Role based Access Control** (**RBAC**) and policies and locks for managing and providing governance for resources.

Another major aspect of governance is cost, usage, and information management. Organization management would always want to be kept updated about their cloud consumption and cost. They would like to identify which team, department, or unit is using what percentage of their total cost. In short, they want to have reports based on various dimensions about consumption and cost. Azure provides a tagging feature that can help provide this kind of information to the management on the fly.

In this chapter, we will cover the following topics:

- Azure RBAC
- Azure policies
- Azure locks
- Azure tags

Azure tags

Tags in a dictionary is defined as *a label attached to someone or something for the purpose of identification or to give other information.* Azure allows tagging of resource groups and resources with name-value pairs. Tagging helps in logical organization and categorization of resources. Azure also allows tagging 15 name-value pairs for resource groups and its resources. Although resource group is a container for resources, tagging resource group does not mean tagging of its constituent resources. Resource groups and resources should be tagged based on their usage, which will be explained later in this section. Tags work at a subscription level. Azure accepts any name-value pairs and so it is important for an organization to define both the names and their possible values.

But why is tagging important? In other words, what problems can be solved using tagging. Tagging has the following benefits:

- **Categorization of resources**: An Azure subscription is used by multiple departments and roles within an organization. It is important for the management to identify the owners of these resources. Tagging helps in assigning identifiers to resources that can represent department or roles.
- **Information management for Azure resources**: Again Azure resources in a subscription can be provisioned by anyone having access to it. Organizations would like to have a proper categorization of resources in terms of their information management policies. The policies can be based on application life cycle management, such as development, testing, and production environments. It could be based on the usage--internal or external facing. It could be based on their priorities and more. Each organization has their own way of defining information categories and for them Azure is no different. Tags help in organizing resources logically.
- **Cost management**: Tagging in Azure can help in identifying resources based on their categorization. Queries can be executed against Azure to identify cost per category according to information management categories defined. For example, the cost of resources in Azure for developing an environment for the finance department and the marketing department can be easily ascertained. Moreover, Azure also provides billing information based on tags. This helps in identifying which teams, departments, or groups are consuming.

Tags have certain limitations in Azure.

Azure allows a maximum of 15 tag name-value pairs to be associated with a resources and resource groups.

Tags are non-inheritable. Tags applied to a resource group do not apply to the individual resources within it. However, it is quite easy to forget to tag resources while provisioning them. Azure policies are the mechanism to ensure that tags are tagged with the appropriate value during provision time. We will consider details of policies later in this chapter. A complete section is devoted to policies.

Tags can be assigned to resources and resource groups using PowerShell, Azure CLI 2.0, Azure resource management templates, Azure portal, and Azure resource manager REST API's.

A sample information management categorization using Azure tags that can be reused is shown here. In this example, department, project, environment, owner, approver, maintainer, start-date, retire-date, and patched-date name-value pairs are used to tag a resource group or resources. It is extremely easy to find all the resources for a particular tag or a combination of tags using PowerShell, Azure CLI, or REST API's.

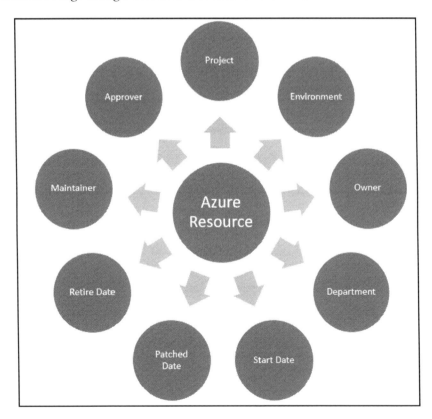

Tags with PowerShell

Tags can be managed using PowerShell, Azure Resource Manager templates, portal, and REST API's. In this section, PowerShell will be used to create and apply tags. PowerShell provides a cmdlet for retrieving and attaching tags to resource groups and resources.

- To retrieve tags associated with a resource using PowerShell, the `Find-AzureRMResource` cmdlet can be used:

  ```
  (Find-AzureRmResource -TagName Dept -TagValue Finance).Name
  ```

- To retrieve tags associated with a resource group using PowerShell, the following command can be used:

  ```
  (Find-AzureRmResourceGroup -Tag @{ Dept="Finance" }).Name
  ```

- To set tags to a resource group, the `Set-AzureRmResourceGroup` cmdlet can be used:

  ```
  Set-AzureRmResourceGroup -Name examplegroup -Tag @{ Dept="IT";
  Environment="Test" }
  ```

- To set tags to a resource, the `Set-AzureRmResource` cmdlet can be used:

  ```
  Set-AzureRmResource -Tag @{ Dept="IT"; Environment="Test" } -
  ResourceName examplevnet -ResourceGroupName examplegroup
  ```

Tags with the ARM template

Azure resource manager template provides also helps in defining tags for each resource. It can be used to assign multiple tags to each resource. This is shown as follows:

```
{
    "$schema":
"https://schema.management.azure.com/schemas/2015-01-01/deploymentTemplate.
json#",
    "contentVersion": "1.0.0.0",
    "resources": [
    {
      "apiVersion": "2016-01-01",
      "type": "Microsoft.Storage/storageAccounts",
      "name": "[concat('storage', uniqueString(resourceGroup().id))]",
      "location": "[resourceGroup().location]",
      "tags": {
```

```
        "Dept": "Finance",
        "Environment": "Production"
     },
     "sku": {
       "name": "Standard_LRS"
     },
     "kind": "Storage",
     "properties": { }
    }
    ]
  }
```

In the previous example, a couple of tags--Dept and Environment are added a storage account resource using Azure resource manager templates.

Resource groups versus resources

It is a must that architects decide the taxonomy and information architecture for Azure resources and resource groups. They should identify the categories on which resources will be classified based on query requirements. However, they must also identify whether tags should be attached to individual resources or resource groups.

If all resources within a resource group need the same tags, then it is better to tag the resource group rather than tagging each resource. It is important to take the queries on tags into consideration before finalizing whether tags should be applied at the resource level or the resource group level. If the queries relate to individual resource types across subscription and resource groups then assigning tags to resources make more sense, however, if identifying resource groups are enough in queries, then tags should be applied to resource groups.

Azure policies

The last section talked about applying tags for Azure deployments. Tags are great for organizing resources; however, there is one more factor and question that was not discussed. How do organizations enforce tags to be applied for every deployment? There should be automated enforcement of Azure tags to resources and resource groups. There is no check from Azure to ensure that appropriate tags will be applied to resources and resource groups. Now, this is not just related to tags--it could be related to any configuration for any resource on Azure. For example, all resources should be deployed only in East US and no resources can be deployed elsewhere.

You might have guessed by now that this section is all about formulating a governance model on Azure. Governance is an important element for Azure because it helps in bringing discipline and cost under control. It also ensures that everyone accessing the Azure environment are aware of organization priorities and processes. It helps in defining the organizational conventions that helps in managing resources.

Each policy can be built using multiple rules and multiple policies can be applied to subscription and resource groups. After the rules are executed and when they are satisfied, it executes an action. The action could be to deny the on-going transaction, audit the transaction, which means writing to logs and allowing it to complete, and append metadata to the transaction if the transaction is missing it.

Examples of policies could be related to the naming convention of resources, tagging of resources, the types of resources that can be provisioned, location of resources, or any combination of these rules.

Built-in policies

Azure provides infrastructure to create custom policies, however, it also provides some out-of-box policies that are frequently needed and used for governance. These policies relate to the allowed location, allowed resource types, and tags. More information for these built-in policies can be found at
`https://docs.microsoft.com/en-us/azure/azure-resource-manager/resource-manager-policy`.

Policy language

Azure policies use JSON language to define and describe policies.

There are two steps in policy adoption. The policy should be defined and then it should be applied and assigned. Policies have scope and can be applied at the subscription and resource group level.

Policies are defined using `if...then` blocks, which is similar to any popular programming language. The `if` block is executed to evaluate the conditions and based on the result from those conditions, the `then` block is executed:

```
{
  "if": {
    <condition> | <logical operator>
  },
```

```
  "then": {
    "effect": "deny | audit | append"
  }
}
```

Azure policies not only allow simple `if` conditions, but multiple `if` conditions can be joined together logically to create complex rules. These conditions can be joined using **AND**, **OR**, and **NOT** operators.

- The AND syntax requires all conditions to be true
- The OR syntax requires one of the conditions to be true
- The NOT syntax inverts the result of the condition

The AND syntax is shown next. It is represented by the `allOf` keyword:

```
"if": {
  "allOf": [
    {
       "field": "tags",
        "containsKey": "application"
    },
    {
      "field": "type",
      "equals": "Microsoft.Storage/storageAccounts"
    }
  ]
},
```

The OR syntax is shown next. It is represented by the `anyOf` keyword:

```
"if": {
  "anyOf": [
    {
       "field": "tags",
        "containsKey": "application"
    },
    {
      "field": "type",
      "equals": "Microsoft.Storage/storageAccounts"
    }
  ]
},
```

The NOT syntax is shown next. It is represented by the not keyword:

```
"if": {
  "not": [
    {
       "field": "tags",
       "containsKey": "application"
    },
    {
      "field": "type",
      "equals": "Microsoft.Storage/storageAccounts"
    }
  ]
},
```

In fact, these logical operators can be combined together as follows:

```
"if": {
  "allOf": [
    {
      "not": {
        "field": "tags",
        "containsKey": "application"
      }
    },
    {
      "field": "type",
      "equals": "Microsoft.Storage/storageAccounts"
    }
  ]
},
```

This is very similar to if conditions in popular programming languages such as C# and Node.js

```
If ("type" == "Microsoft.Storage/storageAccounts") {
    Deny
}
```

It is to note that there is no allow action, although there is a Deny action. It means that policy rules should be written with deny in perspective. Rules should evaluate the conditions and return Deny if they return true.

Allowed fields

The fields that are allowed in policies are as follows:

- `Name`
- `Kind`
- `Type`
- `Location`
- `Tags`
- `Tags.*`
- `Property aliases`

Azure locks

Locks are a mechanism to stop certain activities on resources. RBAC provides rights to users/groups/application in a certain scope. There are out-of-the-box RBAC roles, such as owner, contributor, and reader. With the contributor role, it is possible to delete or modify a resource. How can such activities be prevented despite the user having a contributor role? Here enters Azure locks.

Azure locks can help in two ways:

- It can lock resources such that they cannot be deleted even if you have owner access
- It can lock resource in such a way that neither it can be deleted, nor its configuration is modifiable

This is typically very helpful for resources in the production environment where resources should not be modified or deleted accidentally.

Locks can be applied at subscription, resource group, and individual resource levels. Locks follow inheritance between subscription, resource group, and resources. Applying a lock at the parent level will ensure that those at the child level also inherit it. Even resources you add later inherit the lock from the parent. The most restrictive lock in the inheritance takes precedence. Applying a lock at the resource level will also not allow deletion of a resource group containing the resource.

Locks are applied only to operations that help in managing the resource instead of operations that are internal to the resource. Users either need `Microsoft.Authorization/*` or `Microsoft.Authorization/locks/*` RBAC permissions to create and modify locks.

Locks can be created and applied through the Azure portal, Azure PowerShell, Azure CLI, ARM templates, and REST API.

Creating a lock using the ARM template is seen as follows:

```
{
  "$schema":
"https://schema.management.azure.com/schemas/2015-01-01/deploymentTemplate.
json#",
  "contentVersion": "1.0.0.0",
  "parameters": {
    "lockedResource": {
      "type": "string"
    }
  },
  "resources": [
    {
      "name": "[concat(parameters('lockedResource'),
'/Microsoft.Authorization/myLock')]",
      "type": "Microsoft.Storage/storageAccounts/providers/locks",
      "apiVersion": "2015-01-01",
      "properties": {
        "level": "CannotDelete"
      }
    }
  ]
}
```

Creating and applying a lock to the resource using PowerShell is seen as follows:

```
New-AzureRmResourceLock -LockLevel CanNotDelete -LockName LockSite `
  -ResourceName examplesite -ResourceType Microsoft.Web/sites `
  -ResourceGroupName exampleresourcegroup
```

Creating and applying a lock to the resource group using PowerShell is seen as follows:

```
New-AzureRmResourceLock -LockName LockGroup -LockLevel CanNotDelete `
  -ResourceGroupName exampleresourcegroup
```

Creating and applying a lock to the resource using Azure CLI is seen as follows:

```
az lock create --name LockSite --lock-type CanNotDelete \
  --resource-group exampleresourcegroup --resource-name examplesite \
  --resource-type Microsoft.Web/sites
```

Creating and applying a lock to the resource group using Azure CLI is seen as follows:

```
az lock create --name LockGroup --lock-type CanNotDelete \
  --resource-group exampleresourcegroup
```

Azure RBAC

Azure provides authentication using Azure AD for its resources. Once authenticated, it needs to be evaluated and decided when the identity should be allowed to access any resource, all resources, or just the selected resource intended for that user. This activity has traditionally been known as authorization. Authorization evaluates whether the given identity has the necessary permissions to access the resource and if it can perform the intended operation. Anybody having access to an Azure subscription should be given just enough permissions so that the job can be performed. There should not be more than the required permissions assigned to identities to ensure that the attach surface remains minimum.

Authorization is popularly also known as Role-based Access Control. RBAC in Azure refers to the assigning of permissions to identities (users/groups/applications) at a scope. The scope could be subscription, resource group, or individual resources.

RBAC helps in creation and assignment of different permissions to different identities. This helps in segregating duties within teams rather than everyone having every permission. It helps in making people responsible for their job because others might not even have access to perform it. It is to be noted that providing access as higher scope automatically ensures that the child resources inherit those permissions. For example, providing read access on a resource group ensures that all resources within it will be with read permissions for the given identity.

Azure provides three general purpose built-in roles. They are as follows:

- Owner role which has full access to all resources
- Contributor role which has access to read/write resources
- Readers role which has only read permissions on resources

There are more roles provided by Azure, but they are resource specific. Examples include network contributor and security manager.

To get all roles provided by Azure for all resources, execute the `Get-AzureRmRoleDefinition` command in the PowerShell console.

Each role definition has certain allowed and not allowed actions. For example, owner role has all actions permitted and none of the actions are prohibited. Prohibited actions take precedence on all actions:

```
PS C:\Users\rimodi> Get-AzureRmRoleDefinition -Name "owner"
Name              : Owner
Id                : 8e3af657-a8ff-443c-a75c-2fe8c4bcb635
IsCustom          : False
Description       : Lets you manage everything, including access to
resources.
Actions           : {*}
NotActions        : {}
AssignableScopes  : {/}
```

Each role comprises of multiple permissions. Each resource provides a list of operations. The operation supported by a resource can be obtained using the `Get-AzureRmProviderOperation` cmdlet. This cmdlet takes the name of the provider and resource for retrieving the operations:

```
Get-AzureRmProviderOperation -OperationSearchString "Microsoft.Insights/*"
```

This will result in the following output:

```
PS C:\Users\rimodi> get-AzureRmProviderOperation -OperationSearchString
"Microsoft.Insights/*" | select operation
Operation
---------
Microsoft.Insights/Register/Action
Microsoft.Insights/AlertRules/Write
Microsoft.Insights/AlertRules/Delete
Microsoft.Insights/AlertRules/Read
Microsoft.Insights/AlertRules/Activated/Action
Microsoft.Insights/AlertRules/Resolved/Action
Microsoft.Insights/AlertRules/Throttled/Action
```

```
Microsoft.Insights/AlertRules/Incidents/Read
Microsoft.Insights/MetricDefinitions/Read
Microsoft.Insights/eventtypes/values/Read
Microsoft.Insights/eventtypes/digestevents/Read
Microsoft.Insights/Metrics/Read
Microsoft.Insights/LogProfiles/Write
Microsoft.Insights/LogProfiles/Delete
Microsoft.Insights/LogProfiles/Read
Microsoft.Insights/Components/Write
Microsoft.Insights/Components/Delete
Microsoft.Insights/Components/Read
Microsoft.Insights/AutoscaleSettings/Write
Microsoft.Insights/AutoscaleSettings/Delete
Microsoft.Insights/AutoscaleSettings/Read
Microsoft.Insights/AutoscaleSettings/Scaleup/Action
Microsoft.Insights/AutoscaleSettings/Scaledown/Action
Microsoft.Insights/AutoscaleSettings/providers/Microsoft.Insights/MetricDef
initions/Read
Microsoft.Insights/ActivityLogAlerts/Activated/Action
Microsoft.Insights/DiagnosticSettings/Write
Microsoft.Insights/DiagnosticSettings/Delete
Microsoft.Insights/DiagnosticSettings/Read
Microsoft.Insights/LogDefinitions/Read
Microsoft.Insights/Webtests/Write
Microsoft.Insights/Webtests/Delete
Microsoft.Insights/Webtests/Read
Microsoft.Insights/ExtendedDiagnosticSettings/Write
Microsoft.Insights/ExtendedDiagnosticSettings/Delete
Microsoft.Insights/ExtendedDiagnosticSettings/Read
```

Custom roles

Roles are created by combining multiple permissions. For example, a custom role can consist of operations from multiple resources as follows:

```
$role = Get-AzureRmRoleDefinition "Virtual Machine Contributor"
$role.Id = $null
$role.Name = "Virtual Machine Operator"
$role.Description = "Can monitor and restart virtual machines."
$role.Actions.Clear()
$role.Actions.Add("Microsoft.Storage/*/read")
$role.Actions.Add("Microsoft.Network/*/read")
$role.Actions.Add("Microsoft.Compute/*/read")
$role.Actions.Add("Microsoft.Compute/virtualMachines/start/action")
    $role.Actions.Add("Microsoft.Compute/virtualMachines/restart/action")
$role.Actions.Add("Microsoft.Authorization/*/read")
```

```
$role.Actions.Add("Microsoft.Resources/subscriptions/resourceGroups/read")
$role.Actions.Add("Microsoft.Insights/alertRules/*")
$role.Actions.Add("Microsoft.Support/*")
$role.AssignableScopes.Clear()
$role.AssignableScopes.Add("/subscriptions/c276fc76-9cd4-44c9-99a7-4fd71546
436e")
$role.AssignableScopes.Add("/subscriptions/e91d47c4-76f3-4271-
a796-21b4ecfe3624")
New-AzureRmRoleDefinition -Role $role
```

How is it different from RBAC?

Locks are not the same as RBAC. RBAC helps in allowing or denying permissions on resources that are intrinsic to the resource. These permissions relate to performing operations such as read, write, and update on resources. Locks, on the other hand, relates to disallowing permissions to configure or delete the resource.

Examples of implementing Azure governance features

In this section, we will go through a sample architecture implementation for a fictitious organization that wants to implement Azure governance and cost management features.

Background

Company Inc is a worldwide company that is implementing a social media solution on Azure IaaS. They use web servers and application servers deployed on Azure virtual machines and networks. Azure SQL server acts as the backend database.

Role-based access control

The first task is to ensure that the appropriate teams and application owners can access their resources. It is recognized that each team has different requirements. For the sake of understanding, Azure SQL is deployed in a separate resource group compared to the Azure IaaS artifacts.

The administrator assigns the following roles for the subscription:

Role	Assigned to	Description
Owner	The administrator	Manages all resource groups and subscription.
Security manager	Security administrators	This role allows users to look at the Azure security center and the status of the resources.
Contributor	Infrastructure management	Managing virtual machines and other resources.
Reader	Developers	Can view resources, but cannot modify. Developers are expected to work on their development/testing environments.

Summary

Governance and cost management is one of the top priorities for companies moving to the cloud. Having an Azure subscription with pay-as-you-go can harm the company budget because anyone having access to the subscription can provision as many resources they feel like. Some resources are free while others are expensive. It is important for organizations to keep control on their cloud costs. Tags help in generating billing reports. These reports could be based on departments or projects, or owners or any other criteria deemed fit. While cost is important, governance is equally important. Azure provides locks, policies, and RBAC to formulate governance. Policies ensure that resource operations can be denied or audited, locks ensure that resources cannot be modified or deleted, and RBAC ensures that employees have optimal permissions for performing their jobs. With all these four features, companies can have sound governance and cost control on their Azure deployments.

DevOps on Azure will the focus on next chapter in which some of its important concepts and implementation techniques will be discussed.

10
DevOps on Azure

Software development is a complex undertaking comprising of multiple processes, tools and involves people from different departments. They all need to come together and work in a cohesive manner. With so many variables, the risks are high while delivering to the end customers. One small omission or misconfiguration and the application might come crashing down. This chapter is about adopting and implementing practices that reduce this risk considerably and ensure that high quality software can be delivered to the customer again and again.

Before getting into the details about DevOps, let's understand problems faced by software companies that are addressed by DevOps.

- Organizations are rigid and do not welcome change
- Rigid and time-consuming processes
- Isolated teams working in silos
- Monolithic design and big bang deployments
- Manual execution
- Lack of innovation

In this chapter, we will go detail about the following:

- DevOps
- DevOps practices
- Configuration management
- Continuous integration
- Continuous deployment
- Continuous delivery
- Visual Studio Team Services

- DevOps preparation
- DevOps for PaaS solution
- DevOps for virtual machine (IaaS) based solutions
- DevOps for container (IaaS) based solutions
- Azure automation
- Azure tools for DevOps

What is DevOps?

Today there is no consensus in the industry regarding the definition of DevOps. Every organization has formulated their own definition of DevOps and have tried to implement it. They have their own perspective and think they have implemented DevOps if they have their automation in place, configuration management enabled, by using agile processes or any other combination.

DevOps is about the delivery mechanism of software systems. It is about bringing people together, making them collaborate and communicate, working together towards a common goal and vision. It is about taking joint responsibility, accountability, and ownership. It is about implementing processes that foster collaboration and a service mindset. It enables delivery mechanisms that bring agility and flexibility within the organization. Contrary to the popular belief, DevOps is not about tools, technology, automation. These are enablers that help in collaboration, implemention of agile processes and faster and better delivery to the customer.

There are multiple definitions available on the internet for DevOps and they are neither wrong nor incorrect. DevOps does not provide a framework or methodology. It is a set of principles and practices that, when employed within an organization, engagement, or project, achieves the goal and vision of both DevOps and the organization. These principles and practices do not mandate any specific process, tools and technologies and environment. DevOps provides the guidance which can be implemented through any tool, technology, and process, although some of the technology and processes might be more applicable to achieve the vision of DevOps principles and practices.

Although DevOps practices can be implemented in any organization that provides services and products to customers, going forward in this book, we will look at DevOps from the perspective of software development and the operations department of any organization.

So, what is DevOps? DevOps is defined as:

It is a set of principles and practices bringing both developers and operations teams together from the start of the software system for faster, quicker, and efficient end-to-end delivery of the software system to the end customer, again and again in a consistent and predictable manner reducing time to market, thereby gaining competitive advantage.

Read out loudly the preceding definition of DevOps and if you look at it closely, it does not indicate or refer to any specific processes, tools or technology. It is not prescribing any particular methodology or environment.

The goal of implementing DevOps principles and practices in any organization is to ensure that the demands of stakeholders (including customers) and expectations are met efficiently and effectively.

The customer's demands and expectations are met when:

- Customer gets the features they want
- Customer gets the feature when they want
- Customer gets faster updates on features
- Quality of delivery is high

When an organization can meet the above expectations, customers are happy and remain loyal to the organization. This in turn increases the market competitiveness of the organization which results in a bigger brand and market valuation. It has a direct impact on the top and bottom line of the organization. The organization can invest further on innovation and customer feedback, bringing about continuous changes to its system and services to stay relevant.

The implementation of DevOps principles and practices in any organization is guided by its surrounding ecosystem. This ecosystem is made of the industry and domains the organization belongs to.

DevOps is based on a set of principles and practices. We will look into details about these principles and practices later in this chapter. The core principles of DevOps are the following:

- Agility
- Automation
- Collaboration
- Feedback

The core DevOps practices are the following:

- Continuous integration
- Configuration management
- Continuous deployment
- Continuous delivery
- Continuous learning

DevOps is not a new paradigm, however it is gaining a lot of popularity and traction in recent times. Its adoption is at its highest level and more and more companies are undertaking this journey. I purposely mentioned DevOps as a journey because there are different levels of maturity within DevOps. While successfully implementing continuous deployment and delivery are considered as the highest level of maturity in this journey, adopting source code control, agile software development is considered as a beginning.

One of the first thing DevOps talks about is *breaking the barriers between the developers and the operations team*. It brings about the close collaboration aspect between multiple teams. It is about breaking the mindset that the developer is responsible for writing the code only and passing it on to operations for deployment once it is tested. It is also about breaking the mindset that operations have no role to play in development activities. Operations should influence the planning of the product and should be aware of the features coming up as release. They should also continually provide feedback to the developers on the operational issues such that they can be fixed in subsequent releases. They should influence the design of the system for better operational working of the system. Similarly, the developers should help the operations in deployment of the system and solve incidents when they arise.

The definition talks about *faster, quicker, and efficient end to end delivery of systems to stakeholders*. It does not talk about how fast, quick, or efficient the delivery should be. It should be fast or quick enough depending on the organization domain, industry, customer segmentation, and more. For some organizations, fast enough could be quarterly while for others it could be weekly. Both types are valid for DevOps point of view and they can deploy relevant processes and technologies to achieve the same. DevOps does not mandate it. Organizations should identify the best implementation of DevOps principles and practices based on their overall project, engagement, and organization vision.

The definition also talks about *end-to-end delivery*. It means that from the planning and delivery of the system to the services and operations should be part of the DevOps implementation. The processes should be such that it allows for greater flexibility, modularity, and agility in the application development life cycle. While organizations are free to use the best fit process--**Waterfall**, **Agile**, **Kanban**, and more, typically, organizations tend to favor agile processes with iterations-based delivery. This allows for faster delivery in smaller units which are far more testable and manageable compared to large big delivery.

DevOps talks about *end customers again and again in a consistent and predictable manner*. This means that organizations should continually deliver to customers with newer and upgraded features using automation. We cannot achieve consistency and predictability without the use of automation. Manual work should be reduced to none to ensure a high level of consistency and predictability. The automation should also be end to end, to avoid failures. This also indicates that the system design should be modular allowing faster delivery as they are reliable, available, and scalable. Testing plays a great role in consistent and predictable delivery.

The end result of implementing the before-mentioned practices and principles is that the organization is able to meet the expectations and demands of customers. The organization is able to grow faster than the competition and further increase the quality and capability of their product and services through continuous innovation and improvement.

DevOps practices

DevOps consists of multiple practices each providing distinct functionality to the overall process. The following figure shows the relationship between them. Configuration management, continuous integration, and continuous deployment form the core practices that enables DevOps. When we deliver software services combining these three services, we achieve continuous delivery. Continuous delivery is a capability and maturity of an organization dependent on the maturity of configuration management, continuous integration, and continuous deployment. Continuous feedback at all stages forms the feedback loop that helps in providing superior services to the customers. It runs across all DevOps practices. Let's deep dive into each of these capabilities and DevOps practices:

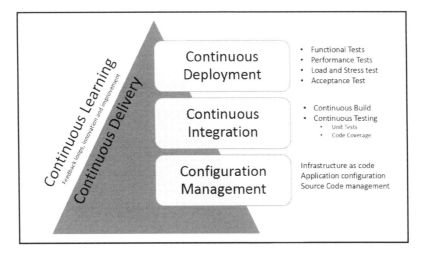

Configuration management

Business application and services need an environment on which they can be deployed. Typically, the environment is an infrastructure comprising multiple servers, compute, network, storage, containers and many more services working together such that business applications can be deployed on top of them. Business applications are decomposed into multiple services running on multiple servers either on-premise or on the clouds and each service has its own configuration along with requirements related to infrastructure configuration. In short, both infrastructure and application is needed to deliver systems to customers and both of them have their own configuration. If the configuration drifts, the application might not work as expected leading to downtime and failure. Moreover, as ALM process dictates the use of multiple stages and environment, an application would be deployed to multiple environments with different configurations. The application will be deployed to the development environment for developers to see the result of their work. The application will be deployed to multiple test environments with different configurations for functional tests, load and stress tests, performance tests, integration tests and more, it would also be deployed to the pre-production environment to conduct user acceptance tests and finally onto the production environment. It is important that an application can be deployed to multiple environments without undertaking any manual changes to its configuration.

Configuration management provides a set of processes and tools and they help in ensuring that each environment and application gets its own configuration. Configuration management tracks configuration items and anything that changes from environment to environment should be treated as a configuration item. Configuration management also defines the relationships between the configuration items and how changes in one configuration item will impact the other configuration item.

Configuration management helps in the following:

- **Infrastructure as Code**: When the process of provisioning of infrastructure and its configuration is represented through code and the same code goes through the application life cycle process, it is known as Infrastructure as Code. Infrastructure as code helps in automating the provisioning and configuration of infrastructure. It also represents the entire infrastructure in code that can be stored in a repository and version controlled. This allows the users to use the previous environment configurations when needed. It also enables provisioning of an environment multiple times in a consistent and predictable manner. All environments provisioned through this way are consistent and equal in all ALM stages.

- **Deployment and configuration of application**: Deployment of an application and its configuration is the next step after provisioning of infrastructure. Examples of application deployment and configuration is to deploy a `webdeploy` package on a server, deploy a SQL server schemas and data (bacpac) on another server, change the SQL connection string on the web server to represent the appropriate SQL server. Configuration management stores values for the application configuration for each environment on which it is deployed.

The configuration applied should also be monitored. The expected and desired configuration should be consistently maintained. Any drift from this expected and desired configuration would render the application as not available. Configuration management is also capable of finding the drift and re-configuring the application and environment to its desired state.

With automated configuration management in place, nobody in the team has to deploy and configure the environments and applications on production. The operations team is not reliant on the development team or long deployment documentation.

Another aspect of configuration management is source code control. Business applications and services comprise code and other artifacts. Multiple team members work on the same files. The source code should be up to date at any point of time and should be accessible by only authenticated team members. The code and other artifacts by themselves are configuration items. Source control helps in collaboration and communication within the team since everybody is aware of what the other person is doing and conflicts are resolved at an early stage.

Configuration management can be broadly divided into two categories:

- Inside the virtual machine
- Outside the virtual machine

The tools available for configuration management inside the virtual machine are discussed next.

Desired State Configuration

Desired State Configuration (**DSC**) is a new configuration management platform from Microsoft build as an extension to PowerShell. DSC was originally launched as part of WMF 4.0. It is available as part of **Windows Management Framework** (**WMF**) 4.0 and 5.0 for all Windows server operating systems preceding Windows 2008 R2. WMF 5.1 is available out of the box on Windows Server 2016, and Windows 10.

Chef, Puppet, and Ansible

Apart from DSC, there are a host of configuration management tools, such as Chef, Puppet, and Ansible supported by Azure. Details about these tools are not covered in this book.

The tools available for configuration management outside of a virtual machine are:

Azure Resource Manager templates

ARM templates are the primary means of provisioning resources in ARM. ARM templates provide a declarative model through which resources, their configuration, scripts, and extensions are specified. ARM templates are based on **JavaScript Object Notation** (**JSON**) format. It uses the JSON syntax and conventions to declare and configure resources. JSON files are text based, user friendly, and easily readable files. They can be stored in a source code repository and have version control on them. They are also means to represent infrastructure as code that can be used to provision resources in Azure resource groups again and again, predictably, consistently, and uniformly. A template needs a resource group for deployment. It can only be deployed to a resource group and the resource group should exist before executing template deployment. A template is not capable of creating a resource group.

Templates provide the flexibility to be generic and modular in their design and implementation. Templates provide the ability to accept parameters from users, declare internal variables, help in defining dependencies between resources, links resources within the same or different resource groups, and also execute other templates. They also provide scripting language type expressions and functions that make them dynamic and customizable at runtime.

Continuous integration

Multiple developers write code that is eventually stored in a common repository. The code is normally checked in or pushed to the repository when the developer has finished developing his feature. This can happen in a day or might take days or weeks. Some of the developers might be working on the same feature and they might also follow the same practices of pushing/checking-in code in days or weeks. This can cause issues with the quality of code. One of the tenet of DevOps is to fail fast. Developers should check-in/push their code to the repository often and compile the code to check if he/she has not introduced any bug and that the code is compatible with the code written by his/her fellow member. If the developer does not follow this practice, then the code on their machine will grow very large and will be difficult to integrate with other's code. Moreover, if the compile fails, it is difficult and time consuming to fix the issues arising out of it.

Continuous integration solves these kinds of challenges. Continuous integration helps in compilation and validation of the code pushed/checked-in by a developer by taking it through a series of validation steps. Continuous integration creates a process flow consisting of multiple steps. Continuous integration is comprised of continuous automated build and continuous automated tests. Normally the first step is compilation of the code. After successful compilation, each step is responsible for validating the code from a specific perspective. For example, unit tests can be executed on the compiled code, code coverage can be executed to check which code paths are executed by unit tests. These could reveal if comprehensive unit tests are written or there is scope to add further unit tests. The end result of continuous integration is deployment packages that can be used by continuous deployment for deploying them to multiple environments.

Developers are encouraged to check-in their code multiple times in a day instead of doing so after days or weeks. Continuous integration would initiate the execution of the entire pipeline immediately as soon as the code is checked-in or pushed. If compilation succeeds, code tests and other activities that are part of the pipeline are executed without error, the code is deployed to a test environment and integration tests are executed on it. Although every system demands its own configuration of continuous integration, a minimal sample continuous integration is shown in following figure.

Continuous integration increases the productivity of the developers. They do not have to manually compile their code, run multiple types of tests one after another, and then create packages out of it. It also reduces the risk of getting bugs introduced in the code and the code does not get stale. It provides early feedback to the developers about the quality of their code. Overall, the quality of deliverables is high and deliverables are delivered faster by adopting continuous integration practice:

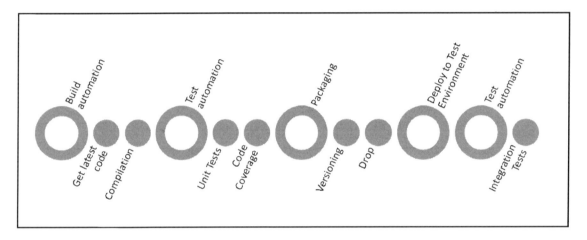

Build automation

Build automation consists of multiple tasks executing in sequence. Generally, the first task is responsible for fetching latest source code from the repository. The source code might comprise multiple projects and files. They are compiled to generate artifacts like executable, dynamic link libraries, assemblies and more. Successful build automation reflects that there are no compile time errors in code.

There could be more steps in build automation depending on the nature and type of project.

Test automation

Test automation consists of tasks that are responsible for validating different aspects of code. These tasks are related to testing code from a different perspective and are executed in sequence. Generally, the first step is to run a series of unit tests on the code. Unit testing refers to the process of testing the smallest denomination of a feature validating its behavior in isolation from other features. It can be automated or manual however the preference is towards automated unit testing.

Code coverage is another type of automated testing that can be executed on the code to find out how much of code is executed while running the unit tests. It is generally represented as a percentage and refers to how much code is testable through unit testing. If the code coverage is not close to 100%, it is either because the developer has not written unit tests for that behavior or the uncovered code is not required at all.

Successful execution of test automation resulting in no significant code failure should start executing the packaging tasks. There could be more steps in test automation depending on the nature and type of project.

Packaging

Packaging refers to the process of generating deployable artifacts such as MSI, NuGet and `webdeploy` packages, database packages, versioning them, and storing them at location such that they can be consumed by other pipelines and processes.

Continuous deployment

By the time the process reaches continuous deployment, continuous integration has ensured that we have fully working bits of an application that can now be taken through different continuous deployment activities. Continuous deployment refers to the capability of deploying business applications and services to pre-production and production environments through automation. For example, continuous deployment could provision and configure the pre-production environment, deploy application to it and configure. After conducting multiple validations, such as functional tests, performance tests on pre-production environment, the production environment is provisioned, configured and the application is deployed to production environments through automation. There are no manual steps in the deployment process. Every deployment task is automated. Continuous deployment can provision the environment and deploy the application for a bare metal deployment while it could reuse the existing environment and conduct only the application deployment if the environment already exists. It is always better to conduct bare metal green field deployment however; business justification can make the demand for brown field deployments.

All the environments are provisioned through automation using Infrastructure as Code. This ensures that all environments, whether it's development, test, pre-production, production and any other environment is the same. Similarly, the application is deployed through automation ensuring that it is also deployed uniformly across all environments. The configuration across these environments could be different for the application.

Continuous deployment is generally integrated with continuous integration. When continuous integration has done its work by generating the final deployable packages, continuous deployment kicks in and starts its own pipeline. This pipeline is called the **release pipeline**. Release pipeline consists of multiple environments with each environment consisting of tasks responsible for provision of environment, configuration of environment, deploying applications, configuring applications, executing operational validation on environments and testing the application on multiple environments. We will look at release pipeline in greater details in the next chapter and also the chapter on continuous deployment.

Employing continuous deployment provides immense benefits. There is a high level of confidence in the overall deployment process which helps in faster and risk-free releases on production. The chances of anything going wrong comes down drastically. The team would have lower stress levels and rollback to the previous working environment is possible if there are issues in the current release:

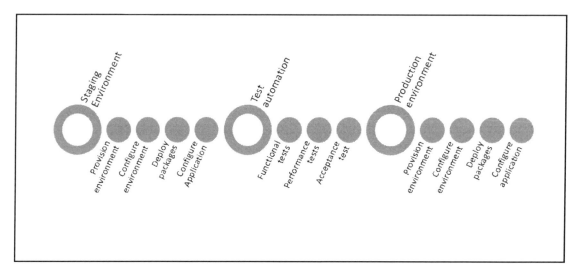

Although every system demands its own configuration of release pipeline, a minimal sample of continuous deployment is shown in the preceding figure. It is important to note that generally provisioning and configuring of multiple environments is part of the release pipeline and approvals should be sought before moving to the next environment. The approval process might be manual or automated depending on the maturity of the organization.

Test environment deployment

The release pipeline starts once the drop is available from continuous integration and the first step it should take is to get all the artifacts from the drop. After which, it might create a completely new bare metal test environment or reuse an existing one. This is again dependent on the type of project and nature of testing planned to be executed on this environment. The environment is provisioning and configured. The application artifacts are deployed and configured.

Test automation

After deploying an application, a series of tests can be performed on the environment. One of the tests executed here is functional tests. Functional tests are primarily aimed at validating the feature completeness and functionality of the application. These tests are written from requirements gathered from the customer. Another set of tests that can be executed are related to scalability and availability of the application. This typically includes load test, stress tests, and performance tests. It should also include operational validation of the infrastructure environment.

Staging environment deployment

This is very similar to the test environment deployment with the only difference is that the configuration values for the environment and application would be different.

Acceptance tests

Acceptance tests are generally conducted by stakeholders of the application and this can be manual or automated. This step is a validation from the customer point of view about the correctness and completeness of application functionality.

Deployment to production

Once the customer provides its approval, the same steps as that of the test and staging environment deployment are executed, with the only difference that the configuration values for the environment and application are specific to the production environment. A validation is conducted after deployment to ensure that the application is running according to expectation.

Continuous delivery

Continuous delivery and continuous deployment might sound similar to many readers; however, they are not the same. While continuous deployment talks about deployment to multiple environments and finally to the production environment through automation, continuous delivery practices is the ability to generate application packages in a way that are readily deployable in any environment. For generating artifacts that are readily deployable, continuous integration should be used to generate the application artifacts, a new or existing environment should be used for deploying these artifacts, conduct functional tests, performance tests and user acceptance tests through automation. Once these activities are successfully executed with no errors, the application package is referred as readily deployable. Continuous delivery comprises continuous integration along with deployment to an environment for final validations. It helps in getting feedback faster from both the operations as well as from the end user. This feedback can then be used to implement subsequent iterations.

Continuous learning

With all the before mentioned DevOps practices, it is possible to create great business applications and deploy them automatically to the production environment, however, benefits of DevOps will not last for long, if continuous improvement and feedback principles are not in place. It is utmost important that real-time feedback about the application behavior is passed on as feedback to the development team from both end users and the operations team.

Feedback should be passed to the teams providing relevant information about what is going well and importantly, what is not going well.

Applications should be built with monitoring, auditing, and telemetry in mind. The architecture and design should support these. The operations team should collect the telemetry information from the production environment, capture any bugs and issues and pass it on the development team such that they can get fixed in subsequent releases. The same has been shown in the following figure.

Continuous learning helps in making the application robust and resilient to failures. It helps in making sure that the application is meeting the requirements of the consumers:

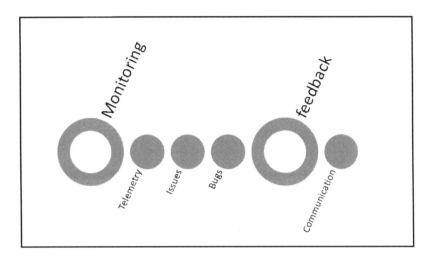

Visual Studio Team Services

Now, it's time to focus on another revolutionary online service, **Visual Studio Team Services** (**VSTS**), that enables continuous integration, continuous deployment and continuous delivery seamlessly. In fact, it would be more appropriate to call it a suite of services available under a single name. VSTS is a PaaS provided by Microsoft and hosted on the cloud. The same service is available as **Team Foundation Services** (**TFS**) on-premise. All examples used in this book uses VSTS.

According to Microsoft, VSTS is a cloud-based collaboration platform that helps teams in sharing code, tracking work and shipping software. VSTS is the new name and earlier it was known as **visual studio online** (**VSO**). VSTS is an enterprise software development tool and service that enables organizations in providing automation facilities to their end-to-end application life cycle management process from planning to deployment of application and getting real-time feedback from software systems. This increases the maturity and capability of an organization to deliver high quality software systems to their customers again and again.

Successful software delivery involves efficiently bringing numerous processes and activities together. These include executing and implementing various agile processes, increasing collaboration among teams, seamless, and automatic transition of artifacts from one phase of the ALM to another phase, and deployments to multiple environment. It is important to track and report on these activities to measure and take action and improve delivery processes. VSTS makes it simple and easy. It provides a whole suite of services that enables the following:

- Collaboration among every team member by providing a single interface for the entire application life cycle management.
- Collaboration among development teams using source code management services
- Collaboration among test teams using test management services
- Automation validation of code and packaging through continuous integration using build management services
- Automating validation of application functionality, deployment, and configuration of multiple environments through continuous deployment and delivery using release management services
- Tracking and work item management using work management services

The following figure shows all the services available from the VSTS top navigation bar:

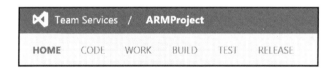

A project in VSTS is a security boundary and logical container that provides all the services we mentioned in the previous section. VSTS allows for the creation of multiple projects within a single account. By default, a repository is created with the creation of a project, however, VSTS allows for the creation of additional repositories within a single project. The relationship between the VSTS account, project and repository is shown in the following figure:

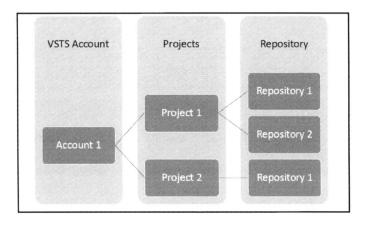

Relationship between VSTS Account. projects and repositories

VSTS provides two types of repositories

- GIT
- **Team Foundation Version Control (TFVC)**

It also provides the flexibility to choose between GIT or TFVC source control repository. There can be a combination of TFS and TFVC repositories available within a single project.

Team Foundation Version Control

TFVC is the traditional and centralized way of implementing version control in which there is a central repository and developers work on it directly in connected mode to check-in their changes. If the central repository is offline or not available, developers cannot check-in their code and have to wait for it to be online and available. Other developers can see only the checked in code. Developers can group multiple changes into a single change set for checking-in code changes that are logically grouped to form a single change. TFVC locks the code files that are undergoing edits. Other developers can read the locked-up file but they cannot edit it. They must wait for the prior edit to complete and release the lock before they can edit. The history of check-ins and changes are maintained on the central repository while the developers have the working copy of the files but not the history.

TFVC works very well with large teams that are working on the same projects. This allows control over the source code at a central location. It also works the best when the project is for a long duration since the history is managed at a central location. TFVC has no issues working with large and binary files.

GIT

GIT on the other hand is a modern distributed way of implementing version control where the developers can work on their own local copies of code and history in offline mode. Developers can work offline on their local clone of code. Each developer has a local copy of code and entire history and they work on their changes with this local repository. They can commit their code to the local repository. They can connect to the central repository for synchronization of their local repository on a need basis. This allows every developer to work on any file since they would be working on their local copy. Branching in GIT does not create another copy of the original code and is extremely fast to create.

GIT works well with a smaller team. With larger teams, there is a substantial overhead to manage multiple pull requests to merge the code on a central repository. It also works best for smaller duration project as the history would not get too large to be downloaded and manageable on every developer's local repository. Branching and merging is a breeze with advance options.

GIT is the recommended way of using source control because of the rich functionality it provides. We will use GIT as the repository for our sample application in this book.

Preparing for DevOps

In this chapter from henceforth, focus will be on process and deployment automation using different patterns in Azure. These include the following:

- DevOps for IaaS solutions
- DevOps for PaaS solutions
- DevOps for container based solution

Generally, there are common shared services not unique to any one application. Their services are consumed by multiple applications from different environments such as development, testing, and production. The life cycle of these common shared services is different from other applications. Therefore, they have different version control accounts, a different codebase, build and release management. They have their own cycle of plan-design-build-test and release.

The resources that are part of this group are provisioned using ARM templates, PowerShell, and DSC configurations.

The overall flow for building these common components is shown next:

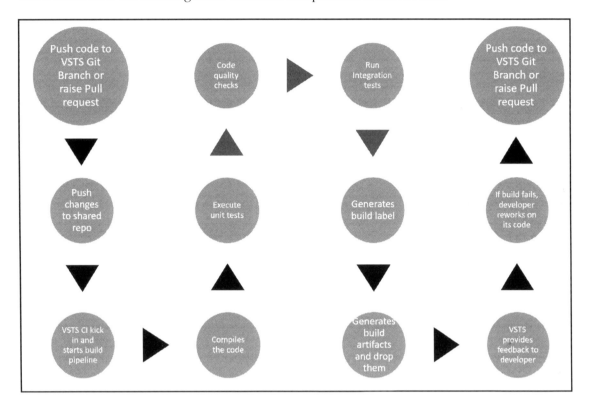

The release process is shown in the following diagram:

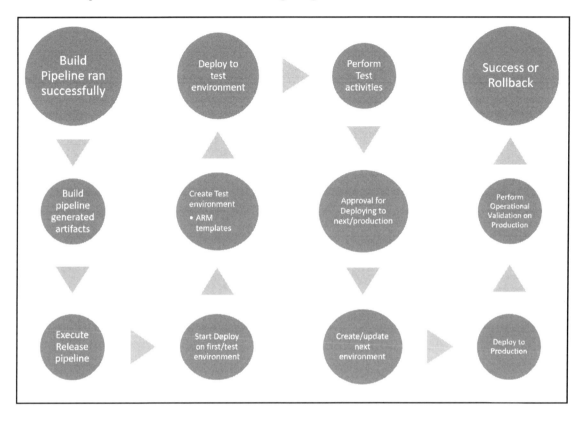

To get on the DevOps journey, it is important to understand and provision the common components and services before starting any software engagement, product, or service.

Provision VSTS account

A version control system is needed to collaborate at code level. VSTS helps in providing both centralized and decentralized versions of control systems. VSTS also provides orchestration services for building and executing build and release pipelines. It is a mature platform to organize all DevOps related version control, build and release and work-item related artifacts. After account is provision, a VSTS project should be created to hold all project related artifacts.

A VSTS account can be provisioned by visiting `https://www.visualstudio.com`.

Provision Azure key vault

It is not advisable to store secrets, certificates, credentials, and other sensitive information in code configuration files in files, databases or any other general storage system. It is advised to store this important data into a vault that is specifically designed for storing secrets and credentials. Azure key vault provides such a service. Azure key vault is available as a resource and service from Azure.

Provisioning a configuration management server

A configuration management server providing storage for configurations and applying those configurations to different environments is always a good strategy for automating deployments. DSC on custom virtual machines, DSC from Azure automation, Chef, Puppet, Ansible are some of the options and can be used on Azure seamlessly for both Windows as well as Linux environments. This book uses DSC as a configuration management tool for all purposes and it provides a pull server that holds all configuration documents (MOF files) for the sample application. It also maintains the database of all virtual machines and containers that are configured and registered with pull server to pull configuration documents from it. The local configuration manager on these target virtual machines and containers periodically checks the availability of new configurations as well as drifts in current configuration and reports back the same to the pull server. It also has inbuilt reporting capabilities that provides information about nodes that are compliant as well as those which are non-compliant within a virtual machine. A pull server is a general web application hosting DSC pull server endpoint.

Provisioning log analytics

Log analytics is an audit and monitoring service provided by Azure to get real time information about all changes, drifts, events occurring within virtual machines and containers. It provides a centralized workspace and dashboard for IT administrators for viewing, searching, and conducting drill-down searches on all changes, drifts and events occurring on these virtual machines. It also provides agents that are deployed on target virtual machines and containers. Once deployed, these agents start sending all changes, events and drifts to the centralized workspace.

Azure storage account

Azure storage is a service provided by Azure to store files as blobs. All scripts and code for automating the provisioning, deployment and configuration of infrastructure and sample application are stored in a VSTS `git` repository and are packaged and deployed in an Azure storage account. Azure provides PowerShell script extension resources that can automatically download DSC and PowerShell scripts and execute them on virtual machines during execution of Azure resource manager templates. This storage acts as a common storage across all deployments for multiple applications.

Images

Both virtual machine and container images should be built as part of the common services build and release pipeline. Tools such as Packer, Docker build can be used to generate these images.

Monitoring tools

All monitoring tools, such as Azure Monitor, application insights, log analytics, OMS, system center operations manager should be provisioned and configured during the release pipeline of common services.

Management tools

All management tools, such as Kubernetes, DC/OS, Docker Swarm, ITIL tools should be provisioned at this stage.

DevOps for PaaS solutions

The typical architecture for Azure PaaS app services is based on the solution shown next:

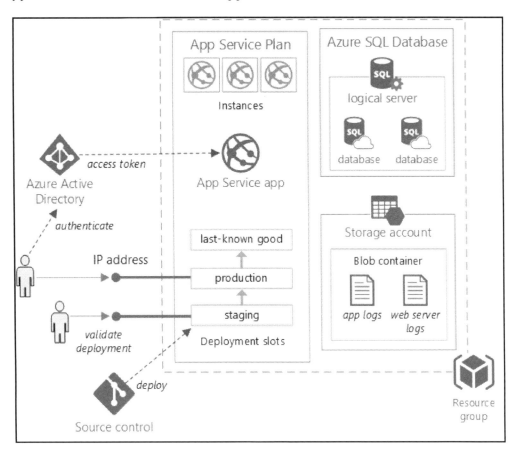

The architecture shows some of the important components, such as Azure SQL, storage accounts, version control system, and more that participate in Azure app services based cloud solution architecture. These artifacts should be created using Azure resource manager templates. These ARM templates should be part of the overall configuration management strategy. It can have its own build and release management pipelines very similar to the one shown in the previous section:

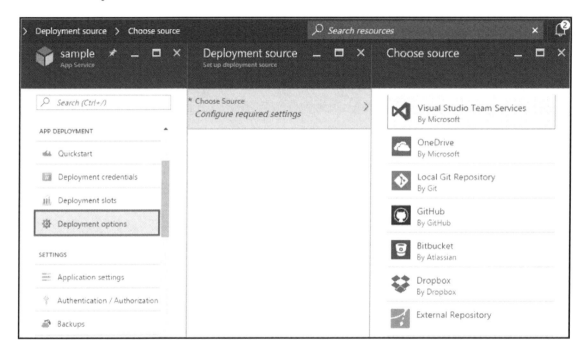

The ARM template should also configure continuous deployment by configuring **Deployment options**.

Azure app services

Azure app service provides managed hosting services for cloud solutions. It is a fully managed platform for provisioning and deploying cloud solutions. App services takes away the burden of creating and managing infrastructure and provides minimum **service level agreements (SLA)** for hosting your cloud solutions. They are open and let users decide the choice of language they want to use for building their cloud solutions and flexible to host the cloud solution on either Windows or Linux operating systems. Creating an app service and hosting cloud solutions provision virtual machines behind the scene that are completely managed by Azure, and users do not see them at all. Multiple different types of cloud solutions such as web application, mobile backend API's, API endpoints, containers can be hosted seamlessly on Azure app services.

Deployment slots

Azure app service provides deployment slots that makes deployment to them seamlessly and easy. There is a production and staging slot and it lets users swap them easily. This helps in first deploying the custom cloud solution to staging and after all checks and tests, they can be swapped to production if found satisfactory. However, in case of any issue in production after swapping, the previous good values from the production environment can be reinstated by swapping again.

Azure SQL

Azure SQL is SQL PaaS service provided by Azure to host databases. Azure provides a secure platform to host databases and takes complete ownership to manage the availability, reliability and scalability of the service. With Azure SQL, there is no need to provision custom virtual machines, deploy a SQL server and configure it. Instead, Azure team does these behind the scenes and manages them on our behalf. It also provides a firewall service enabling security and only an IP address allowed by the firewall can connect the server and access the database. The virtual machines provisioned to host web applications have distinct Public IP addresses assigned to them and they are added to Azure SQL firewall rules dynamically. Azure SQL server and its database is created while executing the Azure resource manager template. It is to be noted that generally management virtual machines should execute such tasks.

Build and release pipeline

Azure app services provide out of box services for continuous deployment and they should be used for deploying custom cloud solutions as shown next. Details about account, repository, branch should be provided. Azure app services would connect to the repository and pull the latest source code from the provided branch and execute the build steps of compiling and generating deployable artefacts. It will also deploy to staging deployment slots automatically.

Visual Studio at the developer's end should be configured to connect to the version control system. The build process should start by Azure app services, whenever a developer checks in or pushes his code to the repository branch.

DevOps for virtual machine (IaaS) based solutions

The typical architecture for IaaS virtual machine based solution is shown next:

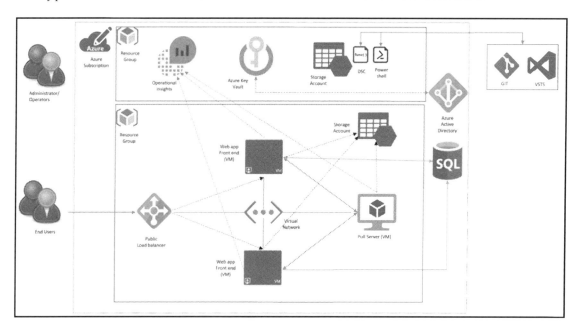

Azure virtual machine

Azure virtual machines hosting web applications, application servers, database, and other services are provisioned using ARM templates. Each virtual machine has a single network card with a public IP assigned to it. They are attached to a virtual network and have a private IP address from the same network. The public IP for virtual machines is optional since they are attached to a public load balancer. These virtual machines are based on a Windows 2016 server image. Operational insights agents are installed on virtual machines for monitoring the virtual machines. PowerShell scripts are also executed on these virtual machines downloaded from a storage account available in an other resource group to open relevant firewall ports, download appropriate packages and install local certificates to secure access through PowerShell. The web application is configured to run on the provided port on these virtual machines. The port number for the web application and all its configuration is pulled from the DSC pull server and dynamically assigned.

Azure public load balancer

A public load balancer is attached to some of the virtual machines for sending requests to them in a round robin fashion. This is generally needed for front-end web applications and APIs. A public IP address and DNS name can be assigned to load balancer such that it can serve internet requests. It accepts HTTP web requests on different port and routes the same to the virtual machines. It also probes on certain ports on HTTP protocols with some provided application paths. **Network Address Translation (NAT)** rules can also be applied such that they can be used to login into the virtual machines using remote desktops.

An alternative resource to Azure public load balancer is the Azure application gateway and depending on the scenario, can be used and deployed.

Build pipeline

A typical build pipeline for an IaaS virtual machine based solution is shown next. A release pipeline starts when a developer pushes his code to the repository. The build pipeline starts automatically as part of continuous integration. It compiles and builds the code, executes unit tests on it, code quality checks and generates documentation from code comments. It deploys the new binaries into the dev environment (note that development environment is not newly created), changes configuration, executes integration tests and generated build labels for easy identification. It then drops the generated artifacts to a location accessible by the release pipeline. In case there are issues during the execution of any step in this pipeline, the same is communicated to the developer as part of build pipeline feedback such that they can re-work and submit their changes again. The build pipeline should fail or pass based on the severity of issues found and that is dependent on organization to organization:

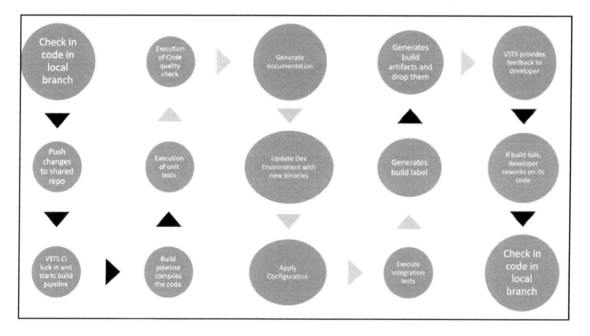

Release pipeline

A typical release pipeline for an IaaS virtual machine based deployment is shown next. A release pipeline starts after completion of the build pipeline. The first step for the release pipeline is to gather the artifacts generated by the build pipeline. They are generally deployable assemblies, binaries and configuration documents. The release pipeline executes and creates or updates the first environment which generally is a test environment. It uses Azure Resource Manager templates to provision all IaaS and PaaS services and resources on Azure and configures them as well. They also help executing scripts and DSC configuration after virtual machines are created as post-creation steps. This helps configuring the environment within the virtual machine and the operating system. At this stage, application binaries from the build pipeline are deployed and configured. Different automated tests are performed to check the working on solution and if found satisfactory, the pipeline moves to deployment to next environment after obtaining necessary approvals. The same steps are again executed on the next environment including the production environment. At last, operational validation tests are executed on production to ensure that the application is working as expected and there are no deviations. At this stage, if there are any issues or bugs, they should be rectified and the entire cycle should be repeated; however if it does not happen within a stipulated timeframe, the previous known snapshot should be restored on the production environment to minimize downtime:

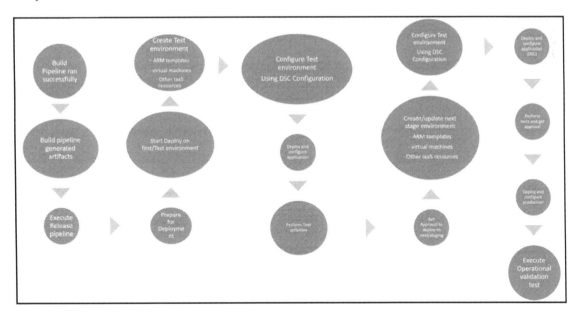

DevOps for container based (IaaS) solutions

The typical architecture for IaaS container based solution is shown next:

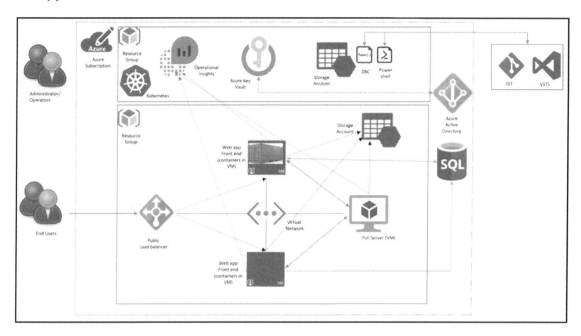

Containers

Containers is also a virtualization technology, however, they do not virtualize physical servers. Instead, containers is an operating system level virtualization. What it means is that containers share the operating system kernel provided by its host among themselves along with the host. Running multiple containers on a host (physical or virtual) share the host operating system kernel. There is a single operating system kernel provided by the host and used by all containers running on top of it.

Containers are also completely isolated from their host and other containers much like a virtual machine. Containers uses Windows storage filter drivers and sessions isolation for providing isolation of operating system services, such as filesystems, registry, processes, and networks. Each container gets its own copy of operating system resources.

Docker

Docker provides management features to Windows containers. It comprises two executables:

- Docker daemon
- Docker client

Docker daemon is the workhorse for managing containers. It is a Windows service responsible for managing all activities on the host related to containers. Docker client interacts with Docker daemon and is responsible for capturing inputs and sending them across to Docker daemon. Docker daemon provides the runtime, libraries, graph drivers, engines to create, manage and monitor containers, and images on the host server. It also provides capabilities to create custom images that are used for building and shipping applications to multiple environments.

DockerFile

DockerFile is a primary building block for creating Windows container images. It is a simple text based human readable file without any extension and is named DockerFile. Although there is a mechanism to name it differently, generally it is named as DockerFile. DockerFile contains instructions to create a custom container image from base image. These instructions are executed sequentially from top to bottom by the Docker daemon, the engine behind all activities related to Windows containers. The instructions refer to the command and their parameters understood by Docker daemon. DockerFile enables infrastructure as code practices by converting the application deployment and configuration into instructions that can be versioned and stored in a source code repository.

Build pipeline

There is no difference from the build perspective between the container and a virtual machine based solution. The build step remains the same. Please refer to the earlier section for build pipeline details.

Release pipeline

A typical release pipeline for an IaaS container based deployment is shown next. The only difference between this and the release pipeline is container image management and creation of containers using DockerFile and Docker compose. Advance container management utilities, such as Docker Swarm, DC/OS, and Kubernetes can also be deployed and configured as part of the release management. However, it is to be noted that these container management tools should be part of the shared services release pipeline as discussed earlier:

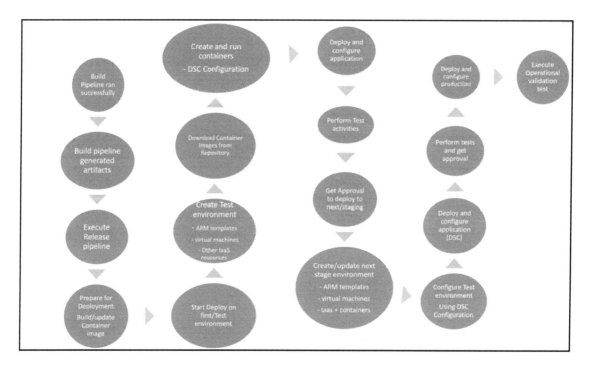

Azure automation

Azure automation is Microsoft's platform for all automation implementation with regard to cloud, on-premise and hybrid deployments. Azure automation is a mature automation platform that provides rich capabilities in terms of the following:

- Defining assets, such as variables, connections, credentials, certificates, and modules
- Implementing runbooks using Python, PowerShell scripts, and PowerShell workflows
- Providing user interfaces to create runbooks
- Managing the full runbook life cycle including build, test, and publish
- Scheduling of runbooks
- Ability to run runbooks anywhere--on cloud or on-premise
- DSC as a configuration management platform
- Manage and configure environments, machines--Windows and Linux, applications, and deployment
- Ability to extend Azure automation by import custom modules

Azure automation provides a DSC pull server that helps in creating a centralized configuration management server consisting of configurations for nodes/virtual machines and their constituents.

It implements the hub and spoke pattern wherein nodes can connect to the DSC pull server and download configurations assigned to them and re-configure themselves to reflect their desired state. Any changes and deviation within these nodes are auto-corrected by DSC agents the next time they run. This ensures that administrators do not need to actively keep monitoring the environment to find any deviations.

DSC provides a declarative language in which you define the intent and configuration but not how to run and apply those configurations. These configurations are based on PowerShell language and eases the process for configuration management.

In this section, we will look into a simple implementation of using Azure automation DSC to configure a virtual machine to install and configure web-server (IIS) and create an index.htm file that informs users that the website is under maintenance.

Provision Azure automation account

Create a new Azure automation account from Azure portal or PowerShell within an existing or a new resource group. Astute readers will find in the next image that Azure automation provides menu items for DSC. It provides the following:

- **DSC nodes**: It lists down all the virtual machines and containers that are enlisted with the current Azure automation DSC pull server. These virtual machines and containers are managed using configurations from the current DSC pull server in consideration.
- **DSC configurations**: It lists down all the raw PowerShell configurations imported and uploaded to the DSC pull server. They are in human readable format and are not in a compiled state.
- **DSC node configurations**: It lists down all compiles of DSC configurations available on the pull server to be assigned to nodes--virtual machines and containers. A DSC configuration produces MOF files after compilations and they are eventually used to configure nodes.

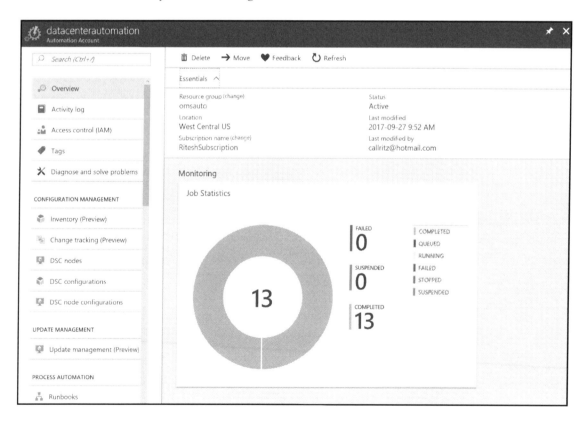

Author DSC configuration

The next step is to write a DSC configuration using any PowerShell editor to reflect the intent of configuration. For this sample, a single configuration `ConfigureSiteOnIIS` is created. It imports the base DSC module `PSDesiredStateConfiguration` consisting of resources used within the configuration. It also declares a node `webserver`. When this configuration is uploaded and compiled, it will generate a `DSCConfigurationNodes` named `ConfigureSiteOnIISwebserver`. This configuration then can be applied to nodes.

The configuration consists of a few resources. These resources configure the target node. The resources install a web-server, ASP.NET and framework and creates an `index.htm` file within `inetpub\wwwroot` directory with content to show that the site is under maintenance. For more information about writing DSC configuration, refer to `https://docs.microsoft.com/en-us/PowerShell/dsc/configurations`.

```
Configuration ConfigureSiteOnIIS {
    Import-DscResource -ModuleName 'PSDesiredStateConfiguration'
    Node WebServer {
      WindowsFeature IIS
        {
            Name = "Web-Server"
            Ensure = "Present"
        }
      WindowsFeature AspDotNet
        {
            Name = "net-framework-45-Core"
            Ensure = "Present"
            DependsOn = "[WindowsFeature]IIS"
        }
      WindowsFeature AspNet45
        {
            Ensure          = "Present"
            Name            = "Web-Asp-Net45"
            DependsOn = "[WindowsFeature]AspDotNet"
        }
      File IndexFile
        {
            DestinationPath = "C:\inetpub\wwwroot\index.htm"
            Ensure = "Present"
            Type = "File"
            Force = $true
            Contents = "<HTML><HEAD><Title> Website under
construction.</Title></HEAD><BODY> `
            <h1>If you are seeing this page, it means the website is under
maintenance and DSC Rocks !!!!!</h1></BODY></HTML>"
        }
```

```
        }
    }
```

Importing DSC configuration

The DSC configuration is still not known to Azure automation. It is available on some local machines. It should be uploaded to Azure Automation DSC Configurations. Azure automation provides `Import-AzureRMAutomationDscConfiguration` cmdlet to import the configuration to Azure automation.

```
Import-AzureRmAutomationDscConfiguration -SourcePath
"C:\DSC\AA\DSCfiles\ConfigureSiteOnIIS.ps1" -ResourceGroupName "omsauto" -
AutomationAccountName "datacenterautomation" -Published -Verbose
```

The DSC configuration on Azure after applying configuration to node should look as shown next:

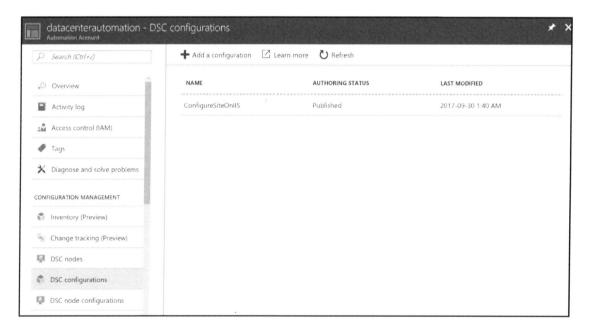

Compiling DSC configuration

After the DSC configuration is available in Azure automation, it can be asked to be compiled. Azure automation provides another cmdlet for the same. Use `Start-AzureRmAutomationDscCompilationJob` cmdlet to compile the imported configuration. The configuration name should match exactly the name of the configuration uploaded. Compilation creates a MOF file named after the configuration and node name together, which in this case is `ConfigureSiteOnIIS. webserver`.

```
Start-AzureRmAutomationDscCompilationJob -ConfigurationName
ConfigureSiteOnIIS -ResourceGroupName "omsauto" -AutomationAccountName
"datacenterautomation" -Verbose
```

The DSC nodes configuration on Azure after applying the configuration to the node should look as shown next:

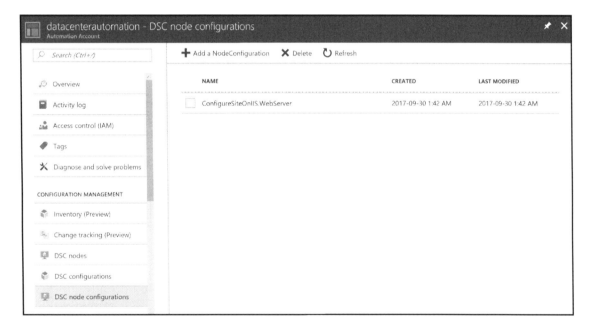

Assigning configuration to nodes

Now, the compiled DSC configurations can be applied to nodes. Use `Register-AzureRmAutomationDscNode` to assign the configuration to a node. The `NodeConfigurationName` parameter identifies the configuration name that should be applied to the node. This is a powerful cmdlet which can also configure the DSC agent that is `localconfigurationmanager` on nodes before they can download configurations and apply the same. There are multiple `localconfigurationmanager` parameters that can be configured and details about the same are available at `https://docs.microsoft.com/en-us/PowerShell/dsc/metaconfig`.

```
Register-AzureRmAutomationDscNode -ResourceGroupName "omsauto" -
AutomationAccountName "datacenterautomation" -AzureVMName testtwo -
ConfigurationMode ApplyAndAutocorrect -ActionAfterReboot
ContinueConfiguration -AllowModuleOverwrite $true -AzureVMResourceGroup
testone -AzureVMLocation "West Central US" -NodeConfigurationName
"ConfigureSiteOnIIS.WebServer" -Verbose
```

The DSC nodes on Azure after applying the configuration to the node should look as shown next:

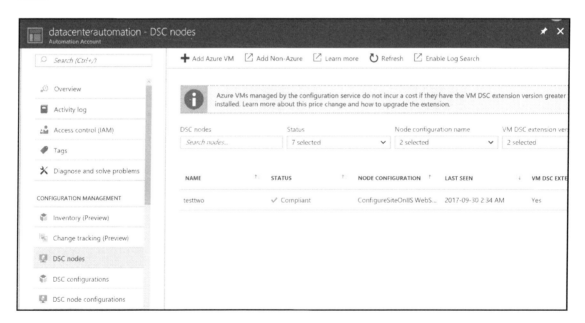

Browse the server

If appropriate, Network security groups and firewalls are opened and enabled for port 80 and a public IP is assigned to the virtual machine, the default website can be browsed using the IP address. Otherwise, log in to the virtual machine that is used for applying the DSC configuration and navigate to `http://localhost`.

It should show a page as shown next:

This is the power of configuration management that without writing any significant code, authoring a configuration once can be applied multiple times to the same and multiple servers and be assured that they will be running in the desired state without any manual intervention.

Azure for DevOps

As mentioned before, Azure is a rich and mature platform providing the following:

- Multiple choices of languages
- Multiple choices of operating system
- Multiple choices of tools and utilities
- Multiple patterns for deploying solutions (virtual machines, app services, containers, micro-services)

With so many options and choices, Azure is the following:

- **Open cloud**: It is open for both open source, Microsoft and non-Microsoft products, tools, and services
- **Flexible cloud**: It provides flexibility to both users and developers to feel comfort in using whatever their existing skillset and knowledge is based on
- **Unified management**: Provides seamless monitoring and management features

All the features mentioned before are important for successful implementation of DevOps for any project or engagement. The next image shows the open source tools and utilities that can be used for different phases in application life cycle management and overall DevOps. This is just a small representation of all tools and utilities and there are much more options available.

- Jenkins, Hudson, Grunt, and Gradle tools for constructing build pipeline
- Selenium for testing
- Chef, Puppet, Jenkins, Hudson, Grunt and Gradle and more for deployment or configuration management
- Nagios for alerting and Monitoring
- Jira and Redmine for managing processes

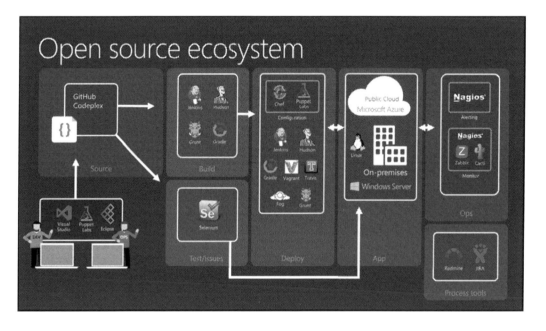

The next image shows Microsoft tools and utilities that can be used for different phases in the application life cycle management and overall DevOps. This is again just a small representation of all tools and utilities and there are much more options available.

- VSTS build orchestration for constructing a build pipeline
- Microsoft test manager, Pester for testing
- Desired State Configuration, PowerShell, ARM templates and more for deployment or configuration management
- Log analytics, application insights, and **System Center Operations Manager (SCOM)** for alerting and monitoring
- VSTS and **System Center Service Manager** for managing processes

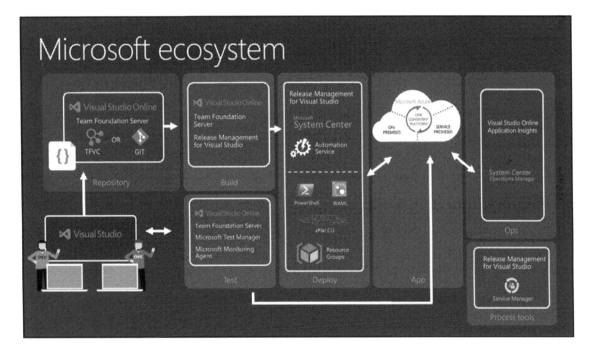

Summary

DevOps is gaining lots of traction and momentum in the industry. Most organizations have realized its benefits and are looking forward to implementing DevOps. This is happening while most of them are moving to the cloud. Azure as a cloud model is rich and mature in providing DevOps services, making it easy for such organizations to implement DevOps. In this chapter, DevOps was discussed at length along with its core practices, such as configuration management, continuous integration, continuous delivery, and deployment. We also discussed different PaaS based, virtual machines IaaS, and a container IaaS based cloud solution along with their respective Azure resources, build and release pipelines. Configuration management was the core part of this chapter and we discussed DSC services from Azure automation and using pull servers to configure virtual machines automatically. Finally, the openness and flexibility of Azure regarding varied open source choice of languages, tools, and operating system was discussed.

Cost is one of the most important drivers to move to cloud and there are opportunities to save and manage cost even on cloud. Next chapter on cost management provides details about cost administration and minimization on Azure.

11
Cost Management

The primary reason corporates are moving to cloud is cost saving. There is no upfront cost for having an Azure subscription. Azure provides **pay-as-you-go** payment mechanism meaning that based on consumption, Azure starts metering the usage and provides monthly invoices. There is no upper limit for Azure consumption. Azure provides unlimited resources and anybody having access to Azure can keep creating as many resources as they want. In such circumstances, it is important for companies to keep a close watch on Azure consumption and its usage. Although they can create policies to set organizational standards and conventions, there is also a need to get Azure billing and consumption information readily. Moreover, they want to employ best practices for consuming Azure resources such that the returns are maximized. For this, architects need to have knowledge about Azure resources and features, their corresponding costs, and cost benefit comparison between features and solution demand.

In this chapter, we will cover the following:

- Azure billing
- Invoicing
- Usage and quotas
- Usage and billing API
- Azure pricing calculator
- Best practices

Understanding billing

Azure is a service utility that has the following advantages:

- No upfront costs
- No termination fees
- Billing based on per minute
- Payment based on consumption-on-the-go

In such circumstances, it is very difficult to estimate the upfront cost of consuming Azure resources. Every resource in Azure has its own cost model and charge based on storage, usage, and time-span. It is very important for the management, administration, and finance department to keep track of usage and costs. Azure provides the necessary usage and billing reports, such that the organization management and administrators can generate a cost and usage report based on multiple criteria's.

Azure portal provides detailed billing and usage information through the billing feature, which can be accessed from the master navigation blade.

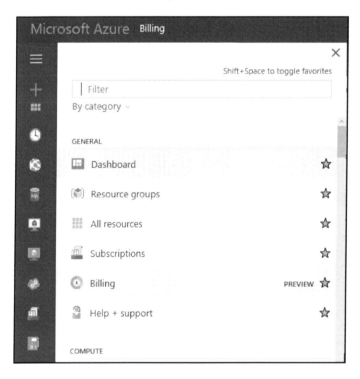

It provides a sub menu to generate reports on both costs and billing:

Clicking on the **Subscriptions** menu on this blade provides a list of all subscriptions that the user has access for generating reports:

Clicking on the subscription name in this list will provide a dashboard through which the complete billing, invoice, usage, consumption, policies, resource groups, and resources can be found. The chart in this overview section provides a cost percentage by resource and also burn rate:

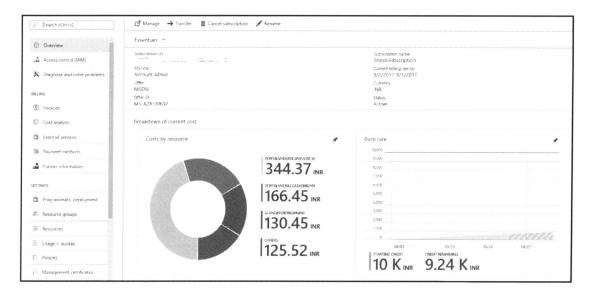

Clicking on the chart shows details of cost based on each resource. Here there are multiple storage accounts provisioned on Azure and cost for the same is shown. Using this screen, multiple types of reports can be generated by providing different criteria's and different combinations of these criteria for the following:

- Resource types
- Resource group
- Timespan
- Tag

Tags are particularly of interesting nature. Queries based on tags like department, project, owner, cost center, or any other name-value pair can be used to display relevant cost. You can also download the cost report as a CSV file using the **Download** button:

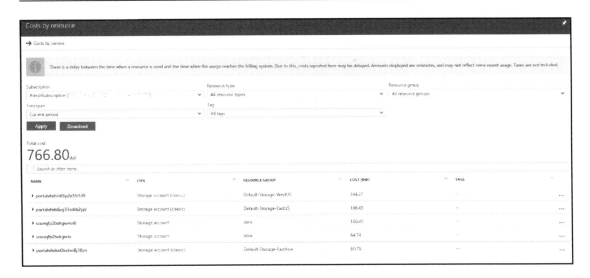

Clicking on individual resource provides the daily cost consumption for the resource:

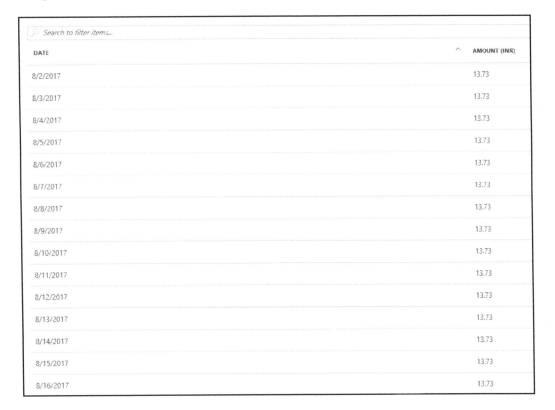

Invoicing

The Azure **Billing** feature also provides information about invoices that are generated monthly.

Clicking on the **Invoices** menu provides a list of all invoices generated:

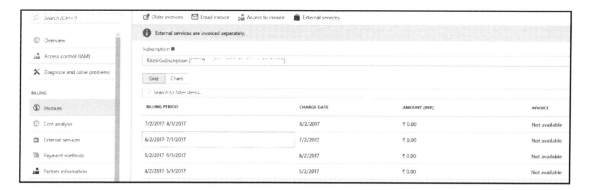

Clicking on any of the invoices provides details about that invoice:

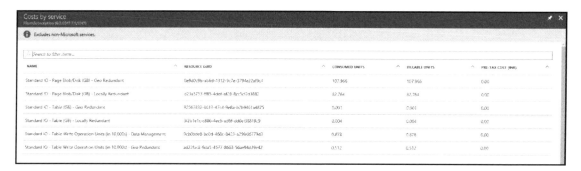

There is also an alternate way to download invoice details. The invoice details are available by logging into `https://account.azure.com` and downloading the invoice details:

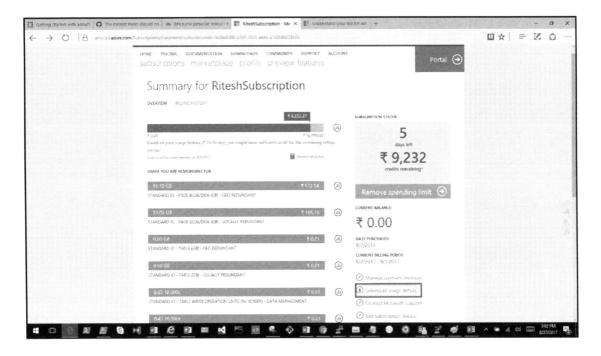

Enterprise agreement customers

Enterprise customers that have a enterprise agreement can utilize `https://ea.azure.com` to download their usage and billing reports. There is also a new Power BI content pack released recently that can be utilized to view Azure usage and costs through reports and a dashboard in Power BI.

 More information about this is available at `https://azure.microsoft.com/en-us/blog/new-power-bi-content-pack -for-azure-enterprise-users/`.

Usage and quotas

Each subscription has a limited quota for each resource type. For example, there could be a maximum of 60 public IP addresses provisioned with an MSDN Microsoft account. Similarly, all resources have a maximum default limit for each resource type. These resource type numbers for a subscription can be increased by contacting Azure support or clicking on the **Request Increase** button.

The usage and quota information is available from the **usage + quotas** sub menu of the **Subscription** menu:

This blade shows all resource types provisioned in subscription along with their location and counts. Here the quota for classic storage accounts is 100 and currently three classic storage accounts have been consumed.

There are filter criteria's available based on location, providers, usage, and quotas. Custom reports based on these filter criteria can be generated.

Resource providers

Resources are based on resource types and they are available from resource providers. There are numerous providers available in Azure and they provide the necessary resource types needed by users to create their instances. For example, the **Microsoft.Compute** resource provider provides virtual machines resource types. Using virtual machines resource types, instances of virtual machine can be created.

Resource providers are required to be registered with Azure subscriptions. Resource types will not be available in a subscription if resource providers are not registered. To get a list of providers that are available, the ones that are registered and the one's not registered and to register non-registered providers or vice-versa, this dashboard can be used:

Usage and billing API

Although the portal is a great way to find usage, billing, and invoice information manually, Azure also provides the following:

- **Invoice download API**: Use this API to download invoices
- **Resource usage API**: Use the Azure resource usage API to get the estimated Azure consumption data
- **RateCard API**: Use the Azure Resource RateCard API to get the list of available Azure resources and estimated pricing information for each

These APIs can be used to programmatically retrieve details and create customized dashboard and reports. Any programming or scripting language can use these API and create a complete billing solution.

Azure pricing models

Azure has multiple pricing models. It virtually has a model for almost every type of customer. From free accounts for students and developers to pay-as-you-go, from enterprise agreements to cloud solution provider partner model. Apart from these account types, there are add-on pricing and discounts like reserved VM instances and Azure hybrid benefits.

Azure hybrid benefits

When a virtual machine is provisioned on Azure, there are two types of cost are involved. These two types of cost are the resource cost for running the virtual machine and operating system license cost. Although enterprise agreement customers get some discounts compared to other accounts fro the pricing perspective, Azure provides another offer for them. It is known as Azure hybrid benefits. In this scheme, existing enterprise agreement customers can bring their on-premise licenses for operating system for creating virtual machine on Azure and Azure will not charge any cost of the license. The cost savings can be as high as 40 percent using this scheme. Enterprise agreements customers should also have software assurance to avail this benefit and is application for both windows standard and datacenter edition. Each 2-processor license or each set of 16-core licenses are entitled to two instances of up to 8 cores or one instance of up to 16 cores. The Azure hybrid benefit for standard edition licences can only be used once either on-premises or in Azure. Data center edition benefits allow for simultaneous usage both on-premises and in Azure.

Azure reserved VM instances

Customers can reserve a fixed number of virtual machines in advance for one year to three years by committing the same to Azure for both Windows and Linux operating system. Azure provides up to 72 percent discount on these virtual machines based on pay-as-you-go pricing model. Although there is an up-front commitment, there is no obligation to use them. These reserved instances can be canceled at any point in time. It can even be clubbed with Azure hybrid benefits offering to further reduce the license cost for these virtual machines.

Pay-as-you-go accounts

These are general Azure accounts which are billed monthly to customers. Customers do not commit any usage and they are free to use any resource based on their needs. Resource costs are calculated based on their resource usage and uptime. This, however, depends on the type of resource. Each resource has its own cost model. There is also no upfront cost associated with these accounts. Generally, there are no discounts available in this scheme.

Enterprise agreements

Customers already have agreements with Microsoft can add their Azure tenant as part of enterprise agreements. Customers can avail great discounts if they are part of enterprise agreements. Customers just need to commit upfront annual monetary commitment and they can be added to this scheme. Customers are free to consume this commitment the way best suited to them. Please refer to `https://azure.microsoft.com/en-in/pricing/enterprise-agreement/` for more information.

Cloud Solution Provider

Cloud Solution Provider (CSP) is a model for Microsoft partners. CSP enables partners to have end-to-end ownership of the customer life cycle and relationship for Microsoft Azure. Partners can deploy their solutions on cloud and charge customers using this scheme. Please refer to `https://azure.microsoft.com/en-in/offers/ms-azr-0145p/` for more information.

Azure pricing calculator

Azure provides a cost calculator for users and customers to estimate their cost and usage. This calculator is available at `https://azure.microsoft.com/en-in/pricing/calculator/`.:

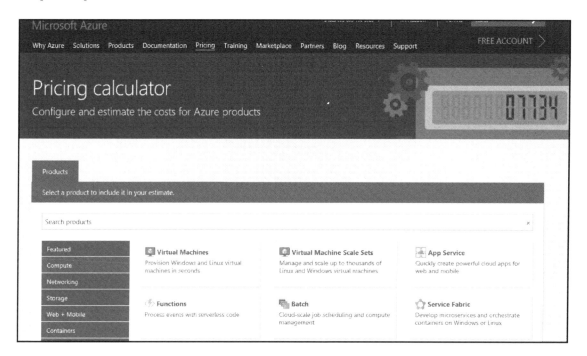

Users can select multiple resources from the left menu and they will be added to the calculator. In the following example, a virtual machine is added. Further configuration with regard to virtual machine region, operating system, type, tier, instance size, number of hours, and count is provided to calculate its cost:

Similarly, cost for Azure functions for virtual machine memory size, execution time, and execution per seconds is shown next:

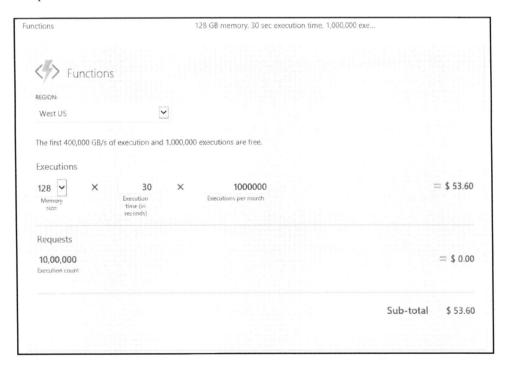

Azure provides different levels and plans of support, which are as follows:

- **Default support**: It is free
- **Developer support**: 29 dollars per month
- **Standard support**: 300 dollars per month
- **Profession direct**: 1000 dollars per month

Finally, the overall estimated cost is displayed:

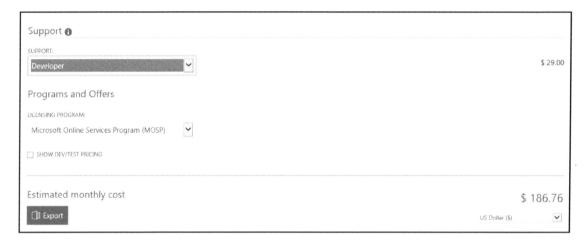

It is important that architects understand each Azure feature used in the overall architecture and solution. The success of Azure calculator depends on which resources are selected and their configuration. Any misrepresentation would lead to bias and wrong estimates and would be different than the actual billing.

Best practices

Architects needs to put in additional effort to understand their architecture and Azure components utilized. Based on the active monitoring, audits, and usage, they should determine the offering from Microsoft in terms of Sku, size, and features. This section will detail some of the best practices to be adopted from a cost optimization perspective.

Compute best practices

Compute refers to services that help in execution of services. Some of the best practices related to compute are as follows:

- Choose the best location for your compute services such as virtual machines. Choose a location where all Azure features and resources are available together in the same region. This will avoid egress traffic.
- Choose the optimal size for virtual machines. A bigger size virtual machine costs higher than a smaller size and even a bigger size virtual machine might not be required at all.
- Resize virtual machines during times of demand and reduce their size when demand subsides. Azure release newer VM sizes as an on-going activity frequently. If a new size that is available is better suited, then it must be used.
- Shutdown compute services during off hours or when they are not needed. This is for non-production environments.
- Deallocate virtual machines compared to shutting them down. This will release all resources and meters for their consumption will stop.
- Use development/testing labs for development and testing purposes. They provide policies and auto-shutdown and auto-start features.
- With virtual machine scale sets, start will lower the number of virtual machines and scale out when the demand increases.
- Choose the correct size (small, medium, large) for application gateways. They are backed up by virtual machines and can help reduce costs with optimal size. Also, choose the basic tier application gateway if a web application firewall is not needed.
- Choose the correct tiers for VPN gateways (basic VPN, standard, high performance, ultra performance).
- Minimize network traffic between Azure regions by co-locating resources in the same region.
- Use load balancer with public IP to access multiple virtual machines rather than assigning a public IP to each virtual machine.
- Monitor virtual machines and find its performance and usage metrics. Based on it, determine if you want to upscale or out scale the virtual machine. It could also result in down-sizing and reducing the virtual machines.

Storage best practices

Storage also has a major impact from overall cost perspective:

- Choose the appropriate storage redundancy type (GRS, LRS, RA-GRS). GRS is costlier than LRS.
- Archive storage data to cool or archive the access tier. Keep data in the hot tier that is frequently accessed.
- Remove blobs that are not required.
- Delete the virtual machine operating system disks explicitly after deleting the virtual machine if they are not needed.
- Storage accounts are metered based on their size, write, read, list, and container operations.
- Prefer standard disks over premium disks. Use premium disks only if business demands so.
- Use CDN and caching for static files instead of fetching it from storage every time.

PaaS best practices

Some of the best practices if PaaS is the preferred deployment model are the following:

- Choose appropriate Azure SQL tier (basic, standard, premium RS, premium) and appropriate performance levels.
- Choose appropriately between single databases and elastic databases. If there are a lot of databases, it is cost-efficient to use elastic databases compared to single databases.
- Re-architect your solutions to use PaaS (serverless, microservices in containers) compared to IaaS solutions. These PaaS solutions take away maintenance costs and are available on per minute consumption basis. If you do not consume these services, there is no cost in spite of your code and services being available round the clock.
- There are resource-specific cost optimizations and it is not possible to cover all of them in a single chapter. Readers are advised to read documentation related to each feature cost and usage.

General best practices

Some of the general best practices from cost perspective are the following:

- Cost of resources are different across regions. Try using a region with minimal cost. This is obviously depended on business justification.
- Enterprise agreements provide maximum discounts. If you are not on EA, try to be on EA for cost benefits.
- If Azure costs can be pre-paid then it provides discounts for all kinds of subscription.
- Delete or remove unused resources. Figure out resources that are underutilized and reduce their Sku or size. If they are not needed, then delete them.
- Use Azure advisor and take its recommendations seriously.

Summary

Cost management and administration is an important activity when dealing with the cloud. This is primarily because the monthly expense could be very low, but can be very high if proper attention is not provided to it. Architects should design their application in such a manner, that it minimizes the cost. They should use appropriate Azure resources, appropriate Sku, tier, size, and know when to start, stop, scale up, scale out, scale down, scale in, transfer data, and more. Proper cost management will ensure that actual expenses meet the budgetary expenses.

The next and final chapter of this book deals will monitoring and auditing capabilities on Azure.

12
Monitoring and Auditing

"If you can't measure it, you can't improve it"

- Lord Kelvin

Imagine a situation where you have architected a solution that is deployed over the cloud as well as on an on-premise data center, consisting of multiple services such as IaaS and PaaS, multi-tier, multi-layer application components. It is based on a highly optimized architecture in terms of availability, scalability, security, performance and more. It is in production now. Now, also imagine that there is no monitoring facility baked into the solution.

There are a few challenges here, they are as follows:

- The availability, scalability, security, and reliability of the solution is not known at any point of time.
- The operations team has no clue about whether the solution is working as expected or not until the users and customers start calling them.
- The performance of the solution degrades over time but the team does not have the current performance metrics to compare to anything.
- Solution and operations teams do not have much information to diagnose, troubleshoot issues.
- Security checks cannot be performed.
- Solution and operations teams do not have any clue about things that can be improved and made better for the customer. There is a lack of innovation.

The issues mentioned before are enough to start thinking about incorporating monitoring in solutions, no matter where and how they are deployed and designed.

In this chapter, we will look at monitoring from the following points:

- Architectural perspective
- Important resources from Azure for monitoring
- Application insights
- Log analytics
- Alerts
- Automating alerts to execute runbooks
- Integrating Power BI

Monitoring

Monitoring is an important architectural concern that should be part of any solution whether big or small, mission critical or not, cloud or not. It should not be avoided at any cost.

Monitoring refers to the act of keeping track of solutions and capturing various telemetry information, processing them, identifying the ones that qualify for alerts based on rules, and raise them. Generally, an agent is deployed within the environment that keeps monitoring it and keeps sending the telemetry information to a centralized server where the rest of the processing of generating alerts and notifying stakeholders happen.

Monitoring helps in taking both proactive as well as reactive actions and measures on the solution. It is also the first step towards auditability of the solution. Without availability of monitoring log records, it is difficult to audit the system from various perspectives such as security, performance, availability and more.

Monitoring helps in identifying availability, performance and scalability issues before it happens. Hardware failure, software misconfiguration, patch update challenges can be known much before they impact users, using monitoring. Performance degradation can be fixed before it happens.

Reactively, the logs help in finding areas and locations that are causing issues, help in identifying the issues and enable faster and better fixation.

Teams can identify patterns of issues using monitoring telemetry information and help eliminate them by innovating newer solutions and features.

Azure is a rich cloud environment that provides multiple rich monitoring features and resources to monitor not only cloud-based deployment, but also on-premise deployment along with other cloud providers.

Azure monitoring

The first question that should be answered is *What must we monitor?*. This question becomes more important for solutions that are deployed on the cloud because of constrained control over it.

There are some important components that should be monitored. They include the following:

- Custom applications
- Azure resources
- Guest OS (virtual machines)
- Host OS (Azure physical servers)
- Azure infrastructure

There are different Azure logs and monitoring for the mentioned components.

Azure activity logs

Previously known as audit logs and operational logs, these are control plane events in the Azure subscription. They provide information and telemetry information at the subscription level instead of individual resource level. They track information about all changes that happen at the subscription level such as creation, deletion, update of resources using **Azure Resource Manager** (**ARM**). They help in knowing the identity (service principal, users, groups) and performing an action (write, update) on resources (for example, storage, virtual machines, SQL) at any given point of time. They provide information about resources that are modified in their configuration but not their inner working and execution.

Azure diagnostic logs

The information originating within the inner working of Azure resources are captured and are known as **diagnostic logs**. They provide telemetry information about the operations of resources that are inherent to the resource. Not every resource provides diagnostic logs and whoever provides logs in their own content is completely different from other resources. Diagnostic logs are configured for each resource individually. Examples of diagnostic logs include storing a file in a container in a blob service in a storage account.

Azure application logs

The application logs can be captured by application insights resources and can be managed centrally. They help in getting information about the inner working of custom applications, such as their performance metrics, availability and more and get insights from them for their better manageability.

Guest and host OS logs

Both guest and host operating system logs are surfaced to users using Azure monitor resource. They provide information about working, status of the host and the guest operating system.

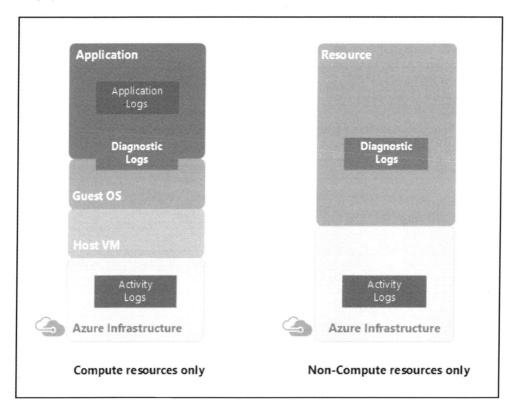

The important resources from Azure related to monitoring are the following:

- Azure monitor
- Azure application insights
- Log analytics previously known as **operational insights**

There are other tools such as **System Center Operations Manager (SCOM)** that are not part of the cloud feature but can be deployed on IaaS-based virtual machines to monitor any workload on Azure or on an on-premise data center.

Azure monitor

Azure monitor is a central tool and resource that provides complete management features for setting monitoring on an Azure subscription. It provides management features for activity logs, diagnostic logs, metrics, application insights, and log analytics. It should be treated as a dashboard and management resource for all other monitoring capabilities.

Azure application insights

Azure application insights help in bringing centralized, Azure-scale monitoring, logs and metrics capabilities to custom applications. Custom applications can start sending metrics, logs and other telemetry information to Azure application insights. It also provides rich reporting, dashboarding and analytics capabilities to get insights from incoming data and act on them.

Azure log analytics

Azure log analytics provide centralized processing of logs and generating insights and alerts from them. Activity logs, diagnostic logs, application logs, event logs, and even custom logs can send information to log analytics which can further provide rich reporting, dashboarding, and analytics capabilities to get insights from incoming data and act on them.

Application insights

As the name suggests, Azure application insights provide insights within the working of an application. The insights relevant for a web application would include incoming number of requests per second, requests failed per second, hardware usage in terms of CPU utilization, memory availability and more. Application insights provide a dashboard, reports and charts to view various metrics related to the application. This helps in viewing and understanding the trends in terms of usage of the application, its availability, number of requests and more to take both precautionary as well as reactive actions on the application. Trends information can be used to find out things not working in favor of the application and things working fine over a period.

The first step in working with application insights is to provision this service on Azure in a resource group that has all general and management services consumed by all applications. If you remember, we had created a similar resource group named `Win2016devOps` that houses all common services such as Azure key vault, application insights, operational insights, and storage account to hold scripts and templates used across environments and applications.

Provisioning

As mentioned before, the first step in consuming application insights services is to provision it on Azure.

Application insights can be provisioned manually using the Azure portal, Azure REST APIs, PowerShell, and ARM templates.

1. Log in to the Azure portal and subscription using the appropriate credentials and navigate to an existing resource group or create a new resource group. Click on the **Add** button.

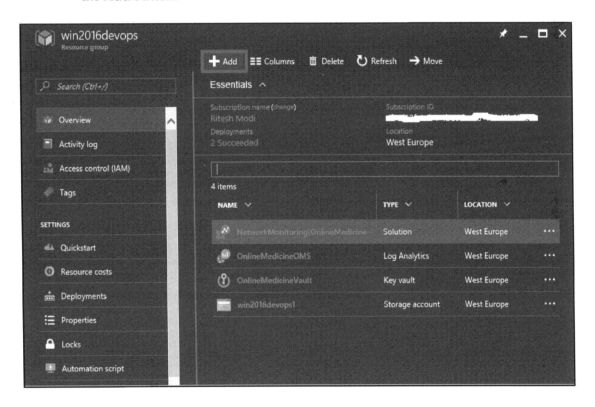

2. Type `Application Insights` in the search box in the resultant blade. The first link should refer to application insights, click on it to create a new application insight service instance. Click on the **Create** button to get started.

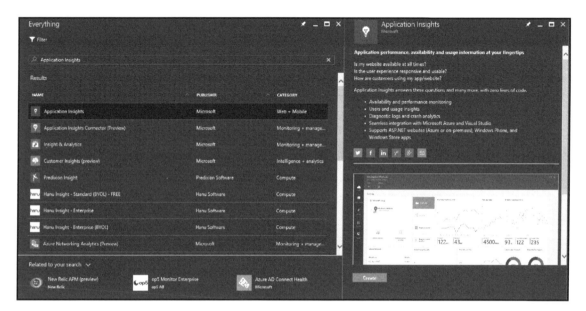

3. The resultant blade will ask for the application insight service instance name, the type of application, subscription name, resource group name, and location of the service. Provide the appropriate details and click on the **Create** button. This will provision the service.

4. Now navigate to the service that shows the essential properties, such as its **Instrumentation Key** highlighted in the following figure. The key will be different in every instance and generally copied and used in Visual Studio. Please note that some of the information has been blacked out due to security reasons.

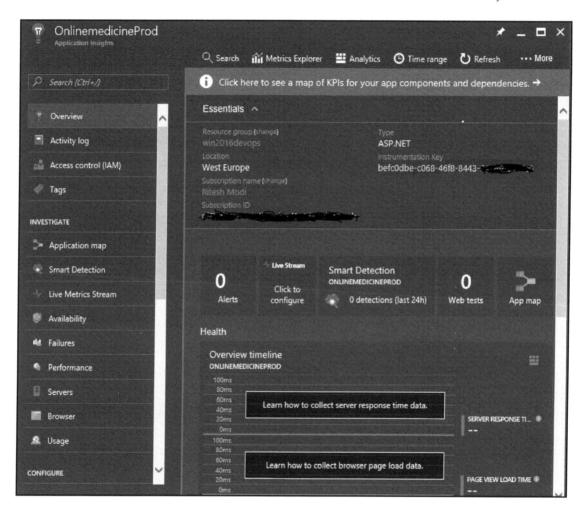

Log analytics

Application insights is used for monitoring the application, however, it is equally important to monitor the environment on which the application is hosted and running. This involves the infrastructure such as virtual machines, Docker container, and its related components.

Provisioning

Log analytics, also known as the **Operational Management Suite (OMS)**, must be provisioned on Azure before it can be used to monitor the virtual machines and containers. Again, similar to the application insights, operational insights can be provisioned through the Azure portal, PowerShell, REST API, and resource group manager templates. An operational insights workspace is a security boundary that can be allowed to be accessed by certain users. Multiple workspaces should be created for the isolation of users and their corresponding access to environment telemetry data.

The JSON script used for provisioning an operational insights workspace is shown next.

```
{
    "apiVersion": "2015-11-01-preview",
    "type": "Microsoft.OperationalInsights/workspaces",
    "name": "[parameters('workspaceName')]",
    "location": "[parameters('deployLocation')]",
    "properties": {
      "sku": {
        "Name": "[parameters('serviceTier')]"
      }
    }
}
```

The `name`, `location`, and `sku` information is needed to provision a workspace and values for them are provided using parameters.

The workspace after provisioning is shown in following figure:

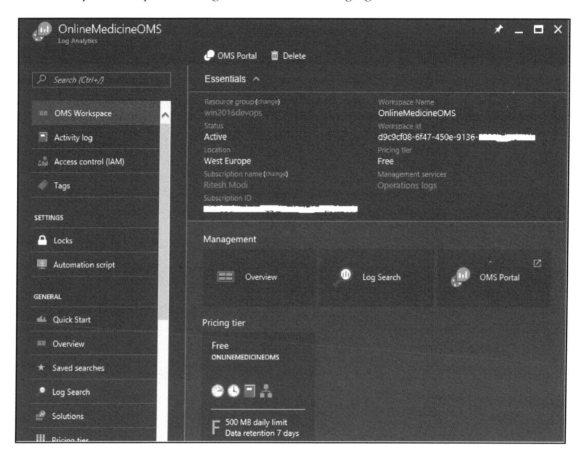

Click on the OMS portal section to open the workspace portal. This portal is used to view all telemetry information captured by operational insights, configure operational insights and providing dashboard features and functionality.

The home screen of operational insights is shown following:

The **Settings** section shows that four data sources are connected. These are four virtual machines connected to the OMS workspace from both the test and production environment. A different strategy of having a separate workspace for each environment can be adopted and it is left to readers to decide the best for their applications and solutions. Operational insights can be configured using the setting tile.

OMS agents

You may have noticed, no assembly or code changes are done to the application for consuming operational insights. Operational insights depend on the installation of an agent on virtual machines. These agents keep collecting telemetry data from these hosts and keep sending them to the Azure operational insights workspace where they are stored for a specified period of time depending upon the `sku` chosen. These agents can be installed manually on virtual machines. Azure resource management virtual machine extensions install agents automatically, immediately after provisioning the virtual machines. The JSON code for provisioning of an agent on a virtual machine is shown in the following:

```
{
        "apiVersion": "2015-06-15",
        "type": "Microsoft.Compute/virtualMachines/extensions",
        "name": "[concat(variables('vmName'),copyIndex(1),'/omsscript')]",
        "location": "[resourceGroup().location]",
        "dependsOn": [
"[concat('Microsoft.Compute/virtualMachines/',variables('vmName'),copyIndex
(1))]",
        "[resourceId('Microsoft.Compute/virtualMachines/extensions',
concat(variables('vmName'),copyIndex(1)),'powershellscript')]"
        ],
        "copy": {
          "count": "[parameters('countVMs')]",
          "name": "omsloop"
        },
        "properties": {
          "publisher": "Microsoft.EnterpriseCloud.Monitoring",
          "type": "MicrosoftMonitoringAgent",
          "typeHandlerVersion": "1.0",
          "settings": {
            "workspaceId": "[parameters('WorkspaceID')]"
          },
          "protectedSettings": {
            "workspaceKey": "[listKeys(variables('accountid'),'2015-11-01-
preview').primarySharedKey]"
          }
        }
    }
```

The workspace ID and account ID are available from the settings tile of the OMS workspace and the copy element is used to deploy it to multiple virtual machines. This resource is a child resource of the virtual machine resource ensuring that this extension is executed whenever a virtual machine is provisioned or updated.

The configuration related to **Workspace ID** and **Account ID** is shown next. The primary key is used as **Account ID** for configuring the agents using ARM templates.

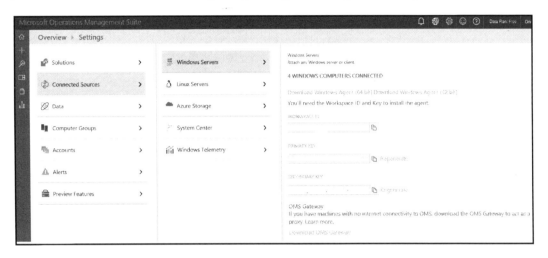

Search

The OMS workspace provides search capabilities to search for specific log entries, export all telemetry data to Excel and/or Power BI, and search language specific to OMS.

A **Log Search** screen is shown next.

Solutions

Solutions in OMS are additional capabilities that can be added to the workspace capturing additional telemetry data that is not captured by default. When these solutions are added to the workspace, appropriate management packs are sent to all the agents connected to the workspace in the context of configuring themselves for capturing solution specific data from virtual machines and containers, and then start sending it to the OMS workspace.

The following screenshot shows the solution gallery and capacity and performance solution on the OMS workspace. Clicking on any solution and subsequently clicking on the **Add** button adds the solution in context to the workspace.

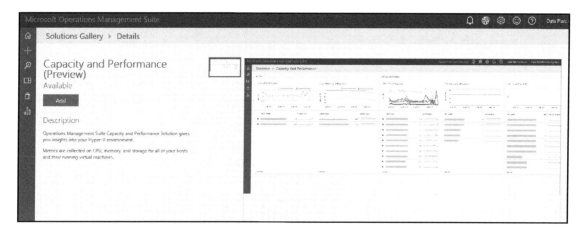

Azure provides lots of OMS solutions for tracking and monitoring different aspects of environments and application. At the minimum, a set of solutions that are generic and applicable to almost any environment should be added to the workspace.

- Capacity and performance
- Agent health
- Change tracking
- Containers
- Security and audit
- Update management
- Network performance monitoring

Alerts

Log analytics provides provisions to generate alerts on the ingested data. It does so by running a pre-defined query composed of conditions on the incoming data. If it finds any or a group of records that falls within the ambit of the said query, it generates an alert. Log analytics provides a highly configurable environment for determining the conditions for generating alerts, time windows from which the query should return the records, time windows when the query should be executed, and action to be undertaken when the query returns results as alerts.

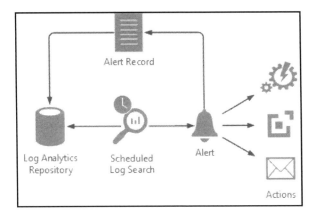

The first step in configuring an alert is to create a saved search. A saved search is simply a search query against log analytics.

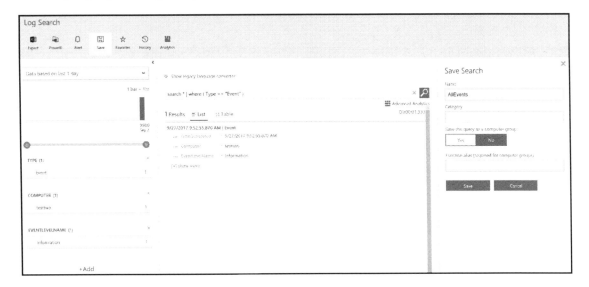

Save the query by providing a name for it. After saving the query, click on the **Alert** button from the **Log Search** menu. It provides the user an interface for defining and adding a new alert rule.

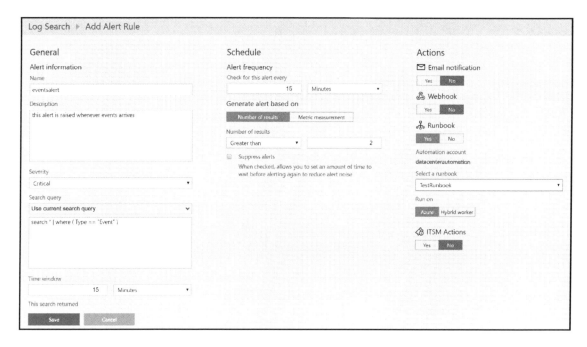

Within the single screen, all configurations related to an alert rule can be performed. Provide a name, description, severity, query to be executed as part of the rule evaluation within their respective fields.

The time window helps in specifying the data interval on which the query should be executed. From the given screenshot, whenever the rule is executed, it processes data from last 15 minutes.

The schedule section helps in configuring the frequency of rule execution. It helps in answering the question *How frequently should the query run?* From the given screenshot, the rule is executed every 15 minutes. The time window should be more than the alert frequency. The alerts can be further configured based on the number of results found. It need not be that an alert is generated for every instance of data found based on the query. It can further be quantified to accumulate a certain quantity of results before raising the requests. The alerts can also be generated based on metric measurements. Additional configuration to suppress alerts can be done. It helps in creating a time interval that should elapse before executing the action. In this case, alerts are generated but action is taken only after the configured elapsed interval.

The actions section helps in the configuration aspect of things that should follow an alert. Generally, there should be a remedial and/or notification action. Log analytics provides four different ways to create a new action. They can be combined in any combination. An alert will execute all configured actions.

- **Email notification**: This is the simplest and sends an email to the configured recipients:

- **Webhook**: Webhook helps in executing any arbitrary external process using a HTTP POST mechanism. For example, a REST API can be executed or service manager/ServiceNow APIs can be invoked to create a ticket:

- **Runbooks**: This action executes Azure automation runbooks. In the next section, we will see the entire process of executing an Azure automation runbook.
- **ITSM actions**: ITSM solutions should be provisioned before using this option and it helps in connecting and sending information to ITSM systems.

Executing runbooks on Alerts

One of the actions provided by a log analytics alert is to execute the Azure automation runbook. This facility of executing runbooks on an alert provides immense power to act on the alert to remediate it as well as inform the relevant stakeholders using notifications.

1. The first step in executing a runbook in response to an alert, is to create an **Azure Automation Account**:

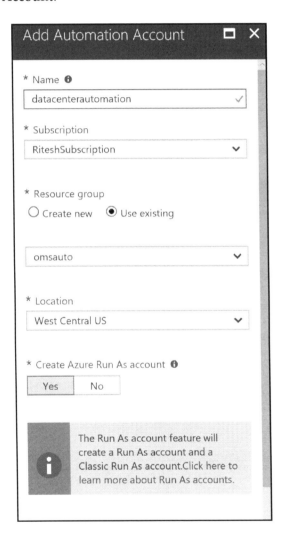

2. After the account is provisioned, create a runbook just to prove that it can be executed as part of the alert generation. In this case, the runbook sends an email as part of the notification. It uses Azure automation credential to send an email using O365 SMTP server. Users should have a valid O365 account before sending email using Azure automation.

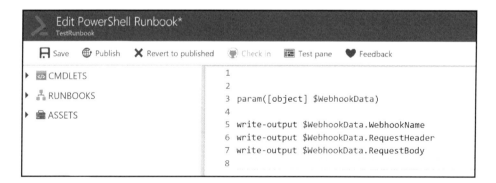

```
1
2  $Cred = Get-AutomationPSCredential -Name "o365"
3      if ($Cred -eq $null)
4      {
5          Write-Output "Credential entered: o365 does not exist in the automation service. Please create one `n"
6      }
7      else
8      {
9          $CredUsername = $Cred.UserName
10     }
11
12 $requestID = Random
13
14 $body = "<HTML><HEAD><META http-equiv=""Content-Type"" content=""text/html; charset=iso-8859-1"" /><TITLE></TITLE></HEAD>"
15 $body += "<BODY bgcolor=""#FFFFFF"" style=""font-size: Small; font-family: TAHOMA; color: #000000""><P>"
16 $body += "Please choose one of the options<br />"
17 $body += "<a href='https://azureforarchitects.azurewebsites.net/api/getjobdone?status=decline&requestID=11'>" + "Decline" + "</b><br />"
18 $body += "<a href='https://azureforarchitects.azurewebsites.net/api/getjobdone?status=approved&requestID=11'>" + "Approve" + "</b><br />"
19 $body += "If you approve request will provision a new virtual machine for user.."
20
21 Send-MailMessage `
22     -To "callritz@hotmail.com" `
23     -Subject "You have asked approval for a VM !!" `
24     -Body "Your request has been sent to approver. Please wait for a response !!" `
25     -UseSsl `
26     -Port 587 `
27     -SmtpServer 'smtp.office365.com' `
28     -From admin@callritzhotmail.com `
29     -BodyAsHtml `
30     -Credential $Cred
31
32 Write-Output "Mail is now send `n"
33 Write-Output "-----------------------------------------------------------------"
34
```

3. It is to be noted that this is just a demonstration. The runbook can also accept parameters and log analytics alerts and send a single parameter of the type, object. This parameter contains all the data pertaining to the source of the alert, details about the alert, and information that is available with log analytics:

Edit PowerShell Runbook*
TestRunbook

🖫 Save ⊕ Publish ✕ Revert to published Check in Test pane ♥ Feedback

▸ CMDLETS
▸ RUNBOOKS
▸ ASSETS

```
1
2
3  param([object] $WebhookData)
4
5  write-output $WebhookData.WebhookName
6  write-output $WebhookData.RequestHeader
7  write-output $WebhookData.RequestBody
8
```

4. The data is in the JSON format and a `ConvertFrom-JSON` cmdlet can be used to create PowerShell objects.

5. The next step is to configure a log analytics configuration such that it can connect to the Azure automation account. For this, a solution **Automation & Control** needs to be enabled and deployed:

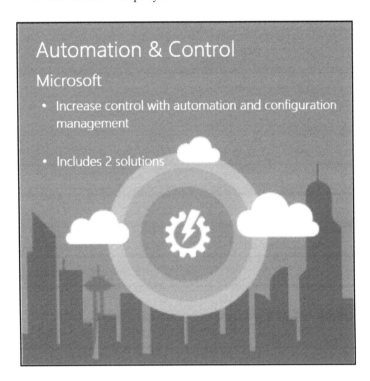

6. The **Solutions Gallery** window--clicking on this tile will navigate to its configuration window. Click on **Configure Workspace** to deploy it:

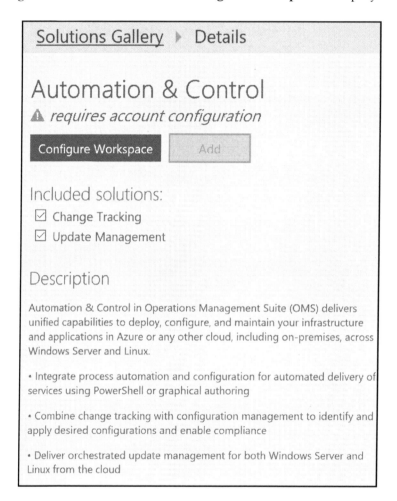

7. Select the newly created Azure **Automation Account** as part of the deployment of the solution:

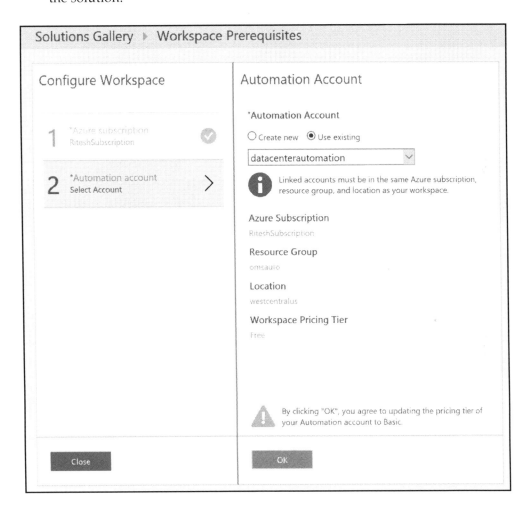

8. After deployment of the solution, navigate to the settings window within the log analytics workspace and ensure that the Azure automation settings show details about the Azure **Automation Account**. This ensures that the log analytics workspace is connected to the Azure **Automation Account**:

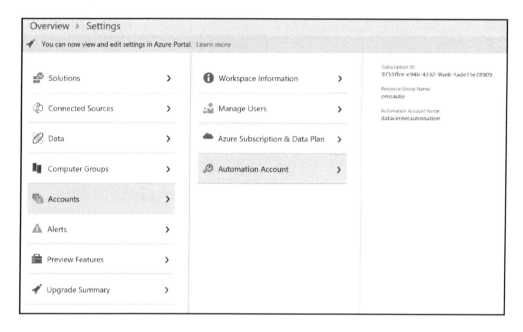

9. Now the runbook should be available while configuring the alert action runbook:

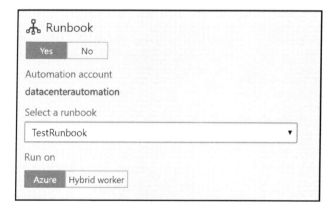

Integrating Power BI

Gathering data and storing it at a central repository is an important aspect. However, there should be tools and utilities to process the data and generate insights out of it. Power BI is a Microsoft-provided service specifically meant for visualization and generating insights from raw data.

Power BI can be enabled using the **Settings** menu just such as the configuration for Azure automation. The connection to Power BI should be made from the **Settings** menu. Once, this connection is made, it can be used to send log analytics data to Power BI.

Log analytics provides two different ways to interact with Power BI. First it needs to be enabled from the **Settings** menu.

Like alerts, the Power BI menu option is available from the log search top level menu. Clicking on it helps in configuring the Power BI connectivity. A scheduler runs periodically to execute search queries and send the resultant data to Power BI. The data is stored as datasets in Power BI and can be used to generate charts, reports, and dashboards:

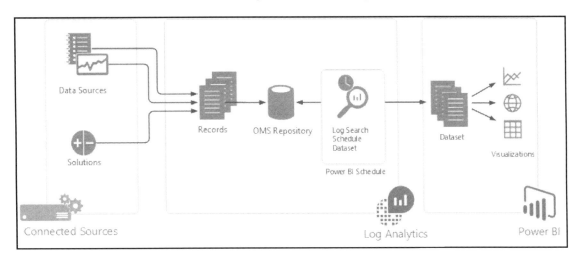

The other way to get data into Power BI from log analytics is to use **Power Query** language within Power BI. The same is shown here. This is scaffolding the code provided by log analytics.

The exported **Power Query Formula Language** (**M Language**) can be used with the Power Query in Microsoft Excel and Power BI Desktop.

For Power BI Desktop follow the instructions:

1. Download Power BI Desktop from
   `https://powerbi.microsoft.com/en-us/desktop/`.
2. In the Power BI Desktop select **Get Data** | **Blank Query** | **Advanced Query Editor**.
3. Paste the M Language script into the **Advanced Query Editor** and select **Done**.

```
let AnalyticsQuery =
let Source =
Json.Document(Web.Contents("https://management.azure.com/subscripti
ons/9755ffce-
e94b-4332-9be8-1ade15e78909/resourceGroups/omsauto/providers/Micros
oft.OperationalInsights/workspaces/data
centermonitoring/api/query?api-version=2017-01-01-preview",
[Query=[#"query"="search * | where ( Type == ""Event"" )  ",#"x-ms-
app"="OmsAnalyticsPBI",#"timespan"="PT24H",#"prefer"="ai.response-
thinning=true"],Timeout=#duration(0,0,4,0)])),
TypeMap = #table(
{ "AnalyticsTypes", "Type" },
{
{ "string",   Text.Type },
{ "int",      Int32.Type },
{ "long",     Int64.Type },
{ "real",     Double.Type },
{ "timespan", Duration.Type },
{ "datetime", DateTimeZone.Type },
{ "bool",     Logical.Type },
{ "guid",     Text.Type }
}),
DataTable = Source[tables]{0},
Columns = Table.FromRecords(DataTable[columns]),
ColumnsWithType = Table.Join(Columns, {"type"}, TypeMap ,
{"AnalyticsTypes"}),
Rows = Table.FromRows(DataTable[rows], Columns[name]),
Table = Table.TransformColumnTypes(Rows,
Table.ToList(ColumnsWithType, (c) => { c{0}, c{3}}))
in
Table
in AnalyticsQuery
```

Summary

Monitoring is an important architectural aspect for any solution. It is also the first step towards auditability. It enables operations to manage the solution, both reactively and proactively. It helps provide necessary records for troubleshooting and fixing issues that might arise from platforms and applications. There are many resources in Azure specific to implementing monitoring for Azure, other clouds, and on-premise data centers. Application insights, OMS, and log analytics are some of the important resources in this regard. Needless to say, it is a must for making your solutions and products better by innovating based on insights from monitoring data.

Index

functions as a service (FaaS) 192
functions
  connected architecture, creating with 216, 218, 220

G

Geo-redundant storage (GRS) 42
GIT 254
guest and host OS logs 300

H

high availability 146, 147
High Availability
  about 58
  affecting factors 59
  Application High Availability 67
  architectural considerations 74
  best practices 77, 78
  computing 63, 64, 65
  data related best practices 79
  deployment related best practices 78
  monitoring related best practices 79
  PaaS High Availability 66
  Storage High Availability 65
  versus disaster recovery 60
  versus scalability 60
  virtual machine High Availability 63
Host Container System Shim (HCSShim) 23
hybrid networks 39

I

IaaS scalability 89
IaaS security
  about 106
  attack surface area, reducing 110
  firewalls 108, 109
  jump servers, implementing 111
  Network Security Groups 106
  Network Security Groups (NSGs) 107
identity 132, 136
Infrastructure as a Service (IaaS) 8, 9
Infrastructure as Code (IAC) 16
ingestion 133, 136
integrity 103
intelligent cloud

Azure Command-Line Interface (CLI) 25
Azure portal 24
Azure Resource Manager templates 26
Azure REST API 26
  interacting with 24
  PowerShell 25
internal load balancing 70
Internet information service (IIS) 73
Internet of Things (IoT) 128, 129
Internet Service Provider (ISP) 7
Invoice download API 287
invoicing 284
IoT architecture
  about 129, 130
  analytics 134
  capture 132
  connectivity 130, 131, 132
  identity 132
  ingestion 133
  presentation 135
  storage 133
  transform 133
IoT hubs
  about 138, 139
  device registration 139, 140
  message management 141
  protocols 139
  reference link 139
  scalability 144
  security 143

J

JavaScript Object Notation (JSON) 26, 244
jump servers
  implementing 111

K

Kudu console 192

L

load balancing 62, 67
Locally redundant storage (LRS) 42
locks 20

M

machine learning 138
Massively Parallel Processing (MPP) 181
message management
  about 141
  cloud, to device messaging 142, 143
  device, to cloud messaging 141, 142
Message Queue Telemetry Transport (MQTT) 131
messaging patterns
  about 45
  architectural concerns 45
  competing consumers 46
  priority queue 47
  queue-based load leveling pattern 47, 48
Microsoft.Compute Namespace 17
monitoring
  about 33, 298
  Azure monitoring 299

N

Network Address Translation (NAT) 263
Network Security Groups (NSGs)
  about 106, 107
  design 108
networking limits
  reference 32

O

on demand functions 206
Online Analytics Processing (OLAP) 179
Online Transaction Processing (OLTP) 179
operational insights 301
operational management suite 30
Operational Management Suite (OMS) 307
Operations Management Suite (OMS)
  about 112
  animalware assessment 112
  detections 112
  notable issues 112
  security domains 112
  threat intelligence 112
optical character recognition (OCR) 205
owner 19

P

PaaS best practices 294
PaaS High Availability 66
PaaS scalability 85
  scaling down 87
  scaling in 88
  scaling out 88
  scaling up 87
PaaS security
  about 111
  Azure SQL 117, 118
  Operations Management Suite (OMS) 112
  storage 113, 114, 116, 117
PaaS
  disadvantages 189
pay-as-you-go payment mechanism 279
performance and scalability patterns 49
performance
  versus scalability 83
permission 19
physical servers
  disadvantages 188
Plain old simple object (POCO) 195
Platform as a Service (PaaS) 10
policies 20
PolyBase 180
port forwarding 72
Power BI
  integrating 323
Power Query Formula Language (M Language) 323
Power Query language 323
PowerShell 25
PowerShell Gallery 25
premium storage 40
presentation 135, 138
principles, serverless technology
  event driven 191
  execute quickly 191
  lower cost 191
  single responsibility 191
priority queue pattern
  about 47
  reference 47
protocols 139

public load balancing 69, 70

Q

queue storage 41
queue-based load leveling pattern 48

R

Raspberry Pi online simulator
   reference link 139
RateCard API 287
Read-access geo-redundant storage (RAGRS) 42
reader 19
redundancy 61
release pipeline 248
RemoteSigned 110
Representational State Transfer (REST) 26
resource groups 18
resource instances 18
resource providers 17, 286, 287
resource types 18
Resource usage API 287
resources, for enabling load balancing
   application gateways 63
retry pattern
   about 52
   reference 53
   strategies 52
role definition 19
Role-Based Access Control (RBAC) 15, 177
roles 19
runbook
   executing, on Alerts 317, 318, 320, 321, 322

S

scalability
   about 82, 144
   reference 82
   Sku edition 144
   units 146
   versus High Availability 60
   versus performance 83
scaling down 84
scaling in 85
scaling out 84
scaling up 84

scaling
   about 83
   best practices 97, 98, 99
scheduled functions 206
Secure Access Signature (SAS) 41
security
   about 102, 143
   authentication 102
   authorization 102
   confidentiality 102
   in IOT 143
   integrity 103
   life cycle 103, 104
serverless technology
   principles 191
serverless
   about 190
   history 188, 189
service 58
service level agreement (SLA) 47, 58, 152, 190, 261
sharding 156
shared access signature (SAS) 114
short messaging service (SMS) 206
Sku edition
   about 144
   free 144
   Standard (S1) 144
   Standard (S2) 144
   Standard (S3) 144
Software as a Service (SaaS) 10
Spark 137
SQL Server Analysis Services (SSAS) 179
standard storage 40
stock keeping units (SKU) 86
storage account
   architectural considerations 43
   concurrency features 44
storage best practices 294
Storage High Availability 65
Storage Service Encryption (SSE) 41
storage services
   about 40
   blob storage 41
   file storage 41